Reform, Inclusion and Teacher Education

This ground-breaking book considers current perspectives on special education reform in the Asia-Pacific region. With major changes being proposed under current education reform, how can teachers cope? This book responds to this by critically examining the region's responsibilities within a global framework and by drawing on local and international research on best practices for special and inclusive education reform.

Reform, Inclusion and Teacher Education offers a context-sensitive approach adapted to the unique challenges faced in the Asia-Pacific region. It provides manageable, realistic, and achievable goals, given the local challenges and needs across this region. The book is helpfully divided into three different sections of education reform:

- "Education reform in the Asia-Pacific region" reviews broad trends and issues in special education across the region, including Australia, China, Hong Kong, India, Korea and Taiwan.
- "Preparing teachers to work in inclusive classrooms" focuses on curricula and pedagogical practices for teacher education. This section considers best practice in preparing teachers for inclusive schooling, and the impact of teachers' attitudes and concerns on education reform.
- "Effective special and inclusive practices" draws upon evidence-based research to provide best practice models to assist in developing inclusive school communities. The focus is on practical strategies for supporting principals and teachers from kindergarten to Year 12 to become more inclusive.

Each section addresses a list of objectives and questions, suggests best practice pedagogy, and concludes with a support section with useful resources and suggested professional development activities. This book will interest pre- and in-service teachers, teacher educators, tertiary lecturers in education and postgraduate students.

Chris Forlin is Head of the Division of Special Education in the Department of Educational Psychology Counselling and Learning Needs at The Hong Kong Institute of Education.

Ming-Gon John Lian is the Director of the Centre for Advancement in Special Education (CASE) at The University of Hong Kong.

This book is written in collaboration with the Centre for Advancement in Special Education (CASE). CASE was established by The University of Hong Kong with the aim of advancing research and services in special education and serving as an agent and catalyst for more effective and high quality education for individuals with learning difficulties or other disabling conditions.

Reform, Inclusion and Teacher Education

Towards a new era of special education in the Asia-Pacific region

Edited by
Chris Forlin
and
Ming-Gon John Lian

Routledge
Taylor & Francis Group
LONDON AND NEW YORK

First published 2008
by Routledge
2 Park Square, Milton Park, Abingdon, Oxon OX14 4RN

Simultaneously published in the USA and Canada
by Routledge
270 Madison Ave, New York, NY 10016

Routledge is an imprint of the Taylor & Francis Group, an informa business

Typeset in Galliard by
Book Now Ltd
Printed and bound in Great Britain by
TJ International Ltd, Padstow, Cornwall

British Library Cataloguing in Publication Data
A catalogue record for this book is available from the British Library

Library of Congress Cataloging in Publication Data

Reform, inclusion, and teacher education: towards a new era of special and inclusive education in Asia-Pacific regions/[edited by] Chris Forlin and Ming-Gon John Lian.

p. cm.

[etc.]

1. Children with disabilities—Education—Asia. 2. Special education—Asia. 3. Inclusive education—Asia. 4. Teachers—Training of—Asia. I. Forlin, Chris. II. Lian, Ming-Gon John.

LC4037.A2R426 2008

371.905—dc22

2007049702

ISBN10: 0–415–46448–X (hbk)
ISBN10: 0–415–46447–1 (pbk)
ISBN10: 0–203–89531–2 (ebk)

ISBN13: 978–0–415–46448–2 (hbk)
ISBN13: 978–0–415–46447–5 (pbk)
ISBN13: 978–0–203–89531–3 (ebk)

Contents

Illustrations

Figures

Tables

Contributors

Adrian Ashman is Professor of Education at the University of Queensland, Australia. He has an extensive publication and research record and international profile in the fields of intellectual disability and special needs education.

Mei-Lan Au is an Assistant Professor at the Hong Kong Institute of Education, Department of Curriculum and Instruction. Her current research focuses on curriculum, pedagogy and assessment approaches to cater for diversity and promote inclusion.

Anne Bellert works as a Learning Support Officer (Inclusion) for the Lismore Diocese, New South Wales. Anne has extensive experience supporting students who experience learning difficulties and their teachers. She is completing her PhD at the University of New England.

Kaili Chen currently teaches in the Division of Learning, Development and Diversity, Faculty of Education, The University of Hong Kong. Her research interests include emotional/behavioral disorders, social skills training, girls with behavior difficulties, curriculum adaptations, and intervention programs.

Stella Chong is an Assistant Professor in the Department of Educational Psychology, Counselling and Learning Needs at the Hong Kong Institute of Education. Her research and publications address multicultural education, inclusive and special education.

Ishwar Desai is an Honorary Senior Fellow in the Faculty of Education at the University of Melbourne and Director of Desai Consulting Pty Ltd. He has extensive experience in research, teaching, consultancy and capacity building in special education and inclusion.

Chris Forlin is Head of the Division of Special Education in the Department of Educational Psychology Counselling and Learning Needs at the Hong Kong Institute of Education. She has published extensively on research in the area of special and inclusive education and consulted internationally on curriculum and pedagogy for inclusion.

Christie Gilson is a Fulbright Fellow who is completing her PhD in special education at the University of Illinois at Urbana-Champaign. Her teaching, advocacy, and research efforts focus on alleviating attitudinal and physical barriers for people with disabilities.

Lorraine Graham is the Associate Director (Student Diversity) in the National Centre of Science, Information and Communication Technology, and Mathematics Education for Rural and Regional Australia (SiMERR) at the University of New England. She has a particular interest in intervention research.

Neil Humphrey is a Senior Lecturer and Course Director of the MEd Psychology of Education at the University of Manchester, United Kingdom. His research focuses upon social and emotional aspects of learning and inclusive education for pupils with special educational needs. Dr Humphrey has published widely on these topics.

Keith Humphreys has written for EQUALS (Entitlement and Quality Education for Pupils with Severe Learning Difficultes) in England, has been a Special Schools Inspector and Head of Special Education at Northumbria University. His current international special education consultancies are with The University of Hong Kong, the Government of Malta and special schools in the United Kingdom.

Yong-Wook Kim is Professor of the Department of Special Education at the Daegu University, Korea. He has published extensively on research in the area of learning disabilities and led inclusive education nationally as General Director of the Korea National Institute of Special Education.

Bruce Allen Knight is the Associate Dean (Research and Innovation) of the Faculty of Arts, Humanities and Education at Central Queensland University. He has published extensively and is a Fellow of the International Academy of Research in Learning Disabilities.

Ming-Gon John Lian is the Director of the Centre for Advancement in Special Education (CASE) at The University of Hong Kong. His research areas include moderate to severe, multiple disabilities, curriculum development, parental involvement, and assistive technology.

Tim Loreman is Associate Professor of Education at Concordia University College of Alberta. His research and publications address inclusive education and teacher education. Tim maintains a busy professional schedule comprised of teaching, international and national speaking engagements, writing, and research.

Anuradha Naidu currently works as a part-time special needs teacher at Watchdog Early Learning and Development Centre, Hong Kong. As a practitioner, she has contributed to the development of special and inclusive education services in India as well as to the implementation of policy.

Michelle Pearce has extensive experience as a special education teacher, principal and consultant, acting as an advisor for teachers and schools in both private and government systems in Australia. She is currently completing her doctoral thesis on the inclusive teacher in the secondary school context.

Kenneth Poon is Assistant Professor at the Early Childhood and Special Needs Academic Group, National Institute of Education, Nanyang Technological University, Singapore. He publishes, consults, and trains internationally in the field of Autism Spectrum Disorders.

Richard Rose is Professor and Director, Centre for Special Needs Education and Research at the University of Northampton and Marden Visiting Fellow at the Hong Kong Institute of Education. His research has been published in a number of books and journals.

Umesh Sharma is Senior Lecturer in the Faculty of Education at Monash University in Australia. His area of research interest includes teacher preparation for inclusive education, attitude measurement, scale development, inclusive curricular strategies and positive behavior support.

Hsin-Yi Wang is Assistant Professor in Chia Nan University of Pharmacy and Science in Taiwan. She has dedicated herself to providing quality education for children with disabilities, and focused her research on early intervention, inclusive education and teacher development.

Pamela Wolfberg is Associate Professor of special education and directs the Autism Spectrum program (Project Mosaic) at San Francisco State University. She has published extensively and leads worldwide efforts to develop inclusive peer play programs for children with autism.

Wu-Tien Wu is Professor Emeritus of special education at Taiwan Normal University. He has been the leader of numerous professional organizations both in Taiwan and abroad. He has published over 300 papers/books in the areas of special education and counselling.

Xu Jiacheng is Dean of Special Education College of Beijing Union University. His research focuses on the quality of life of people with intellectual disability. He has published more than 30 papers and research reports in the area of special education and rehabilitation.

Editorial board

All chapters in the text have been peer reviewed by two academics or practitioners in the field of special and inclusive education. The reviewers formed the editorial board for this text.

Foreword

The publication of this book is particularly timely. It comes at a time when education systems around the world are focused on the challenge of achieving the goal of "education for all", as defined by the United Nations organizations. Within this overall policy agenda, the issue of how best to reach out to learners with impairments, and many others who are defined as having special educational needs, must be seen as a priority, not least because too often they remain marginalized within existing arrangements.

The book is an important contribution to the field that has traditionally been referred to as special education or, sometimes, special needs education. Its chapters draw on the innovations of many professionals in responding to the challenges of responding to children who experience educational difficulties during an era of unprecedented change. In particular, it focuses on three key issues that are relevant to the Asia-Pacific region, namely, the impact of overall education reform efforts, the challenge of inclusion and the implications for teacher education.

In the last decade or so, education reforms have been a high priority in many countries. The central focus of these reforms has been on "raising standards", defined in terms of improved test scores. Unfortunately, the evidence from some countries, including my own, suggests that this can have perverse as well as positive consequences, with the most disadvantaged groups of learners being further penalized for "failing" to achieve. This is why it is so vital that the field of special education should review its purposes and practices. This book focuses specifically on what this means for education systems in the Asia-Pacific region. It should, therefore, command wide attention amongst policy-makers and practitioners.

It is impossible to consider the future contributions of special education without referring to the idea of inclusive education. In some countries, inclusive education is thought of as an approach to serving children with disabilities within general education settings. Internationally, however, it is increasingly seen more broadly as a reform that responds to diversity amongst all learners. This approach was endorsed in 1994 by the Salamanca World Conference on Special Needs Education. Arguably the most significant international document that has ever appeared in the field of special education, the Salamanca Statement argues that regular schools with an inclusive orientation are the most effective means of combating discriminatory attitudes, building an inclusive society and achieving education for all. Furthermore, it suggests that such schools can provide an effective education for the majority of children and improve the efficiency and ultimately the cost-effectiveness of the entire education system. Thus, the aim is to ensure that *all* children enjoy equal opportunities in education, irrespective of race, gender, socio-economic background or impairment. Such a major shift in thinking is, of course, very challenging. It requires a redefinition of the role of special education, as well as new forms of organization and practice across education systems. It also points to a need for research initiatives that will provide a sound theoretical base for advancement. Most importantly, it calls for collaboration and networking among professionals, within and across countries and regions, in order to share experiences and effective practices.

This rich collection of papers from professionals, all focusing on the Asia-Pacific region, not only addresses the impact of reform and inclusion on special education but does so in the important context of teacher education. It is, therefore, a valuable resource for government officials, school administrators, preservice and experienced teachers, and academics whose research is focused on the development of education systems that can serve all children effectively.

I congratulate all of the authors on the breadth of themes that are covered within the book. In my view, it provides an important contribution to thinking in the Asia-Pacific region.

Mel Ainscow
University of Manchester, UK

Preface

Special education reform in the Asia-Pacific region, like elsewhere, has in recent years attempted to espouse the international declarations that promote a more equitable and inclusive perspective to the education of students with disabilities. The move towards inclusive education is, however, extremely contentious in this region as often there is little or no history of inclusive school practice. As education systems endeavor to adopt this international movement towards inclusion, the special education reform process in the Asia-Pacific region needs to address significantly different issues that are unique to its diverse culture and history of education.

This text responds to this by critically examining the region's responsibilities within a global framework and by drawing on local and international research on best practices for special and inclusive education reform. Most importantly, it does not propose a fully inclusive model of education that exactly mirrors the approach taken internationally. Rather, it offers a context-sensitive approach adapted to the unique challenges faced in the Asia-Pacific region. The text draws direction from international reform but relies upon developing its own unique approach to attaining equity. While it is desirable that a greater move towards a more inclusive model should occur, given the contextual barriers that exist in much of the Asia-Pacific region it is acknowledged that this may not be fully realizable at this juncture in the reform process. What this text suggests is a starting point that is manageable, realistic, and achievable, given the local challenges and special needs across this region.

The text is divided into three sections each of which highlights different key issues, providing a current perspective on special education reform across the Asia-Pacific region. It focuses on transformation from an equity concept towards a whole schooling inclusive approach, teacher preparation for this paradigm shift, and practical strategies for developing inclusive school systems across all age and grade levels. This approach takes into consideration the unique cultural, social, and educational characteristics of the Asia-Pacific region.

The first section considers the broad aspect of special education reform and how it is being enacted across the Asia-Pacific region. Special education reform is clearly high on the agenda throughout the region with different approaches being adopted depending upon local contexts and societal needs. Chris Forlin and Ming-Gon John Lian commence in Chapter 1 by providing an overview of contemporary trends and issues surrounding special education reform. The Western trend away from segregated special education towards inclusive education is further reviewed from the perspective of how appropriate this is for the Asia-Pacific region by Wu-Tien Wu, Adrian Ashman and Yong-Wook Kim in Chapter 2. The transition process and the unique challenges being faced are explored citing Taiwan, Australia, Korea, India and China as examples. Readers are cautioned to draw guidance from Western models where inclusion is more firmly established, but they are also advised to critically review the type of reform that best meets the requirements of the Asia-Pacific region. Whether the Western approaches to inclusive education are valid for this region is debated throughout Section 1, with consideration being given to the heavy reliance to date on a dual system of special and mainstream schools and how systemic reform of special education towards a more inclusive approach can manage to provide equitable opportunities for all students. This section also discusses the need for a change to teacher education, which has tended to lag behind the reform process. In Chapter 3 Anuradha Naidu explores why a greater emphasis needs to be placed on establishing a collaborative process that engages teachers from special schools, who have the expert knowledge in supporting students with disabilities, with Non-Government Officers, mainstream teachers and the students themselves in positive dialogue to further inform development. Xu Jiacheng concludes this section in Chapter 4 with an in-depth discussion of the challenges posed by special education reform from the perspective of a new model in China oriented towards support for quality of life.

Section 2 addresses the need for teacher education to be changed by providing examples of programs that have been effective in the Asia-Pacific region. Chris Forlin in Chapter 5 describes the concerns, needs, curriculum, and approaches in preparing personnel for implementing inclusive education. A detailed curriculum for teacher education is proffered and a range of pedagogies are discussed that can be used to implement the curriculum. In Chapter 6 by Hsin-Yi Wang, the focus is on preparing general education teachers for working with early childhood learners who have disabilities, through the use of an Industrial Collaboration model which involves an early intervention program and efforts to enhance positive attitudes, teaching competences, and practical experiences. Kaili Chen and Kenneth Poon in Chapter 7 introduce training of itinerant or resource service providers via a program for supporting inclusive education in Singapore. A case study that investigates trainees' perceptions of the Diploma in Special Education approach as well as their own needs and hopes is explored. Chris Forlin, Mei-Lan Au and Stella Chong in Chapter 8 conclude this section by reflecting upon teachers' attitudes, perceptions, and concerns about inclusive education as potential barriers for education reform in the Asia-Pacific region. Throughout this section, multiple perspectives in teacher education for carrying out inclusive education are addressed with recommendable approaches introduced.

The third section of the text draws upon international best practice for supporting students with disabilities as examples from which the Asia-Pacific region can draw suitable practices. The first four chapters focus on supporting special education reform within a whole school environment, with consideration being given to all types and levels of schooling. Thought is given to what makes a good inclusive teacher by reviewing their attributes, knowledge, skills and attitudes towards learners requiring additional support. Chapter 9 by Keith Humphreys focuses on providing a balanced curriculum suitable for learners within a special school environment. Chapter 10 by Richard Rose discusses how teachers can rise to this challenge in the primary school; while Michelle Pearce in Chapter 11 considers this from the perspective of the secondary school situation. The role of the principal as a catalyst for change and their responsibilities in supporting and promoting inclusive education are discussed in Chapter 12 by Umesh Sharma and Ishwar Desai.

The next four chapters focus on good teaching practices for including learners with disabilities in regular schools. They provide a range of strategies for teachers to use to deliver effective inclusive classroom lessons. The suggestions offer a repertoire of successful and dependable approaches for teachers to employ. Strategies for including those students with disabilities who are most highly represented in mainstream schools in the Asia-Pacific region are discussed in further detail. Bruce Allen Knight, Anne Bellert and Lorraine Graham focus on the specific needs of students with learning difficulties in Chapter 13. They identify research-based approaches to overcome the barriers experienced by these learners. In Chapter 14, Pamela Wolfberg introduces an Integrated Play Groups model for including learners with Autistic Spectrum Disorder (ASD) which inspires teachers to refine and reflect on their teaching practice. Evidence-based strategies are presented in Chapter 15 by Neil Humphrey who considers the inclusion of learners with Attention-Deficit/Hyperactivity Disorder and those with ASD. In Chapter 16 Christie Gilson and Ming-Gon John Lian identify what teachers need to do as learners prepare for transition from school into post-school options. They propose a range of promising practices for transition programs and services that have, hitherto, been largely ignored in schools in the Asia-Pacific region.

The final chapter by Tim Loreman reflects upon special education reform across the Asia-Pacific region. He identifies the main themes emerging from the text and reiterates some of the major challenges faced in the region and concludes by providing potential solutions and possibilities for employing inclusive education as a catalyst for special education reform.

At the end of each of the three sections support materials are provided to enable the reader to access more information about the topics covered in the section. These contain an annotated list of websites and well-chosen texts from the range of books available. In addition, these segments provide support for teacher educators in working with both pre- and in-service teachers and district and school leaders. A wide assortment of activities is provided. These can be used to guide facilitators as they aim to engage learners in finding out more about special and inclusive education reform and practice in their own region, district and school. Many of the activities lend themselves to small group work with answers recorded on paper prior to whole-group discussion. The activities are authentic approaches to problem-based learning and can be contextualized to meet the needs of learners in any given environment.

This text will provide readers with a current perspective of special education reform and how this is impacting across the Asia-Pacific region. Approaches for forwarding the international trend towards more inclusive mainstream schools will provide opportunities for contemplation of what might work in the region. Stressing important issues of concern for other systems will encourage local systems across the region to reflect upon the unique educational needs of their own learners. Identifying best practices that have worked internationally will facilitate regional systems to replicate appropriate models and to develop their own versions that address their distinctive needs. Learning from others is an important aspect to moving forward. Being willing and perceptive enough to adapt what is learned to meet one's own individual needs and to accept responsibility for making decisions that may not reflect an exact replica of what is happening elsewhere marks true reform. We challenge you to read, absorb, examine, reflect and then to translate these ideas into your own decisions that are suitable and feasible for wherever you are in the Asia-Pacific region.

Acknowledgments

We would like to specifically acknowledge the contribution of the Centre for Advancement in Special Education (CASE) in instigating the writing of this book, and for its collaboration in coordinating the collation of so many chapters and authors. It has been a very long journey but the collegiality and patience of all authors has made it a very positive, exciting and rewarding experience for both of us. It has been a great pleasure working with all of the authors and our colleagues at CASE on this meaningful and rewarding project.

Chris Forlin and Ming-Gon John Lian

This book is published in collaboration with the Centre for Advancement in Special Education (CASE), The University of Hong Kong: http://www.hku.hk/case/

Section 1

Education reform in the Asia-Pacific region

1 Contemporary trends and issues in education reform for special and inclusive education in the Asia-Pacific region

Chris Forlin and Ming-Gon John Lian

Chapter objectives

- To investigate education reform for special and inclusive education.
- To consider current reforms in teacher education for inclusion.
- The identification of the impact of cultural diversity on education reform.
- To identify the development of effective special and inclusive practice.
- To consider appropriate support structures for special education reform in the Asia-Pacific region.

Focus questions

1 How is education reform being implemented in the Asia-Pacific region?
2 How can teachers be prepared for the changing paradigm?
3 What makes effective special and inclusive schooling?
4 What strategies need to be employed to support special education reform?

Introduction

Similar to what has been happening internationally, special education in the Asia-Pacific region is undergoing a major reform, resulting in paradigm shifts in the way schools operate and children are educated. Educational opportunities for students with disabilities have in many countries altered dramatically since the introduction of the normalization principle in the early 1970s, the initiation of the first World Conference on Education for All in Jomtein in 1990 [United Nations Educational, Scientific and Cultural Organization (UNESCO), 1990], the development of the influential Salamanca Statement in 1994 (UNESCO, 1994), and the opening of the World Education Forum at Dakar in April 2000. All of these have led to an increased awareness of governments to reconsider inclusive education opportunities for children with special or diverse learning needs who, in many instances, have been educated previously in segregated facilities.

In the Asia-Pacific region major evolutional changes have occurred (e.g. in China, Hong Kong, Macau, Taiwan) or are starting to occur (e.g. in Vietnam, Cambodia, Indonesia) in special education programs for students with disabilities. These include curriculum reform, changes in academic structure, quality-level school program advancement, greater devolution of responsibility to schools and increased local accountability, and the introduction of inclusive education.

In this region education for learners with disabilities was originally offered by missionaries and most of this occurred in the past 40 years. During this time many special education schools were established by non-profit and charity organizations or parental groups, mainly with the aim of providing learners with an opportunity for special needs education. The education of children with disabilities was not seen as the role of government schools, so facilities and staffing relied almost entirely on the generosity and good will of Non-Government Organizations (NGOs) (Forlin, 2007a).

While most education systems in the Asia-Pacific region have been relatively supportive of the move towards a more inclusive approach and are starting to encourage inclusive schools, there still remains a wide continuum of school provision including many segregated special schools now operated by governments or NGOs. There have also been many local and cultural issues that have created tensions when trying to move the inclusive philosophy forward, particularly in systems that have traditionally focused on the importance of examination results, while employing didactic teaching approaches to achieve them.

In addition, reforms to teacher education have frequently not kept pace with these changes, making teacher preparation for inclusion often an *ad hoc* and invariably an add on approach (Forlin, 2007a). Even within these constraints, systems are increasingly reporting positive changes when implementing new reforms, including program enhancement in more appropriate assessment, accessible curriculum, effective teaching pedagogies, increased information/instructional and assistive technology, greater parental involvement, and better home school partnerships, as well as a focus on action research (Rose, 2007).

Equity and justice

Embedded within a rights-based philosophy, the education of students with disabilities has gradually focused more on providing equal education opportunities, which has led in many instances to increased inclusive practices in regular classes. Regular schools, which have conventionally catered for the needs of children within a "normal" intellectual range, aim to include all children within their local community, regardless of special educational need. While this has occurred mainly to date in Western countries, a similar trend is now starting to transpire in many of the Asian jurisdictions (Forlin, 2007a; Rose, 2007).

Gradually, the education of children with disabilities, in many although not all areas, has been accepted as a government responsibility. In addition to special schools, most of the Asia-Pacific region is starting to implement a series of more inclusive programs and these are offered in an increasing number of mainstream schools. These can take the form of resource or smaller sized special focus classes, school-based intervention or remedial programs, peripatetic teaching services, and consultant services, plus related services such as education psychology, audiology and speech therapy (Poon-McBrayer and Lian, 2002).

In the West, where countries have been involved in this paradigm shift for some time, legislation has been enacted that mandates for schools to become more inclusive and to ensure that they provide appropriately for the needs of all children. Such legislation not only aims to ensure fairness of access but also provides direction to schools on responsibilities towards their students, while additionally supporting the rights of parents.

Although as yet legally formalized mandates specifically focused on inclusion do not exist in the Asia-Pacific region, most countries have started to develop policy that reflects the statements in international documents such as the highly significant Salamanca Statement (UNESCO, 1994). In addition, with the exception of Malaysia in 2007, most regions have enacted or are in the process of enacting either laws or acts that incorporate some form of disability discrimination (see Forlin, 2007b for a detailed overview of legislation in the Asia region). By utilizing a disability rights perspective, support for inclusion in law and policy is thus being provided.

Where legislation exists, for example the *Disability Discrimination Ordinance* (Equal Opportunities Commission, 2007) in Hong Kong, the *Law of the People's Republic of China on the Protection of Persons with Disabilities* (National People's Congress, 1986) and the *Regulations on Education for Persons with Disabilities* (Chinese State Council, 1994), together with corresponding rules and regulations (Department For Education and Employment, 2001), regular schools have been directed to accept students with disabilities wherever possible except where there are severe difficulties that cannot be addressed. The degree to which this is implemented, nevertheless, varies greatly because of the many other barriers faced in providing education to children where class sizes are still extremely high and trained teachers difficult to appoint. In many of the Asia-Pacific regions the goal of achieving universal primary education for all is clearly challenging (UNESCO, 2005a, 2005b). In many instances, however, it is the lack of specific legal protection that creates one of the major barriers to providing equal education opportunities for all students. To overcome the difficulties faced when trying to facilitate equality of access by those with disabilities, a broader perspective that goes beyond the school is needed. As Forlin (2006) suggests, this requires:

> a concerted effort at all levels of society and must be acknowledged by the provision of appropriate fiscal spending to enable the desired outcomes to be achieved. Regardless of financial support it is still critical to recognize that this will only be effective if people believe in the value and merit of incorporating diversity in all schools and are prepared to commit to enabling this to happen.
>
> (Forlin, 2006, p. 265)

The Confucian approach to education

Another major factor influencing special education reform in Asia is the Confucian philosophy that has dominated societal decisions over the years. The philosophical underpinning regarding people with disabilities is, according to Confucius, that they should be cared for with tolerance and acceptance (Pang and Richey, 2006). In the early Confucian writings in the Book of Rites (*Liji*) there were many references to people with special needs that related to how they should be treated, for example "People should respect others' parents and treat others' children like their own: All those who are bachelors, widows, orphans, single, handicapped and sick should be supported" (Piao, 1992, p. 35). Education was considered the key to societal change and everyone was deemed to be educable (Pang and Richey, 2006). According to Piao (1991), the support for people with disabilities and the expectation that they should be treated in an honorable way was enacted at least a thousand years before similar human rights perspectives were initiated in the West.

Even though the Confucian philosophy has traditionally advocated an empathetic view towards those with special needs, the movement towards enacting an inclusive educational philosophy has been relatively slow to be adopted in the region (Forlin, 2007a). The emphasis on an inclusive education system is, however, noticeably starting to gain increased momentum as the Asia-Pacific region follows the international trend to embrace the ideology of greater inclusivity. The focus is also no longer on those students who exhibit a specific disability. Inclusion seeks to address the needs of all students who may have difficulty in accessing the mainstream curriculum and attempts to do this within a whole school approach to diversity (Forlin, 2005). This has led in the Asia-Pacific region to an emphasis on an *Education for All* model. According to UNESCO (2005b), this involves:

> the need for education systems to be equitable, inclusive and relevant to local circumstances. Where the access to or the process of education is characterized by gender inequality, or by discrimination against particular groups on ethnic or cultural grounds, the rights of individuals and groups are ignored. Thus, education systems that lack a strong, clear respect for human rights cannot be said to be of high quality. By the same token, any shift towards equity is an improvement in quality.
>
> (UNESCO, 2005b, p. 124)

The coordination of responses towards the achievement of the goals of *Education for All* in the Asia-Pacific region is spearheaded by the Asia and Pacific Regional Bureau for Education (UNESCO, Bangkok). This is supported by the *Asia Education for All* website (http://www.unescobkk.org), which provides data and resources from across the region to aid in research, policy making and the implementation of education programming towards the attainment of quality education for all.

While Special Administrative Regions (SARs) such as Hong Kong and Macau share a Chinese cultural heritage with greater China, their education systems have developed from a completely different perspective (Maosen *et al.*, 2004). Special education reform towards a more inclusive approach has taken many different shapes across the region and requires change at a number of levels. The newly developing disability discrimination legislation, for example, offers a blueprint for ensuring that people with disabilities are able to access equal opportunities across a range of domains. By itself, however, it does not ensure an inclusive education system. Special education reform also requires consideration of policy development, funding mechanisms, resource allocation, system-wide directives, support and most critically, appropriate teacher education. It similarly requires positive people with a disability. Whilst being able to reflect on international changes in special education towards more inclusive education systems, it is critical for the Asia-Pacific region to review these in light of their very different cultural needs and societal expectations.

International reforms in teacher education

A major issue in the Asia-Pacific region continues to be the preparation of teachers for this changing form of special education. In much of the region teachers have limited qualifications and in some systems no formal teacher training at all. Most systems are working towards embedding the preparation of teachers for more inclusive teaching within courses that aim to give them at least a basic introduction to catering for difference (Forlin, 2007a). In order to do this, consideration must be given to the conflicting traditional and progressive approaches to teaching in order to draw from them a new direction that will prepare teachers for the major paradigm shift encountered by implementing an inclusive education philosophy. At the same time, teacher preparation must also address the needs of teachers who continue to work in special schools, especially as their role tends to be moving towards providing greater support for mainstream schools (Forlin, 2007a). Although such changes to special education are being introduced, they are still in their infancy. In many places (such as Hong Kong) recent research has found that teachers believe that they still have had insufficient training for implementing inclusive education (Lian, 2004a) and that they demonstrate a hierarchy of preference in relation to the inclusion of students with different types of special education need (Pearson *et al.*, 2003). Although this phenomenon is not unique to the Asia-Pacific region it does propose specific challenges due to the highly structured mainstream education system.

The traditional perspective on teacher preparation involves a focus on learning content and the transference of knowledge; a progressive perspective needs to be aimed at guiding the development of the whole child who is encouraged to create their own meaning of the world around them. The traditional approach of transmitting knowledge has worked well if classes are homogenous and students are educated using a formal didactic structure, as tends to be found in the Asia-Pacific region. The trend in recent years, however, has been to move towards more Western child-focused approaches such as social constructivism. Systems that have taken this direction have found it much easier to embrace an inclusive approach as constructivist values fit well with the developmental learning philosophy. It is in areas, such as the Asia-Pacific region, where they try to establish inclusive classes while retaining traditional expository instructional teaching approaches that problems arise.

In teacher education, the progressive education philosophy has tended to move away from the importance of promoting content knowledge, which has previously dominated the field, towards a more constructivist approach. According to Null and Ravitch (2006), however, this has not necessarily achieved the appropriate outcomes. This is particularly pertinent in the Asia-Pacific region, where different cultural beliefs and religions are very firmly embedded, and where moves away from segregated special education towards inclusive schools are often incongruent with these tightly held values.

Acknowledging that good teaching is a craft that will improve with practice favors the idea of teachers having students in their classes for whom they consider they are not trained, so that they will learn the techniques by trial and error. Indeed, in situations where this has occurred, such as the remote regions in Australia, teachers have reported the attainment of enhanced skills and practices as a result of needing to accommodate students with very diverse needs (Forlin, 2006). Teachers also require updated access to local support through sites such as the *Federation in Community Support* (FICS) website (http://www2.ied.edu.hk/fpece/fics/), which acts as a central hub to locate support services and programs for students with a wide range of diverse and special learning needs in Hong Kong.

Effective special and inclusive practices

Special education reform across the Asia-Pacific region will inevitably result in key changes to the direction of special education and the expectations and roles for leaders and teachers in both special and mainstream schools. Effective special and inclusive practices will depend upon the combination of these two key groups in establishing, supporting, and maintaining progress. While effective practices cannot be implemented without the instruction of the governments and education systems that provide appropriate policy directions and support, implementation will not be effective without the total commitment of school leaders and teachers from both special and regular education systems who will be required to implement the change. The inclusive mainstream leader and teacher of the future will need to cater for increasingly diverse student populations, which will require new pedagogical approaches. The special education leader and teacher will be required to have not only expert knowledge about the needs of students with disabilities, but will increasingly be called upon to use that knowledge to work collaboratively with mainstream schools to support teachers in accommodating children with higher support needs in their classes. The role of the school leader will become even more important, as according to Beattie

(2002), "In today's schools, we need holistic leaders whose purpose [is] to create [the] structures and framework for collaborative meaning-making and shared vision-building" (p. 219).

Whole school approaches

As indicated by To (cited in Lian, 2004b, p. 66): "Inclusion is not simply placing children with special learning needs into mainstream schools. It is about changing schools for them to be more responsive to the needs of all children." In the Asia-Pacific region such as in Hong Kong they are supporting this approach by adopting a number of initiatives to further the development of special and inclusive education. The establishment of *Resource Schools on Whole School Approach* and *Special Schools cum Resource Centers* are initiatives intended to provide sustainable systems that further and strengthen teachers' skills in addressing the needs of all students.

The focus to date of school reform in the Asia-Pacific region to enable the development of more inclusive schools has been on building a culture and climate of acceptance, setting inclusion policy, and implementing inclusive education, which is closely connected with suggestions proposed by international writers (e.g. Forlin, 2007b). There still appears, however, to be resistance to the inclusive education movement in the Asia-Pacific region. To further the process towards more inclusive school communities, greater consideration needs to be given to the development of appropriate support mechanisms to ensure more positive outcomes.

Strategies to support teachers

In the Asia-Pacific region, international trends towards different ways of supporting students with disabilities have started to be considered seriously by various governments. As these jurisdictions move to promote more inclusive education systems, it is necessary to consider how effective classroom support for these students and other marginalized groups can be developed within existing resources (Forlin, 2007b). The development of appropriate policy taking into account cultural and socio-economic factors to ensure equitable support that can be accessed by all schools must carefully consider this issue. Within the region, issues of class size and traditions of didactic teaching and education priorities driven by academic attainment goals must be measured carefully when attempting to implement different support models.

The development of suitable models of support can be a significant contributory factor in the successful teaching of students with disabilities (Forlin, 2007b; Rose, 2007). A range of models of support, including the use of teaching assistants, mentoring and peer tutoring, and differentiated activity or innovative methods of teaching, have been employed within European contexts and are beginning to be explored in some of the Asian systems. For example, the use of teaching assistants is common in special schools throughout Asia but rarely employed in mainstream schools. Effective inclusive schools will need to adopt a range of support models that recognize student diversity and respond to the needs of teachers. Policies developed in this area will need to recognize cultural issues that will determine which models have greatest applicability in a range of contexts. They will also require consideration of the emerging links between special and mainstream schools. Models from other countries suggest that the development of relationships between special and mainstream schools can be positive in both influencing understanding of student needs and encouraging support mechanisms that assist in the development of inclusion (Groom, 2006). As it would seem most likely that education systems across many of the Asian regions will, in the near future at least, be retaining a continuum of placement options that include fairly substantial numbers of special schools, then opportunities for establishing support links between them and mainstream schools would seem an important way forward.

Conclusion

The evolutional changes in the way students with disabilities are educated have become key factors influencing recent paradigm shifts. Over the years schools in the Asia-Pacific region have developed a competitive education ethos that places academic achievement as the most sought after outcome. Within such a philosophy, special schools have flourished in order to accommodate students who are unable to achieve these academic standards. Initially, these special schools played a major role in enabling students with disabilities to attend school, which had hitherto been denied them.

In more recent years, however, the role of the special school has been challenged by those who believe that this does not provide equal education opportunities for all students. Indeed, some research has reported that students with profound and multiple disabilities are not being catered for appropriately even in special schools because of a lack of understanding about their needs, which stems from a lack of training opportunities and appropriate resources (Simmons and Bayliss, 2007). It is suggested that the wealth of opportunities for adult and peer interaction in inclusive classrooms may give greater support to these students.

Inclusive education as a catalyst for special education reform is a high priority on the agenda of Asia-Pacific governments. Alongside this, the issue of teacher preparation and the need to upskill current teachers has also received much attention. While there would seem little doubt that the region will continue to retain a continuum of placement options, the role of special and mainstream schools will be challenged as governments endeavor to initiate a new dimension to schooling for students with disabilities. Reform for mainstream schooling along the lines of more inclusive practice will inevitably engender parallel forms of reform for special schools, who, with potentially dwindling numbers of students, will need to look outside their traditional domains in order to remain viable. The new era of special education is likely to see a much greater role for special education teachers in supporting and indeed working alongside their mainstream colleagues to cater for the needs of students with disabilities and other special needs, particularly as they make the transition from segregated to mainstream schools.

It would seem that if a more inclusive approach to special education is to work in the Asia-Pacific region, there needs to be a much stronger alignment between special and regular schools, with a genuine collaborative approach being implemented to support all students. Concomitant with this, regular schools will need to reconsider their assessment procedures and seek out alternative modes for recording performance other than by an examination-driven curriculum. Special education is not a physical place; neither is it a curriculum that can only be disseminated by trained specialists. Special education is the education of students with disabilities, wherever they choose to attend school. In the Asia-Pacific region, one of the great strengths is the number of teachers who have worked with students with disabilities, albeit in segregated facilities, for many years.

The new era of special education in this region should aim to capitalize on the knowledge of these teachers by involving them in working closely with teachers in mainstream schools, working alongside education training institutions to provide all teachers with the skills and knowledge to support students with diverse learning needs, and in supporting the transition of students from segregated to more inclusive settings. Such genuine and positive collaborations between special and mainstream schools and training institutions will auger well for the expected special education reform that lingers on the horizon across the Asia-Pacific region.

References

Beattie, M. (2002) "Educational leadership: Modeling, mentoring, making and re–making a learning community", *European Journal of Teacher Education*, 25(2/3): 199–221.

Chinese State Council (1994) *Regulations on Education for Persons with Disabilities*, Beijing, China: Legal System Publisher.

Department For Education and Employment (2001) *Special Educational Needs Code of Practice*, London: DFEE.

Equal Opportunities Commission (2007) *Disability Discrimination Ordinance*. Online. Available; http://www.eoc.org.hk/EOC/GraphicsFolder/ddo.aspx (accessed 8 October 2007).

Forlin, C. (2005) "Implementing an outcomes-focused approach to learning: Implications for inclusive education", *Center for Advancement of Special Education*, 1(2): 3–6.

Forlin, C. (2006) "Inclusive education in Australia ten years after Salamanca", *European Journal of Psychology of Education*, XXI(3): 265–77.

Forlin, C. (2007a) "A collaborative, collegial and more cohesive approach to supporting educational reform for inclusion in Hong Kong", *Asia Pacific Education Review*, 8(2): 1–11.

Forlin, C. (2007b) "Classroom diversity: Towards a whole school approach", in S. N. Phillipson (ed.), *Learning Diversity in the Chinese Classroom: Contexts and Practice for Students with Special Needs*, Aberdeen, Hong Kong: Hong Kong University Press, pp. 95–123.

Groom, B. (2006) "*Enabling inclusion for pupils with social emotional and behavioral difficulties: The role of teaching assistants*", *Proceedings of the Inclusive and Supportive Education Congress*, University of Strathclyde, Scotland 1–4 August.

Lian, M-G. J. (2004a) "Curriculum and assessment adaptations for students with mild to severe and multiple disabilities in Hong Kong", *Asia-Pacific Journal of Inclusive Education*, 1(1): 123–42.

Lian, M-G. J. (2004b) "Inclusive education: Theory and practice", *Hong Kong Special Education Forum*, 7(1): 57–74.

Maosen, L., Taylor, M. J. and Shaogang, Y. (2004) "Moral education in Chinese societies: Changes and challenges", *Journal of Moral Education*, 33(4): 405–28.

National People's Congress (1986) *Compulsory Education Law of the People's Republic of China*, Beijing, China: Law Publishers.

Null, J. W. and Ravitch, D. (eds) (2006) *Forgotten Heroes of American Education: The Great Tradition of Teaching Teachers*, Greenwich, CT: Information Age.

Pang, Y. and Richey, D. (2006) "The development of special education in China", *International Journal of Special Education*, 21(1): 77–86.

Pearson, V., Lo, E., Chui, E. and Wong, D. (2003) "A heart to learn and care? Teachers' responses toward special needs children in Hong Kong", *Disability & Society*, 18(4): 489–508.

Piao, Y. (1991) *Teshu jiaoyu gailun* [*Introduction to Special Education*], Beijing, China: Huaxia Press.

Piao, Y. (1992) *Teshu jiaoyu gailun* [*Introduction to Special Education*], Beijing, China: Huaxia Press.

Poon-McBrayer K. and Lian, M-G. J. (2002) *Special Needs Education: Children with Exceptionalities*, Hong Kong: The Chinese University Press.

Rose, R. (2007) "Curriculum considerations in meeting special educational needs", in L. Florian (ed.), *The International Handbook of Special Education*, London: Sage, pp. 295–306.

Simmons, B. and Bayliss, P. (2007) "The role of special schools for children with profound and multiple learning difficulties: Is segregation always best?", *British Journal of Special Education*, 34(1): 19–24.

United Nations Educational, Scientific and Cultural Organization (1990) *World Declaration on Education for All and Framework for Action to Meet Basic Learning Needs* (Jomtien Declaration), New York.

United Nations Educational, Scientific and Cultural Organization (1994) *The Salamanca Statement and Framework for Action on Special Needs Education*, Salamanca, Spain.

United Nations Educational, Scientific and Cultural Organization (2005a) *Education For All.* Online. Available at: http://www.unesco.org/education/efa/ (accessed 21 June 2006).

United Nations Educational, Scientific and Cultural Organization (2005b) *Education for All Global Monitoring Report 2005, The Quality Imperative*, Paris.

2 Education reforms in special education

Wu-Tien Wu, Adrian Ashman and Yong-Wook Kim

Chapter objectives

- To identify the education reforms that have affected the learning outcomes of students with disabilities.
- To discuss the origin of inclusive education.
- To consider practices in Taiwan, Australia, and Korea.
- To review the positive aspects of adopting Western ideas into the Asia-Pacific region.

Focus questions

1 What is the origin of inclusive education?
2 What are the developments for inclusive education in Taiwan, Australia, and Korea?
3 Is the Western style of inclusive education valid for the Asia-Pacific region?

Introduction

Education reform has a significant impact on policies, strategies, and teaching practices in most countries, with the provision of equal education opportunities for all students becoming one of the hottest topics. The most critical impact of education reforms on special education is the overwhelming acceptance of inclusive education policies and practices, together with increased accountability for students' learning outcomes. These changes have brought great challenges to administrators, teachers, and parents.

In this chapter we sketch a number of education reforms that have affected the learning outcomes of students with disabilities in selected areas within the Asia-Pacific region. This chapter is not intended to be a definitive statement about education reform or education histories in the selected countries but a mechanism to comment about ways in which systematic reform and teacher education would support equitable opportunities and resource allocation. The chapter outlines briefly the origin of inclusive education and its development in three countries. It concludes by questioning the validity of the Western style of inclusive education for the Asia-Pacific region and argues that policies and practices that have a specific cultural, economic, and political history to other countries cannot be transferred to the Asia-Pacific region without carefully considering the cultural similarities and differences that will necessitate the adaptation of social justice ideals.

Education reform from special to inclusive education

It is easy to become culturally myopic when considering the needs of students in our respective countries, societies, and cultures. Indeed, in education there is an imperative to recognize cultural influences and to be as inclusive of these as possible, while at the same time providing the acculturation and socialization that instills the values and standards of society. It is, therefore, socio-culturally inconsistent to take education policies and practices from one country or culture and apply them to another without considering the extent to which those policies and practices might align with local cultural imperatives.

To a large extent, inclusive education policies and practices have been adopted by education systems in many countries, including those in the Asia-Pacific region, without much consideration being given to their appropriateness to the society and culture from which, and to which, they are being applied. Inclusive education is being applied almost exclusively from the origin location, the United States where the movement towards including students with diverse learning abilities began in 1965 with *The Elementary and Secondary Education Act of 1965* (PL 89-10), not with *The Education for All Handicapped Children Act of 1975* (PL 94-142), which is more commonly cited and more specific. In effect, development in the United States in respect of inclusive education has a history of more than 40 years and has evolved as education reform in general. Both the *Individuals with Disabilities Education Act (IDEA) of 1990*, and the *No Child Left Behind Act (NCLBA) of 2002*, represent an end point of refinement in education policy that has seen the introduction of practices referred to as mainstreaming, integration, and eventually, inclusion.

The movement from segregated education settings for students with special learning needs in the Asia-Pacific regions has taken its lead largely from initiatives begun in the United States. This has come about largely because of the movement of ideas transported by Asian academics and education policy-makers to their own countries in the 1980s. The speed that was characteristic of early North American developments has only limited parallels in the Asia-Pacific area, largely because of significant cultural differences that have maintained two education systems, regular and special education; however, the pace appears now to be accelerating.

The philosophy of inclusive education embodies the notion that student can learn together and learn to live together (Council for Exceptional Children, 1998, 2005). The principle of inclusive education was adopted at the World Conference on Special Needs Education held at Salamanca (United Nations Educational, Scientific and Cultural Organization, 1994) and has been further supported by the UN Standard Rules on the Equalization of Opportunities for Persons with Disabilities, proclaiming participation and equality for all and, therefore, endorsed by UNESCO (2004).

Inclusive education means much more than all students attending a school regardless of their strengths or weaknesses, and becoming part of the school community. It has often been seen as the placement and education of students with disabilities in general education classrooms with students of the same ages who do not have disabilities. Inclusion is thought to engender feelings of belonging among students, teachers, and support staff and the integration of students at all times regardless of the nature or severity of disability. More accurately, inclusion refers to the acceptance of students who experience severe learning difficulties in environments that are close to those that the majority of school-aged students experience, and whose participation in these environments leads to learning and skill development appropriate to their age and intellectual capabilities.

Accountability in special education following the most recent reforms would be related to performance-standard-based curriculum and instructional design, one achievement measure and one school cost system, high quality teacher preparation, and the empowerment of parents. It would move schooling from two systems to one with the purpose of closing the gap between the students with disabilities and their peers and encouraging every child to learn to his or her potential.

In 1997, the Department of Education and Employment in the United Kingdom published a report entitled *Excellence for All Children: Meeting Special Educational Needs*. It stated that every child with a special education need has a right to achieve his or her potential. This report advanced the transition in beliefs from education for all to quality education for all, with the eventual goal of excellence in education (Wu, 1998). This is a great challenge not only to administrators, but also for all educators and parents. Since that time, inclusive education has been the overarching policy for the education of students with special learning needs in the United Kingdom.

Similarly, the government in Hong Kong has also advocated inclusive education practices. Following curriculum reforms in the year 2000, a unified curriculum and assessment framework has been implemented in schools, including those in which there are students with special learning needs. These reforms have posed great challenges to the traditional school-based curricula that have been employed in special schools. It has also had a great impact on the roles of the regular classroom and special education teachers alike, including an increase in the levels of stress reported by teachers (see, e.g. Chan, 1998).

While inclusion is now an established government policy in Hong Kong, there is a need to understand precisely how all stakeholders can operate within a developing education environment. Such environments span the range of inclusive education options from full inclusion to largely segregated settings. It appears that Hong Kong special education teachers face similar pressures and demands when attempting to meet imposed performance standards and dealing with the issue of accountability as their colleagues elsewhere in the world. These same pressures are being felt in other places in the Asia-Pacific region.

Education reform in Taiwan

A national conference on education for students with disabilities resulted in a major statement by the Ministry of Education, Republic of China (ROC) relating to changes in policies and practices in Taiwan. Following that, a report by the Education Reform Committee of the Executive Yuan, ROC (1996) proposed future directions for special education and the amended *Special Education Act Amended of Republic of China* (2001) set important guidelines for the development of special education services. These events have provided direction for a new configuration of special education in Taiwan.

The *Final Report on Education Reform* (Education Reform Committee of the Executive Yuan, ROC, 1996) established five principles:

1 Release of educational restraints.
2 Focus on individual student outcomes.
3 Maintain flexible educational pathways.
4 Improve the quality of education.
5 Establish lifelong learning opportunities.

The accommodation of students with special education needs was addressed in Principle 2 through 11 recommendations, which included the following points:

- Within five years, provide free and appropriate physical/medical examinations for students from birth to age six years for early identification and intervention.
- Increase the school entrance rate of students with disabilities and establish special education indicators.
- Establish an early intervention system for students of ages three to five years, and within five years, extend free education to preschool students from age three years.
- Establish a community-based education placement system and prohibit the establishment of new large-scale special schools.
- Set up resource classroom programs in each and every school and provide qualified teachers, appropriate curricula, equipment, follow-up, and evaluation.
- Enhance teachers' education and in-service training for those working in special and regular education classes.

There is a common belief that improving special education services in terms of quantity and quality is an important issue in education reform in Taiwan. Implementation of government policies mean that education administrators and legislators are taking the recommendations seriously. Arguably, the most important changes flowed from the amendments to the *Special Education Act of Republic of China* (1984). The amended *Special Education Act* (2001) has many key features. These aimed to strengthen special education administration and accountability, professionalize special education staff, and to use a quota system to buoy special education budgets (at least 3 per cent of the total education budget at the central government level and 5 per cent at the local). The Act also proposed extending free education for preschool children with disabilities, while legalizing parental participation and due process. An individualized education program was to be mandatory for all school-age children with a disability. In addition, free related services were to be provided when needed to ensure the student's educational progress. The provision of flexible schooling, curriculum, and instruction options and the adoption of multidisciplinary approaches in diagnosis and treatment were recommended. The focus was on strengthening the support system and providing barrier-free education environments, while extending inclusive education programs.

The immediate impact of the Act has been an increase in the special education budget that has tripled from the fiscal year 1998 and continues to increase with central government support each year. Another impact has been the promotion of inclusive education programs, although not necessarily full inclusion. In recent years in Taiwan, an increasing number of students with disabilities are being enrolled in regular schools with the result that inclusive education programs have increased in number year by year echoing worldwide inclusive education trends. Statistics released by the Ministry of Education, ROC (2005) indicated that the majority of first to twelfth grade students with disabilities (73,372, or 92.5 per cent) have been educated in regular school settings, with the most common options of placement being regular classes with special education services (i.e. the inclusive classes) and resource room programs (i.e. the integrative type) that account for 34 per cent and 33 per cent, respectively, of students with special education needs. One group presents an anomaly (students with an intellectual disability) because the majority of these students (about 50 per cent) have been placed in self-contained special classes in regular schools.

Since 2000, the Ministry of Education has been engaged in a special project called the "12-Year Educational Placement for Students with Disabilities". Inclusive education was thus formally promoted at the senior high school level. A number of support strategies and services have been developed and implemented. In five years (2000–5), the number of students with special education needs enrolled in senior high schools in Taiwan increased from 6,952 to 16,539 and the number involved in inclusive education programs increased from 1,529 to 8,992. Inclusion also became the major practice of education placement in senior high schools accounting for 55 per cent of the total enrollment of such a population, although fewer than that of elementary and junior high levels (80 per cent and 75 per cent, respectively) (Wu, 2006).

To continue the movement towards effective inclusive education, it will be essential to pursue a number of strategies that were incorporated in the *Special Education Act Amended of Republic of China* (1997, 2001). These are as follows:

- Maintaining the least restrictive environment.
- Downsizing inclusive education classes.

- Providing free transportation services.
- Establishing appropriate services for examination.
- Encouraging the development of professional teams.
- Providing teaching aids and related services.
- Involving parents.
- Following due process.

In addition, two policy statements by the Ministry of Education are critical in supporting inclusive education. They are: (a) to require new teachers to complete a 3-credit hour introductory special education course (54 hours in total); and (b) to incorporate special education related subjects/courses in the in-service education programs.

While there are very positive connotations in education reform in Taiwan that should lead to more effective education provisions for students with disabilities, to date there is no systematic nationwide inclusive education program. There is not even such a term in legislative documentation, although the principle and spirit of inclusion are rooted in the *Special Education Act* and related regulations. The idea of inclusion has been widely acknowledged and accepted by the public, whereas the idea of full inclusion still raises doubt in most people's minds, including special education teachers. Inclusive education is being implemented in an informal way and special education scholars continue to play an important initiating and leading role. Inclusive education is likely, therefore, to be in a developmental phase in Taiwan for some time (Wu, 2005a, 2005b).

Education reform in Australia

In Australia over the past 20 years, there have been numerous changes in the provision of education services and support to students with disabilities. Some of these have paralleled developments that have taken place elsewhere in the world, although Australia has largely responded in an idiosyncratic way because its education systems are state, rather than federal, government responsibilities. This means that there are six state and two territory governments legislating ideals and values, with their respective bureaucracies developing and administering policies and practices. In addition, the Australian Government oversees broad education policies and initiatives and provides support to the various governments through grants and funded programs. As such, it is not easy to discuss Australian education reform as there is not a 100 per cent overlap of legislation, policies, and practices, although all governments have pursued inclusive education as a social justice principle.

In most state and territory education bureaucracies the term "special education" has largely disappeared from official documents. The transition to inclusive education principles and practices also led to the disappearance of special education support units and directorates within the responsible government departments. The concept of inclusion, that is, providing relevant and appropriate learning opportunities in regular classes and regular schools, is a fundamental administrative policy. It is generally accepted as the active participation of students in ways that are consistent with their abilities, talents, skills, and the educational demands of the curriculum. Although most forms of service provision for students with disabilities have remained, generally along the lines of Deno's (1970) cascade model, there have been changes in the proportion of students served in special schools, in special classes, and in regular classes. Great variability exists, however, across education systems, sectors, and geographic locations.

Determining what has changed across Australia over the past few years in response to general education reform is difficult. Certainly, there is an emphasis on social justice and common references to the various state anti-discrimination laws. Visiting any education system website, however, will not produce information about the types of reform that might have affected the provision of services to students with disabilities. You will find policy statements along the line of the two shown below, the first from the Queensland Department of Education and the Arts and the second from the New South Wales Department of Education and Training. You will note that even the names (and hence, responsibilities) of the two departments are different.

Education Queensland:

1 Responds optimistically and constructively to the needs of educationally disadvantaged/marginalized students.
2 Uses diversity as a rich resource for building a connected and intellectually challenging curriculum in the classroom.
3 Ensures that students, teachers and community members from diverse groups feel safe and free from discrimination, bias and harassment.
4 Respects student voice and ensures that all students learn *through* democratic processes.
5 Promotes locally negotiated responses to student, family and community needs through effective community engagement processes and cross-agency collaboration.
6 Ensures that all Education Queensland policies and initiatives recognize the centrality of inclusive education practices to quality education.

(Department of Education, Training and the Arts, 2005)

Similarly, for New South Wales:

1.1 The NSW Department of Education and Training will assist people with disabilities to gain the knowledge, skills and understanding they need to successfully participate as citizens by working with its staff and students to achieve the following goals:

1.1.1 Students, staff and customers with disabilities will be provided with the same opportunities as other people to take advantage of the range of education, training and employment opportunities provided by the Department.

1.1.2 The Department will report on its progress in developing and implementing policies and practices to improve access, participation and outcomes for people with disabilities.

1.1.3 The Department will strengthen strategic alliances and have a coordinated approach to the delivery of services for people with disabilities.

(NSW Department of Education and Training, 2006)

How such policies are implemented in the field will depend upon systemic, regional, and local personnel and financial resources.

What has occurred over the past two or three decades can be encapsulated along the following lines. The transition from a two-tiered system of education (i.e. regular, special) that existed into the 1970s provided promise for more effective coordination and a greater number of services available to students with disabilities and their parents/providers. Many idealists held hopes that special schools and even separate special education classes would close with their students making the transfer to regular classes. Certainly, the number of support services have expanded for students in the birth to preschool years and beyond the compulsory education age, and curricula have expanded to include less academic elective subjects. Parents and caregivers were also accepted as partners in the education process. Family-centered services became common for infants and toddlers with disabilities, and for students with exceptional talents. In addition, parent advocacy and support groups grew strongly and constituted an important voice in promoting integration (i.e. bringing students with disabilities into regular classes and schools).

However, the years have not witnessed a decline in the number or importance of special schools. Indeed, it would appear that special schools are becoming larger and more expensive to run than they were in the past. In Queensland, for example, only 35 per cent of special schools have enrollments less than 60 students. The number of special classes in regular schools did fall nationally as a result of the introduction of inclusive education policies but these too would now seem to be stable in number, largely providing support to students with physical and sensory impairments.

It appears as though there is a developing perception among teachers and other education professionals that there is no persuasive evidence to support the closure of special schools. In what was, arguably, the most balanced Australian view of the advantages and disadvantages of inclusion versus segregation for students with disabilities, Jenkinson (1997) put the case that the possibility of gains from the inclusion of students with very high support needs in regular classes would be significantly outweighed by the disadvantages to the students concerned and would be detrimental to other class members. Moreover, providing the level of support required in terms of personnel, or the provision of facilities to ensure the hygiene and safety of the included student would be beyond reasonable expectations. In a recent study by one of the authors and colleagues (Ashman *et al.*, 2002), the overwhelming majority of informants during the community consultation process agreed with this proposition. They expressed the view that inclusion is not an appropriate option for *all* students because of the student's vulnerability in terms of medical condition, or the prospect of non-acceptance by peers in a regular school setting.

While full inclusion of students with suitable support has remained a national education goal and ideal in Australia, many teachers and other education practitioners have questioned the success of inclusive education at the level of the regular classroom. There appears to be little compelling evidence that inclusive education practices provide enduring learning outcomes in academic areas, although there is a body of literature that has supported social benefits to the included students and their normally achieving peers in the same classes (see e.g. Ashman, 2003). Indeed, the changes and the acceptance of inclusive policies and practices have not been without their costs. It has not only brought some satisfaction but also frustration to students, parents or advocates, and teachers because of the demands that inclusion places upon public and private education systems.

Certainly, each government authority and independent education system continues to work towards the provision of realistic education options for students with disabilities. Australia, though, does not have a national law akin to the *IDEA* (1990) or the *NCLBA* (2002) as in the United States, or the *Special Education Act* as in Taiwan and Korea. The various Education Acts in each of the Australian states and territories mandates access to education for school- and preschool-age students.

In the past, and present, the provision of an appropriate educational response to students with disabilities has been achieved through professional responsibility and commitment, rather than through legislation. While it has not been perfect, what happens in Australia for students with disabilities appears to be at least as positive, supportive, and responsive as in other countries.

Education reform in Korea

The Korean Constitution establishes a universal principle that everyone has the right to receive appropriate education based on his/her unique education requirements. As Chapter 31, Section 1 of the Law states, "All citizens have equal rights to education according to their capabilities." This means that the Korean educational system will provide proper education for every individual at each stage of his or her life. It also implies that everyone, whether having a disability or not, has the right to receive an education that he/she desires.

To meet this end, Korean educators and administrators are actively implementing policies, including the revision of related laws and regulations, the enhancement of inclusive education, and the assignment of special education assistants to improve students' educational achievement and to resolve discriminatory elements that may affect students with disabilities. In fact, various methods of support are being promoted to secure the right of learning by students with disabilities and to fortify teachers' responsibilities in inclusive education settings. In Korea, education reform is pressing forward to improve special education environments because it derives from current social/philosophical beliefs that stress the importance of rights, equality, and self-determination of the individual, and emphasize educational obligation.

Since the first special class was opened in the Daegu Chil Sung School in 1971, a growing number of students with disabilities have received special support across Korea. In 2006, for example, 32,506 students with special needs were receiving education in 5,204 special classes placed in kindergarten to Year 12 programs throughout the country. There were also 6,741 students with disabilities who received general education in fully inclusive settings. This means that about 63 per cent of 62,538 students with disabilities were receiving education in general education settings. Every year, more students are expected to participate in inclusive classrooms. This shows that the interest in, and demand for, special education is expanding throughout society in general. A number of support plans have been developed and implemented to support an improvement in the quality of inclusive education, including the following:

1 To foster the qualification and competence of inclusive classroom teachers, to expand in-service opportunities for general teachers to carry out inclusive education and to increase awareness and knowledge about disabilities. Many inclusive classroom teachers anticipate in-service programs to help them understand students with disabilities and inclusive education practices. However, time restriction and a lack of training organizations result in only 20 per cent of current inclusive classroom teachers having either received in-service training or special education teacher certification. To help teachers receive the necessary training without restriction of time and location, a web-based training program has been developed. In 2004, about 1,200 teachers completed the web-based training program on inclusive education through the Korea Institute of Special Education (KISE) and, in 2006, about 600 teachers participated in the program.
2 To guarantee the rights of students with disabilities to learn through collaborative instruction and curriculum modification, provided by both general and special education teachers who share the responsibilities. If the focus has been on physical placement and social interactions of students with disabilities in inclusive environments, in the future it must be on a curriculum process that supports inclusion instead. It is impossible to achieve inclusive education without the students with disabilities being actively participating in activities in the inclusive classroom. Therefore, the KISE works diligently to promote curriculum modification and collaborative instruction that will meet the needs of students with disabilities. The KISE also engages in research in instructional modification, develops materials and distributes them to schools around the country.

The incentive for change in school-based practices for students with disabilities comes from the *Special Education Law of Republic of Korea*, which was enacted in 1977 and underwent a major amendment in 1994. The law has contributed much to changing society's perceptions, prohibiting discrimination against students with disabilities, and promoting inclusive and individualized education, therapeutic education, and parent involvement. To satisfy demands from people who are connected to students with disabilities, however, closer attention has been given to special education theories and current trends that stress the dignity and diversity of individuals. The newly revised Law (2007) stresses the importance of fully inclusive education, and focuses on: (a) strengthening responsibilities of the federal government and local self-governing organizations and diversifying special education service delivery systems, including circuit instruction, hospital school, and after school programs; (b) stressing early special education programs for infants and toddlers, higher education, and continuing education, and developing a free appropriate special education service delivery system; and (c) reducing the number of children per class in order to enhance quality of education for students with disabilities.

The success in achieving these goals will depend on teachers' capabilities and competence. Teachers' attitudes and perceptions towards students with disabilities may also affect the social and psychological environment of classrooms. This means that it will be the determining factor for conduct and demeanor of all students in the classroom towards their peers with disabilities. Therefore, colleges providing preservice and in-service education training programs must promote quality in special education and inclusive education and offer classes that deal with these topics. Many tertiary institutions offer classes that promote understanding of special education and inclusive education as electives, and more of these institutions are listing these classes as compulsory to meet the requirements of local schools currently implementing inclusive education.

While these initiatives are very positive and have led to considerable progress at a national level in supporting special education, there is still much to be achieved in Korea. New laws, regulations, and policies related to students with disabilities are being developed, and existing ones are being amended and supplemented. In addition, there are a few matters that still require change.

First, there is a need to acknowledge the diversity in people's characteristics and accept people with disabilities as they are. There is still a tendency or sentiment to view disability as an individualized pathology or disease. Even more, because of fierce competition in college and university entry examinations, middle school and high school staff feel burdened by students with disabilities, view their characteristics as incompetent, and think that they will hinder general students' education (Kim, 2003). Disability awareness programs at the national level will need to be systematically implemented to improve perceptions, so that people with disabilities and the general public can live harmoniously in one healthy society.

Second, there is a need to provide financial support to meet the education requirements of students with disabilities. Until recently in Korea, financial support for special education was provided as "leftovers" from the educational budget after all other allocations were made. To move freely on a school campus, support facilities are required to resolve basic physiological needs, and support services for inclusive education, including easy access to information and assistive technologies, are basic necessities needed to provide equal education opportunities. It is important to view financial support for students with disabilities from a human rights perspective instead of that of investments and returns.

Third, there is a need to restructure schools so that they can provide environments where general students and students with disabilities can coexist. In many ways, there is no substantive difference between the education requirements of students with disabilities and other students. Students with disabilities, regular students and teachers, and special education teachers must be encouraged to accept that they all contribute to the school community. Special education teachers and general teachers must take responsibility for all students.

Up to now, supporting systems, policies, laws and regulations for students with disabilities in Korea have relied mostly on theories and models from other countries. Many of these have not been applicable to Korea's cultural norms and current social trends. Future policies will need to be prioritized taking into consideration the actual life circumstances of people with disabilities within the Korean culture and in accordance with community sentiments. They will need to be implemented successively so that policies and current trends can move forward at the same pace.

Challenges of inclusive education

Mainstreaming brought students with disabilities into general classrooms when it was thought that they did not need tailor-made instruction. It was thus presumed that these students would keep up with their mainstream peers. Integration further recognized that segregation existed and was based on the notion that students with disabilities could learn alongside their peers without disabilities, at least for part of the time. In reality, however, students who were integrated part-time were not truly a part of the class and were often involved in activities very different from those that were engaging the other students in the class. Inclusion implies that general education classes are structured to meet the needs of all students. This is supposed to occur through education strategies developed for a diverse student population and collaboration between educators, so that individualized instruction and supplementary aids and services are provided, as needed, for effective learning (Western Regional Resource Center, 1998).

While inclusive education appears to be a wholly worthwhile ideal for the education of students with disabilities, the reality of success is far less than one might have hoped, or believed, from the rhetoric. The professional literature published during the early years of mainstreaming and integration (i.e. the 1970s and 1980s) gave the impression of wide ranging acceptance. Parents of students with disabilities and some teachers have applauded the opportunities available to students for increased social contact and the potential for improved learning outcomes. Reports of successful integration, however, were often limited to anecdotes, with some writers drawing attention to the limitations in school schedules, timetables, and teaching practices that restricted opportunities for students to take full advantage of regular classroom activities. There was also considerable opposition to mainstreaming. Teachers complained that they were not trained to deal with low-functioning students and that regular classroom practices were unsuitable for students with demanding learning needs (see e.g. Vlachou and Barton, 1994). By the late 1990s, inclusion had become the accepted education model with the associated rhetoric in most Western countries. Nevertheless, special education classes and schools continued to exist.

Over the past two decades a vast amount of professional literature on inclusion has continued to emerge. There are substantial collections relating to the philosophy and values implicit in inclusion. Several writers, for example, have argued that inclusion is a moral imperative that does not require, and cannot wait for, empirical justification (see e.g. Stainback *et al.*, 1996) while others (e.g. Kauffman *et al.*, 1988) have warned against a rush headlong into inclusion because of the lack of support provided by administrators and others responsible for its implementation.

Debate about the education of all students, regardless of their abilities, has continued around the world and is now a major focus in the Asia-Pacific region. Perhaps the best international examples of full inclusion of students with learning difficulties are Italy and some parts of the United States and Canada. These examples show that inclusion *can* be achieved, but it is also evident that there are many ways in which regular classes can be overwhelming and unsatisfactory.

Looking broadly at the literature, there are, however, few studies in which researchers report substantial academic gains by included students and many of these are anecdotal and often emphasize the social aspects of inclusive classrooms (see e.g. Kauffman *et al.*, 1988). Hodges *et al.* (2006), for example, drew attention to the general lack of research on academic outcomes for students with special education needs. While their work specifically targeted mathematics and students with emotional and behavioral disorders, their conclusion reflected the general impression that achievement of included students is of modest interest to researchers. In contrast, there are many reports of positive attitude change towards included students as a result of contact with, and proximity to, good behavior models and also a small number of reports that are less optimistic. Prominent among these are studies involving students with emotional and behavior difficulties who provide significant challenges to classroom harmony. A study by Cook and Semmel (1999) is an excellent example of the difficulties faced by teachers and researchers who aim to improve the classroom social climate. Cook and Semmel (1999) reported a low level of social acceptance of students with learning difficulties among their normally achieving peers. They asked students to identify those with whom they would be willing to work, willing to play, and with whom they would spend time in recreation or leisure out of school as everyday playmates. Peer acceptance scores for students with mild and severe difficulties in each setting were uniformly low; although students with mild disabilities were better accepted in heterogeneous classrooms they remained low as desirable workmates. This outcome is confirmed by several reports in the literature (see e.g. Pavri and Monda-Amaya, 2001).

The comments above must ring alarm bells in Western countries where inclusive education is seen as the educational setting of first choice for students with disabilities, although policy-makers and advocates of inclusion seem not to hear them. It should engender serious reservations in countries where the culture and educational imperatives are vastly different to those in the West, such as in the Asia-Pacific region. It is curious, therefore, that there remains a political imperative for inclusive education when the evidence for its success is as equivocal as it is.

Having said this, inclusion is an important ideal that fulfills community and government obligations to social justice, notably to provide education experiences that meet the needs of all students, individually. As can be seen by the early sections of this chapter, each of the countries mentioned have approached inclusion in somewhat different ways. In Australia, for example, there is no specific legislation that mandates inclusive education as in the United States. It certainly appears as though governments in Taiwan, Korea, and in Hong Kong are edging closer to the United States model than their colleagues and policy-makers in Australia.

The important consideration for education reform internationally is to seek ways of incorporating cultural and community imperatives into education policy and practice. The United States ideal places a huge emphasis on individuality and individual rights, whereby a person's individual rights override those that reflect community values. This appears to be in stark contrast to cultural imperatives in many, if not most, of the Asia-Pacific region, where the sense of family and community is strong.

There is considerable advantage to education reform that offers equality of opportunities regardless of one's physical and intellectual capabilities. Drawing guidance from countries where inclusion is part of the education rhetoric can be of some value but this must not be accepted uncritically as the ideal. The effectiveness of education reform in any country will depend upon the social, cultural, political, and economic environments that will sustain procedures and practices that encourage the consideration and accommodation of individual learning styles and capabilities. These would then need to be translated into teacher training, adapted curricula, and instructional practices that stimulate peer and community acceptance of difference and diversity.

There should be no imperative to strive for full inclusion of students with disabilities. Indeed, a strong argument can be mounted to sustain the view that not every student can, or will, benefit from inclusion in regular education classrooms. Students who display dangerous or aggressive behavior and those with a severe mental health condition may put their safety and that of others at risk if there is not constant monitoring in regular education classes. Similarly, students with life-threatening medical conditions (e.g. severe epilepsy) may also be at risk without regular scrutiny and supervision. This may be difficult to achieve in regular classes where there is one teacher only and the class size is big, as in most of the Asia-Pacific region. It is also questionable whether students with profound intellectual disability or severe multiple disabilities can be provided with the necessary care and attention, and appropriate educational experiences in regular classes.

For these students, special schools and special classes seem to be the most suitable education context. In such a specifically designed setting, services and resources can be concentrated, there is clear staff commitment to providing the best opportunities for students with high support needs, and there is an appropriate staff student ratio that is difficult, if not impossible, to match in regular schools. This does not mean, of course, that these students should be isolated from their non-disabled peers.

Conclusion

There is a common belief that improving special education services in terms of both quantity and quality is the key issue in education reform. It appears that special education in many countries, highly developed countries in particular, has moved beyond the point at which reconsideration might be given to alternatives other than inclusive education. The major goal for education reformers in the Asia-Pacific region will be to tease out the credible policies, processes, and practices that have local cultural connection and which can be adapted to conform to local political and economic agendas.

References

Ashman, A. F. (2003) "Peer mediation and students with diverse learning needs", in R. Gillies and A. F. Ashman (eds), *Cooperative Learning: The Social and Intellectual Outcomes of Learning in Groups,* London: Routledge, pp. 87–102.

Ashman, A., Bayne, B. and Mangan, J. (2002) *Resourcing Methodology, Resourcing Instrument, and Algorithm for Students with Disabilities and Their Schools*, Report submitted to the Inclusive Education Branch, Education Queensland, Brisbane: University of Queensland School of Education.

Chan, D. W. (1998) "Stress, coping strategies and psychological distress among secondary teachers in Hong Kong", *American Educational Research Journal,* 35: 145–63.

Cook, B. and Semmel, M. I. (1999) "Peer acceptance of included students with disabilities as a function of severity of disability and classroom composition", *Journal of Special Education,* 33: 50–61.

Council for Exceptional Children (1998) *IDEA 1997: Let's Make it Work*, Reston, VA.

Council for Exceptional Children (2005) *Philosophy of Inclusive Education*, Reston, VA.

Deno, E. (1970) "Special education as developmental capital", *Exceptional Student,* 37: 229–37.

Department of Education, Training and the Arts (2005) *Inclusive education statement 2005,* Brisbane, Queensland. Online. Available at: http://education.qld.gov.au/studentservices/learning/docs/inclusedstatement2005.pdf (accessed 6 October 2007).

Education Reform Committee of the Executive Yuan, Republic of China (1996) *Final Report on Educational Reform*, Taipei (in Chinese).

Hodges, J., Riccomini, P. J., Buford, R. and Herbst, M. H. (2006) "A review of instructional interventions in mathematics for students with emotional and behavioral disorders", *Behavioral Disorders,* 31: 297–311.

Individuals with Disabilities Education Act (1990) (IDEA, PL 102-119, 1990; IDEA PL 105-17, 1997; IDEA Amendments, 2004) PL 101-476. Online. Available at: http://www.resa.net/sped/parent/the_laws.htm (accessed 8 October 2007).

Jenkinson, J. C. (1997) *Mainstream or Special? Educating Students with Disabilities*, London: Routledge.

Kauffman, J. M., Gerber, M. M. and Semmel, M. I. (1988) "Arguable assumptions underlying the Regular Education Initiative", *Journal of Learning Disabilities*, 21: 6–12.

Kim, Y. W. (2003) "Perception of general teachers and students to included students with disabilities", *Korea Journal of Special Education*, 18: 70–85.

Ministry of Education, Republic of China (2005) *Education Statistics of the Republic of China*, Taipei.

No Child Left Behind Act (2002) PL 107-10. Online. Available at: http://www.ed.gov/policy/elsec/leg/esea02/107-110.pdf (accessed 8 October 2007).

NSW Department of Education and Training (2006) *People with Disabilities – Statement of Commitment*. Online. Available at: https://www.det.nsw.edu.au/policies/general_man/general/spec_ed/PD20050243.shtml (accessed 19 May 2006).

Pavri, S. and Monda-Amaya, L. (2001) "Social support in inclusive schools: Student and teacher perspectives", *Exceptional Student*, 67: 391–411.

Special Education Act Amended of Republic of China (1997, amended 2001) Taipei: Office of the President of Republic of China (in Chinese).

Special Education Act of Republic of China (1984) Taipei: Office of the President of Republic of China (Taiwan) (in Chinese).

Special Education Law of Republic of Korea (1977, 1994) Seoul: Office of the President of Republic of Korea. Online. Available at: http://www.inca.org.uk/2137.html (accessed 8 October 2007).

Stainback, S., Stainback, W. and Ayres, B. (1996) *Schools as Inclusive Communities*, in W. Stainback and S. Stainback (eds) *Controversial Issues Confronting Special Education: Divergent Perspectives*, 2nd edn, Boston: Allyn & Bacon, pp. 31–43.

The Education for All Handicapped Children Act (1975) PL 94-142. Online. Available at: http://www.scn.org/~bk269/94–142.html (accessed 8 October 2007).

The Elementary and Secondary Education Act, USA (1965) PL 89-10. Online. Available at: http://www.kckps.org/disthistory/state_school_history/throckmorton/throckmorton_1945–1967_pt2.htm (accessed 8 October 2007).

UK Department of Education and Employment (1997) *Excellence for All Children: Meeting Special Educational Needs*, London: The Stationery Office.

United Nations Educational, Scientific and Cultural Organization (1994) *The Salamanca Statement and Framework for Action on Special Education Needs*. Online. Available at: http://unesdoc.unesco.org/images/0009/000984/098427eo.pdf (accessed 6 October 2007).

United Nations Educational, Scientific and Cultural Organization (2004) *Inclusive Education*. Online. Available at: http://portal.unesco.org/education/en/ev.php-URL_ID=8229&URL_DO=DO_TOPIC&URL_SECTION=201.html

Vlachou, A. and Barton, L. (1994) "Inclusive education: Teachers and the changing culture of schooling", *British Journal of Special Education*, 21: 105–7.

Western Regional Resource Center, University of Oregon (1998) *Educating Students with Disabilities in General Education Classrooms: A Summary of the Research*, Eugene, OR.

Wu, W. T. (1998) "Educational reform and special education", *Bulletin of Educational Information*, 23: 197–220 (in Chinese).

Wu, W. T. (2005a) *Inclusive Education in Taiwan*, paper presented at the 2005 International Seminar on Inclusive Education in the Asia-Pacific Region. Korea Institute for Special Education, Ansan City, Korea.

Wu, W. T. (2005b) "Review on inclusive education in Taiwan", *Journal of Education Research*, 136: 28–42 (in Chinese).

Wu, W. T. (2006) "Inclusive education as applied to senior high level: The case in Taiwan", paper presented at the 2006 Symposium on Enhacing Inclusive Education in the Asia-Pacific Region, University of Hong Kong, Hong Kong.

3 Collaboration in the era of inclusion

Anuradha Naidu

Chapter objectives

- To highlight the attitudinal shifts that facilitated systemic reform for inclusive education in India.
- To consider the impact of collaboration, alliance-building and stakeholder participation on including people with a disability in education reform.
- To discuss how an authentic inclusive education practice involving a bottom-up process of teacher sensitization, preparation, and reflection was implemented in an Indian context.

Focus questions

1 What are the different perspectives that have determined historically the types of education provisions available for children with a disability in your society?
2 What are the barriers that prevent the successful inclusion of a child with a disability in a mainstream school?
3 How can these barriers be identified and eliminated?
4 What are the provisions under which disability policies will help facilitate inclusive education?

Introduction

Developments in Indian social policy on disability issues in the past decade demonstrate a perspective shift from charity to empowerment. The inclusion of children with disabilities in the mission for "Education for All" follows an amendment to the Indian Constitution in 2001 spearheaded by the disability movement, an alliance of stakeholders comprising persons with a disability, parents, and professionals. Access to schooling is the main focus of this advocacy effort. Stakeholders recognize that new strategies that support bottom-up approaches to education reform must evolve. Special schools are increasingly under pressure to revise their roles and support teacher training, sensitization programs, and the development of assistive technology. India's experiences in the search for inclusive education hold insights for the Asia-Pacific region.

This chapter will reflect on the decade from 1995 to 2006 to highlight the development of leadership and advocacy in the disability movement and the special education sector in India. Both processes have led to creative collaborations of government and civil society organizations. Organizations for people with disabilities and special institutions have shifted perspectives and have influenced the national policy for inclusive education in India. Both processes engage with each other towards a common goal of education reform for inclusion.

India, a land of many cultures

India is a diverse country with many cultures, religions, and languages. India's Constitution, which was formulated and dedicated to the people in 1950 (three years after India's independence from Britain), states that the country is a socialist, secular, democratic republic (*Constitution of India*, 1950). India has a population of 1.028 billion people living in an area of 3.3 million square kilometers in 28 states and six centrally administered territories (*Census of India*, 2001). The Constitution recognizes 22 languages among the hundreds of languages that are spoken; Hindi is the official link language. Six major religions, namely, Hinduism, Islam, Christianity, Buddhism, Sikhism, and Jainism are practiced (*Census of India*, 2001). Additionally, there are several other forms of tribal worship. India is also a geographically diverse country ranging from the coastal plains of the peninsula, the plateaus of central India, smaller mountain ranges, and to the magnificent Himalayas, each supporting local communities with distinct cultures and livelihoods.

The latest statistics available on the literacy levels in India reflect the disparities that one would associate with such diversity. In 2001, the national literacy level was 65.38 per cent. A comparison based on gender shows higher literacy levels for males (75.85 per cent) than for females (54.16 per cent). Comparisons between rural (59.40 per cent) and urban (80.30 per cent) data likewise demonstrate a bias in favor of the latter (*Census of India*, 2001).

Diversity in education

The *National Curriculum Framework* for school education, which guides the education reform process in India, identifies this diversity among the people of India as a contemporary issue that needs to be addressed in the development of curriculum and pedagogy (National Council of Educational Research and Training, 2005). The framework acknowledges that children can become alienated from the education process for linguistic, cultural, and socio-economic reasons. The geographical location of homes in mountainous or remote areas in many instances makes schools inaccessible to children. Poverty is also a variable that pushes children into child labor when in fact they should be in schools. When these factors are not addressed in the central planning process, the disparities of the socio-economic milieu of India are reflected in schools and classrooms by the under-representation of children from disadvantaged communities and social groups. Among the groups identified by the state as disadvantaged and, therefore, needing special focus for their inclusion, are children from the scheduled castes and scheduled tribes (the official terms used to refer to the most socially marginalized communities in India), girl children, working children, migrant children, and children who live on the streets. More recently included in this focus area are children with a disability. The *National Plan of Action* was prepared in response to the Indian Government's ratification of the *Framework of Action for Education For All* at the Dakar Global Conference, 2000 (Ministry of Human Resource Development, 2003). It details the Government of India's plans to address the issue of equity in education alongside universal access, retention, and achievement. Under the Education Ministry's flagship program, known as *Sarva Shiksha Abhiyan* (which aims to provide "Education for All"), special interventions and strategies are planned to ensure the inclusion of girl children, children from socially disadvantaged communities, migrant and working children, and children with disabilities (Ministry of Human Resource Development, 2005a).

With 80 per cent of the Indian population living in rural areas, the barriers to children's inclusion in the educational mainstream could be attributed to inadequate infrastructure, such as the lack of roads, transport, or even toilets for girl children. Domestic duties, such as caring for younger siblings and housework, and even attainment of puberty are often cited as reasons to keep girl children away from schools. Caste-based discrimination in schools, understaffing in schools, and often a curriculum that does not reflect local cultural contexts also alienate children.

Special needs education in India: entrenchment in welfare

The history of special education service provision in India, which goes back to the period of British rule, demonstrates its segregation from the education system from its very genesis. The position paper on the *Education of Children with Special Needs* points out that even as early as the 1880s, Christian missionaries established special schools for the blind and for the deaf. Schools for students with an intellectual disability were similarly set up much later in the mid-twentieth century (National Council of Educational Research and Training, 2006). In contrast to this trend, the integration of children with a disability was recommended throughout the history of education planning in India, first before independence in the *Sergeant Report* in 1944 (National Council of Educational Research and Training, 2006), and later in the *Kothari Committee* in the 1960s (National Council of Educational Research and Training, 2006). Nevertheless, the subject of disability and special education continued to be administered as an issue of welfare. The Welfare Ministry set up segregated services in the form of special employment exchanges, centralized Braille printing presses and scholarships. Further, the state funded initiatives by the non-governmental voluntary sector to provide rehabilitation services, including special education (Hegarty and Alur,

2002). Even as recently as 2001, when the Indian Constitution was amended to guarantee the fundamental right to education for all, the education of children with a disability was perceived as a subject of state welfare. This systemic entrenchment of special education in welfare has resulted in the creation of segregated services that are accessible only to urban communities where these services came to be located. As a consequence, the majority of children with a disability in rural India continue to be excluded from the general as well as the special education provisions. However, casual integration at the primary school level, as distinct from planned and formal initiatives, takes place in India too. In these situations, school teachers have found solutions in their classrooms that address a wide range of diversity. However, there is no formal means to recognize this, except through the work of community-based rehabilitation (CBR) initiatives funded by international donor organizations since the 1990s (Stubbs, 2002).

Special needs in current education policy: conceptual clarity needed

UNESCO (1997) notes that the concept of children with special education needs extends beyond those who may be included in disability categories to cover those who are failing in school for a wide variety of other reasons that are known to be likely to impede a child's optimal progress. In the Indian policy documents, however, the definition of "special needs" varies in different contexts. In some documents, special needs education targets the inclusion of all disadvantaged groups and in others it limits itself to children with a disability. This indicates that conceptual clarity is yet to emerge in policy documents in India as disability moves from a welfare issue with a medical perspective to one of human rights.

For example, in 2000, a National Council of Educational Research and Training (NCERT)–UNESCO regional workshop report on the status of education in India used the term "special needs education" to refer to children of school-going age such as working children, street children, and children who are victims of disaster, social conflict and poverty. The central government's perspective document titled *The National Plan of Action,* however, reflects a narrower focus definition of special needs that limits it to children with a disability. Finally, the most recent of all policy documents, the *National Curriculum Framework* of 2005, states that a student with a disability has an equal right to membership in the same group as all other students. The evolving definitions indicate the contradictions that dialogue and collaboration between the two streams of special and general education will need to resolve. In other parts of the world, the situation has not been dissimilar. Critics of the education reform movement in the North American context clearly argue for a unified system of reform that fully includes all children (Erickson and Thurlow, 1997; as cited in Zatta and Pullin, 2004). A unified system accommodates and supports diverse learners without the unnecessary categorization of students. Researchers have also focused attention on holistic development of schools that are more responsive to the diversity of all learners, rather than a limited focus on a group of students categorized as having special needs or disabilities (Booth and Ainscow, 1998).

Collaboration for national level policy change through self-advocacy

In India, the issues of special needs and disability rights are very closely tied up with each other. In the early 1990s, which was the beginning of the United Nations Economic and Social Commission for Asia and the Pacific (UNESCAP) Decade of the Disabled, the first attempts to develop a cross-disability alliance in India were initiated. Dismayed by the absence of a social policy to ensure equal opportunities for education, employment, and access to basic facilities for India's disabled community (which accounts for 6–7 per cent of the population), a fragmented group, comprising service delivery organizations and disability activists, came together under a non-political banner, known as the Disability Rights Group (DRG). This cross-disability platform, which was strongly influenced by the social model and the human rights approach, began its first campaign with the demand for legislation to protect the rights of people with disabilities as Indian citizens. That initiative influenced a radical shift in the approach to disability and eventually led to the passage of the *Persons with Disabilities (Equal Opportunities, Protection of Rights and Full Participation) Act, 1995.*

Some of the major achievements of this alliance and the networks that have resulted from this process over the past decade are of tremendous significance to the inclusion of persons with a disability in social policy in India. The following are the key outcomes:

- Disability was included as a category of information gathering in the *Census of India* in 2001. This was the first comprehensive attempt at enumeration of people with a disability.
- Employment opportunities have been created in government and private business for people with a disability.
- National and grassroots level advocacy networks, self-help groups of organizations for people with disabilities, parent groups, and Non-Government Organizations (NGOs) have grown in numbers.
- Civil society groups have stepped up advocacy activities to monitor the implementation of the *Persons with Disabilities Act, 1995*, particularly the provisions relating to physical access, employment in the government sector, and more recently inclusive education.
- Children with a disability are now covered under the *Sarva Shiksha Abhiyan* program. This was the outcome of a collaborative advocacy effort by the disability movement in alliance with other social movements and interest groups for the amendment of the Indian Constitution.
- In 2001, the Constitution was amended to include education as a fundamental right.

Together with these outcomes a paradigm shift in the understanding of disability has come to determine a more positive disability culture. Such a culture is beginning to empower people with a disability, celebrate diversity and provide guidelines for the development of inclusive practices in India. People with a disability are among the poorest and most marginalized in India and, therefore, their concerns must be addressed as a development issue and a human rights concern. A positive disability culture must be created, with role models, symbols, and celebrations. In particular, cross-disability alliances have to be strengthened to gain visibility as a social movement.

Collaboration at the grassroots: Building models through action research

In India, NGOs have played a significant role in the delivery of services, including education services for children with a disability (Mukhopadhyay, 2003; Timmons and Alur, 2004). These provisions have been in the form of segregated services, run predominantly on state funding (Hegarty and Alur, 2002), specifically, the central Ministry of Welfare (since renamed as Ministry of Social Justice and Empowerment). There are approximately 3,000 special provisions in the country, serving about 10,000 children. With the increased impact of the social model of disability, the conditions for introspection have been created. First, several NGOs have included persons with a disability on their boards of governance and staff as a step towards inclusion. Second, NGOs working in the area of special education have realized that even after 20 to 25 years of service, their approaches have had little or no impact on their constituency, since nearly 98 per cent of children with a disability are outside the school system (Timmons and Alur, 2004; Ministry of Human Resource Development, 2005a). Third, a growing, articulate lobby of disability activists who have been to special schools have organized themselves either with NGO support or as autonomous groups. These autonomous self-advocacy groups have been critical of the charity focus and the opportunities for inclusion that they lost as a result of segregation in special schools.

Some examples of NGOs that have reworked their strategies towards inclusion are the Spastics Society of India, Bombay (Timmons and Alur, 2004) and the Spastics Society of Northern India, New Delhi. Following a process of stakeholder reflection on their vision and mission, and on staff training, their strategies are orientated to support a paradigm shift towards inclusive education. One effort has been to facilitate reverse inclusion by admitting children without disabilities into special schools. The other is through action research by teachers, which is a process of "identifying effective educational practices and redesigning ways of helping classrooms and schools to become democratic communities of quality learning and teaching" (Burnaford *et al.*, 2001, p. 30). A model of inclusive pedagogy, curriculum differentiations, and assessment strategies for inclusive schools is emerging from these action research experiences; this is guiding the teacher training programs and the technical support offered to mainstream schools.

Collaboration with the government: Implementing policy

Under the *Sarva Shiksha Abhiyan* program, there is increasing evidence of NGO and government collaboration. A review of conference reports of the National Institute of Education Planning and Administration on NGO and government partnerships for inclusive education held in 2003 and 2004 indicates a growing dialogue and the development of models to support inclusion at the district and state levels (Mukhopadhyay, 2003). While the practices cited are not representative of inclusive education in the most progressive sense of the term, nevertheless, these are attempts to either create support services to facilitate inclusion processes in mainstream schools or are a continuum of services that will enable students with a disability access to the mainstream curriculum. The continuum of services that these initiatives have generated also includes home-based programs, pullout programs, and open schooling under the National Institute of Open Schooling. For example, the National Association of the Blind, Delhi, has set up preparatory units, resource centers, a material production centre, and a talking book studio to support the mainstreaming of its students. The Shikshit Yuva Seva Samiti, an NGO involved in village development activities, worked with a state government to sensitize parents, local-level functionaries, and teachers in the community to facilitate enrollment of children with a disability. The Blind People's Association offers courses to train teachers of mainstream schools in collaboration with the Rehabilitation Council of India, a statutory body of the Government of India that regulates courses for rehabilitation professionals (and for special education too). As one of the state directors of the *Sarva Shiksha Abhiyan* pointed out, "Creating special schools is an option but too costly… The idea is to have the neighborhood or village schools provide that special component of education that meets the needs of the disabled children…" (*The Hindu*, 29 June 2005).

Influencing the education system through advocacy

The *Persons with Disabilities Act, 1995*, states that the appropriate governments and the local authorities shall ensure that every child with a disability has access to free education in an appropriate environment till s/he attains the age of 18 and shall endeavor to promote the integration of students with a disability in mainstream schools. Given the lack of awareness of the provisions of the *Persons with Disabilities Act* as well as the issues and problems of people with a disability, however, NGOs and organizations for people with disabilities have collaborated to develop and implement sensitization programs for government functionaries at the national, state and local levels. The focus of these programs has been to not just talk about the legislation, but also to facilitate interactions with positive role models of persons with a disability. Further, in the decade since the promulgation of this Act, redress for a variety of issues has been sought both in the courts as well as with the Office of the Chief Commissioner of Disabilities.

A review of the types of cases relating to the right to education indicates that a majority of them relate to the denial of the litigants' right to avail themselves of the seats reserved in higher education programs. However, one case (Social Jurist v. Union of India and Ors, 2004) related to the formulation of a central education scheme for the provision of accessible transport, buildings and books. Another judgment, passed by the Delhi High Court in 2004, directs the Central Board of Secondary Education to strengthen infrastructure (Pandey *et al.*,

2005). In other words, the concerns of all these arguments have been limited to access to schooling; they do not distinguish between this and access to the curriculum (Naidu, 2005).

The next phase

The case studies cited previously also demonstrate the limitations imposed by the institutional barriers that are entrenched in a medical construction of disability. While the definitions in the perspective documents on education call for the inclusion of all learners of different social categories, children with a disability are eligible for schemes and programs based on medical criteria. For example, the 2001 District Primary Education Program document defines the child with a disability as having one of the following disabilities: visual, hearing, locomotor or intellectual disability. The draft inclusive education scheme of 2003 attempts to address the needs of learners with the following disabilities: visual disability, speech and hearing disability, neuromuscular-skeletal and neurodevelopmental disorders like cerebral palsy, autism and mental retardation, and multiple and learning disability. With the inclusion of learning disabilities and autism, this last list is indicative of the widening definition of need, but the definitions are still medical.

Keeping in mind the systemic entrenchments associated with the administration of special needs education in India, the National Centre for the Promotion of Employment of Disabled People (NCPEDP), an NGO, spearheaded a national campaign in 2004 to demand that the education of people with a disability should be transferred from the Welfare Ministry to the Education Ministry. This came about following the results of a study that revealed that only 0.1 per cent of youth with a disability ever accessed higher education ("Arjun Singh announces...", 2005). The campaign led to a debate in Parliament and the preparation of an *Action Plan for Inclusive Education for Children and Youth with Disabilities* (Ministry of Human Resource Development, 2005b). This plan provides a blueprint for inclusive education of children and youth with a disability from 0 to 21 years, sensitization programs, teacher training, curriculum development, accommodations, and modifications. The other achievement has been the inclusion of people with a disability and the leadership of NGOs in the highest advisory body to the Education Ministry (*The Hindu*, 13 July 2005).

Building alliances with other social movements

In India, there is no doubt that the discourse on special and inclusive education is strongly influenced by both the disability movement and the special school sector and is interpreted to focus on the student with a disability. Regarding the larger issue of "Education for All", the disability movement represented by the cross-disability alliance, the Disability Rights Group, has collaborated with the National Alliance for the Fundamental Right to Education (NAFRE). The two major occasions for collaboration have been for the inclusion of disability in the Constitutional amendment that guarantees the right to education as a fundamental right and the *Right to Education Bill* (Ministry of Human Resource Development, 2005c) that attempts to operationalize the former. But now the time has come to open up the inclusion debate to facilitate a dialogue between the representatives of all social groups, as well as educators both general and special. Unless quality issues of education are addressed, the main subject of inclusion regarding school development and pedagogy that will make education accessible to all will always remain in the background.

A blueprint for inclusive education in India

In the years 2002–7, with the effort to promote inclusion in government schools, there has been a rise in the number of children with moderate to severe disability, including behavioral disorders, autism and deaf blindness, who have enrolled in education services. Parents and advocates of the rights of people with a disability, however, wish to see the development of a continuum of services that will enable all students to benefit educationally. The plan presented below is a blueprint for the development of inclusive education developed by Vidya Sagar, a disability resource centre that entered into a technical partnership with a government municipal corporation to restructure and reorient the municipality's education provision towards inclusion (Naidu *et al.*, 2005). The proposal aimed to create a school climate and culture that would support the inclusion of children in the range of disabilities mentioned above.

Creating a positive school climate and culture through multiple stakeholder collaboration

The plan recommended a consultative process of planning that involved the principal, teachers, special educators, education department staff, school administrative staff, students, parents of children with a disability, people with a disability and community members. This representative sample of stakeholders planned for an audit of the school environment to collectively identify barriers such as architectural, physical, attitudinal and institutional. They used different means such as checklists, discussions and interviews, and access audits. The collaborative process helped identify the strategies to eliminate barriers as well as create readiness in the school community to receive the new students.

Restructuring for responsible inclusion

In the next phase of implementation, a smaller technical team will plan the development of the human, financial, and material resources, keeping the audit results in mind. This team will design training programs to prepare teachers, students, adult volunteers, carers and parents, and develop guidelines for the implementation of inclusive education in a phased manner. Based on an assessment of students' needs, the team will also determine the continuum of services required, placement schedules and transition plans. Channels of communication that will encourage dialogue and facilitate a collaborative school culture may also be considered at this stage. In addition, ways of obtaining financial and other material resources to modify architectural barriers in the school and classroom environment will need to be resolved.

Staff development and training

An initial training of staff, which includes special and general educators, is required to provide teachers with the opportunity to learn through a collaborative process. Teachers need to understand the issues relating to disability from the perspective of conditions and causes, and the ensuing social marginalization. This may be facilitated through technical sessions, interactions with students with a disability and their parents, and through observation. Teacher self-reflection to confront their own negative attitudes will need to remain an ongoing process. The other area of skill development concerns the challenges of handling the inclusive classroom, with the help of strategies such as differentiated instructional designs, collaboration and co-teaching models, and curricular adaptations of content standards. The plan also recommends that teachers take special efforts to involve parents in the inclusion program, particularly in the social inclusion and vocational training aspects.

This is one example of how the bottom-up process of collaboration between stakeholders (persons with a disability, parents, teachers, professionals, and administrators) can facilitate education reform in India. In this case, stakeholders recognized that the question of addressing education quality could be raised through social audits of existing service provisions. As the dialogue gained momentum, all stakeholders realized that technical collaboration would help to prepare the ground for change, enabling a smaller, flexible, grassroots level organization to share its expertise with the larger, bureaucratic, government institution. Bottom-up processes of school development and on-site training generate creative models that provide the needed evidence to support new policy initiatives. These processes need to go alongside policy changes and curriculum restructuring in teacher education.

Conclusion

This chapter has highlighted some of the significant processes that could facilitate the inclusion of children with a disability in mainstream schools. There are two important enduring principles here for educators and administrators to consider and build their practice on. These are, first, the need to interact closely with people with a disability to understand how to view their problem from a social model perspective. Second, collaboration of teachers, parents, people with a disability, and administrators is necessary to develop an appropriate policy as well as practice a culture that will facilitate inclusive education. Learning to work together and to respect differences is a challenge, but a value and a skill that should be the basis to facilitate inclusion in education across all of the Asia-Pacific region.

Teachers also need to reflect on their practice; they need to understand how students with a disability in mainstream classes are learning, and to find out how to help them learn better. Simultaneously, there is a need for similar forms of introspection in special schools. The challenges of inclusion are gradually rendering the traditional special school model of service delivery obsolete and irrelevant. What are the new support services that need to be developed? Where should they be located? These are just some questions that will have to be analyzed through collaborative workshops and strategic planning exercises.

It is also important to enable all stakeholders, especially people with a disability, to share their views and identify issues for internal debate and research. Based on a grassroots dialogue, teachers can initiate a foundational approach to education reform in the classroom. Developing a practice that includes strategies for curriculum modification, accommodations and alternative assessments in the classroom will help to support inclusion in schools by meeting a wide range of student and parent needs. When everybody involved understands how s/he can participate in inclusion, a positive proactive culture begins to emerge.

References

"Arjun Singh announces plan to make education disabled-friendly by 2020" (2005) *Disability News and Information Service*, 3(7). Online. Available at: http://www.dnis.org/(accessed 1 April 2005).

Booth, T. and Ainscow, M. (1998) *From Them to Us: International Study of Inclusion in Education*, London: Routledge Falmer.

Burnaford, G., Fischer, J. and Hobson, D. (2001) *Teachers Doing Research: The Power of Action Through Inquiry*, Hillsdale, NJ: Lawrence Erlbaum.

Census of India (2001). Online. Avaliable at: http://www.censusindia.net/ (accessed 28 September 2007).

Constitution of India (1950) Online. Available at: http://lawmin.nic.in/legislative/Art1–242 (1–88).doc (accessed 28 September 2007).

Hegarty, S. and Alur, M. (2002) *Education and Children with Special Needs: From Segregation to Inclusion*, New Delhi: Sage.

Ministry of Human Resource Development (2003) *Education for All: National Plan of Action*, New Delhi.

Ministry of Human Resource Development (2005a) *Sarva Shiksha Abhiyan*. Online. Available at: http://ssa.nic.in/ (accessed 1 October 2007).

Ministry of Human Resource Development (2005b) *Action Plan for Inclusive Education of Children and Youth with Disabilities.* Online. Available at: http://education.nic.in/INCLUSIVE.asp#INCLUSIVE%20EDUCATION (accessed 27 September 2007).

Ministry of Human Resource Development (2005c) *Right to Education Bill, 2005.* Online. Available at: http://education.nic.in/elementary/RighttoEducationBill2005.pdf (accessed 27 September 2007).

Mukhopadhyay, S. (2003) *Report on the National Seminar on Partnership of Government and Non-Government Organizations for Inclusive Education*, New Delhi: National University of Education Planning and Administration.

Naidu, A. (2005) "Multiple voices, multiple conversations, multiple communications", *Conference Proceedings of the National Conference on Alternative and Augmentative Communication in India*, Chennai, 18–20 December.

Naidu, A., Natarajan, P., Padmanabhan, R. and Shukla, V. (2005) "Shaking it up: An attempt at transformation", *Conference Proceedings of North-South Dialogue III International Conference on Inclusive Education*, New Delhi, 1–4 March.

National Council of Educational Research and Training (2005) *National Curriculum Framework*. Online. Available at: http://www.ncert.nic.in/sites/publication/school curriculum/NCFR%202005/contents1.htm (accessed 1 October 2007).

National Council of Educational Research and Training (2006) *National Focus Group on Education of Children with Special Needs*. Online. Available at: http://www.ncert.nic.in/sites/publication/schoolcurriculum/Position_Papers/pdfs/special_ed_final1.pdf (accessed 1 October 2007).

Pandey, S., Chirimar, P. and D'Souza, D. (2005) *Disability and the Law*, New Delhi: Vedam eBooks.

Stubbs, S. (2002) *Inclusive Education: Where There are Few Resources*, Oslo: The Atlas Alliance.

The Hindu (2005) "69,000 disabled children covered under SSA", 29 June. Online. Available at: http://www.hindu.com/2005/06/29/stories/2005062915130500.htm (accessed 28 September 2007).

The Hindu (2005) "Javed Abidi Nominated to CABE", 13 July. Online. Available at: http://www.hindu.com/2005/07/13/stories/2005071300421300.htm (accessed 27 September 2007).

Timmons, V. and Alur, M. (2004) "Transformational learning: A description of how inclusionary practice was accepted in India", *International Journal of Special Education*, 19: 38–48.

United Nations Educational, Scientific and Cultural Organization (1997) *International Standard Classification of Education*. Online. Available at: http://www.unesco.org/education/information/nfsunesco/doc/isced_1997.htm (accessed 1 October 2007).

Zatta, M. and Pullin, D. (2004) Education and alternate assessment for students with significant cognitive disabilities: Implications for educators, *Education Policy Analysis Archives*, 12(16). Online. Available at: http://epaa.asu.edu/epaa/v12n16/v12n16.pdf (accessed 1 October 2007).

4 Meeting new challenges of special education in China*

Xu Jiacheng

Chapter objectives

- To understand the background and early stage historical development of special education in China.
- To realize the contemporary need for specialized teacher education.
- To identify the existing challenges and possible solutions.
- To investigate the concepts and related issues regarding integrated and supported education.
- To be able to adopt and utilize helpful resources for supported education.

Focus questions

1. What are the contemporary challenges faced by special education practitioners in China?
2. What are the major concepts and key characteristics of integrated and supported education?
3. What are the potential and professional resources for supporting quality of life based special education?
4. What are the necessary basic approaches for specialized teacher education?

Introduction

Specialized teacher education has an intrinsic effect on the development of special education in China. In response to a society undergoing transformation, special education in China is changing quickly, with special education schools as the backbone of the system and special education classes and *suiban jiudu* (隨班就讀) or Learning in Regular Classrooms (LRC) as the mainstream practice. Such a pattern poses new challenges to teacher education. These challenges include the need for a special education curriculum, the development of effective teaching models, the demand for multidisciplinary and allied professionals, and the provision of a barrier-free environment and assistive technologies. This

*This chapter was translated by Andrew Tse.

chapter suggests that special education in China will move towards a type of education oriented towards support for quality of life. In the context of supported education, specialized teacher education should help teachers to: (a) re-define the concept of disability at the humanistic level; (b) develop new concepts in curriculum; (c) invest in multi-faceted curriculum resources; (d) design individualized education plans that are more vigorous and dynamic; (e) construct more open teaching models with the aid of modern assistive technologies; and (f) develop a special education team that is composed of multidisciplinary and allied professionals. The aim is to develop professional competence, evolving from the integration of professional support and support systems. This chapter will also propose the development of school-based training designed for front line teachers, the building of resource centers to consolidate resources in education, health and the community; and the development of new multi-level and multi-form approaches to teacher specialization, in order to expedite the process of teacher specialization in China.

The beginning of special education and teacher specialization

Special education in China has a 130-year history, developing from a care and training model to a single school segregated education model. Beginning in the 1980s, as China moved into an era of reform and increased openness, special education also went through a period of vast change, moving from segregation to inclusion, which in turn gave rise to new challenges. Against such a background, two important questions arise. First, what kinds of new challenges are posed by special education in China today; and second, how does specialized teacher education meet these challenges?

Since 1874, there has been virtually no specialized teacher training system for special education programs in China. Up until the early 1980s, teacher specialization was mainly actualized in the development of communication techniques such as the use of Braille, sign languages and lip reading. Table 4.1 lists special education schools and teacher status during the first 100 years of historical development.

In the area of education for students with visual disabilities, China's first school for the blind converted the Braille alphabet of the West into Kangxi Braille (康熙盲文) based on pronunciation used in the Kangxi Dictionary (康熙詞典). Later, other Braille systems such as the *Wu-Fang-Yuan-Yin* (五方原音), *Ke-Hua-Xin-Mu-Ke-Ming* (客話心目克明), *Xin-Mu-Ke-Ming* (心目克明) and the *Blind-Word According to the National Pronunciation* (國音盲字) were also used (Chen, 2004). In 1953, a new Braille system was designed by Huang Nai (黃乃), a Chinese who was blind. In 1975, a double-spell Braille scheme was proposed by Huang Nai. In 1979, education for children with low vision and total blindness was separated, and large print textbooks and vision aids were used to help students with low vision in their study (Piao, 1996).

Table 4.1 Outline of China's special education schools and teachers during the first 100 years of development

Time (years)	*Institution*	*Number of schools*	*Legislation*	*Teacher status*
Late 1800s–1940s	Church-sponsored special schools and private special schools. Only one public school.	40	No special laws and provisions related to special education teachers.	Mentoring + short-term training.
1950s–1980s	Special education was integrated into the national education system, mainly for blind and deaf people.	319		Mentoring + middle-level normal education + in-service training.

In the area of education for students who are deaf, sign language was the main specialized skill required that differentiated teachers of the deaf from general education teachers. In 1959, the Chinese alphabet scheme for sign language was introduced, followed by research on Chinese syllable sign language and on finger spelling in Chinese. In 1954, the Ministry of Education held a meeting in Beijing to discuss the education system and teaching plans for sign language and decided to conduct teaching experiments in lip reading classes. During this period, the training of special education teachers in China was mainly school based, and conducted in the manner of mentors or teaching apprentices (Li and Zhou, 1999). The progress of teacher specialization training was limited and slow.

Special education and teacher specialization during the social transformation period

In the 1980s, China observed the end of the Cultural Revolution and the implementation of a policy of reform and openness. In the transition from a planned economy to a market economy, special education in China began to develop at a more rapid pace. During this period, special education was first influenced by integrated education, moving gradually from the special school only service delivery system to a new model of having special schools and classes as the backbone, and learning in regular classrooms (LRC) as the mainstream (Chen, 2004). During this time, there were two periods of rapid expansion in the number of special education students and teachers.

It can be seen from Figures 4.1 and 4.2 that, from 1980 to 2004, the number of students and teachers in special schools in China both increased rapidly. The period between 1990 and 1998 saw the fastest growth in the numbers of teachers and students of special schools in China, with student numbers increasing

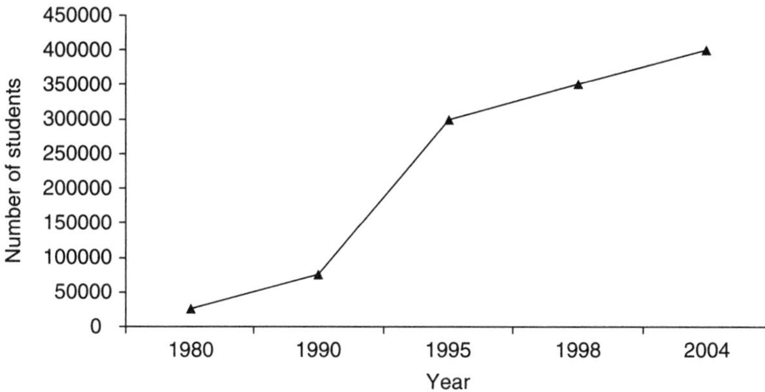

Figure 4.1 Increase in special education students in China from 1980 to 2004. Adapted from China Education Yearbooks for corresponding years.

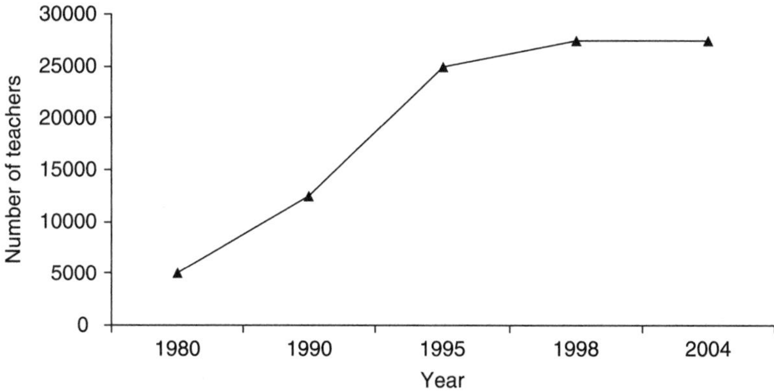

Figure 4.2 Increase in special education teachers in China from 1980 to 2004. The second growth period: Focus on Learning in Regular Classrooms (LRC). Adapted from China Education Yearbooks for corresponding years.

from less than 100,000 to 300,000. This number began to stabilize by year 2000. A similar growth pattern was observed for the number of teachers.

The second period of rapid growth for special education in China was from 2000 to 2004, with special education classes being attached to general education schools and LRC being the mainstream practice. Since the 1990s, implementation of LRC had gradually been adopted and this reached a peak after 2000, by which time the number of students involved reached over 60 per cent of all students receiving special education.

Table 4.2 shows that the number of students in integrated education in China grew rapidly between 1994 and 2006. This expansion of students reflects the

Table 4.2 Number of students in integrated education from 1994 to 2006

	1994	*1996*	*1998*	*2000*	*2002*	*2004*	*2006*
Percentage of the total					68.29	65.35	61.12
Students in special education schools (× 10,000)	21.14	32.11	35.84	37.76	37.45	37.18	36.29
Students in integrated education (× 10,000)	11.53	9.51	22.55	23.93	*117	*103	*93.05

Note: Based on the special education section in the Survey and Statistics of the National Education Development for each year; * are estimated figures.

demand for the corresponding increase in teachers engaged in integrated education in general schools.

The development of special education in China led to a corresponding development of teacher training for special education. From 1986 onwards, a multi-level and multi-form special education teacher training system was gradually developed. This comprised secondary level special education teacher training schools, tertiary level special education teacher training colleges, special education courses offered by regular teacher training colleges, and postgraduate education for special education (Xu, 1998). Figure 4.3 illustrates the special education teacher training system formed in China since the 1980s.

New challanges in special education

The first challenge stems from the growing demand for more special education services. A national survey in 1987 revealed that people with disabilities accounted for 5 per cent of the total population in China, that is, 60 million out of the population of 1.3 billion people in China have one of the five categories of disabilities (i.e. visual disabilities, hearing disabilities, language disabilities, physical disabilities, and intellectual disabilities) and over 6 million of them are of school age. The vast number of special education services has led to an urgent need for training of additional special education teachers.

Another national survey on people with disabilities was conducted in April 2006. The number of people with disabilities was 83.96 million representing 6.34 per cent of the total population. The distribution of disability types within the disabled population is as follows: visual disabilities 14.86 per cent; hearing disabilities 24.16 per cent; language disabilities 1.53 per cent; physical disabilities 29.07 per cent; intellectual disabilities 6.68 per cent; mental disabilities 7.40 per cent; and multiple disabilities 16.30 per cent (National Bureau of Statistics of China, 2006).

The second challenge comes from the integration of special education programs into general schools. Children with blindness, deafness and intellectual

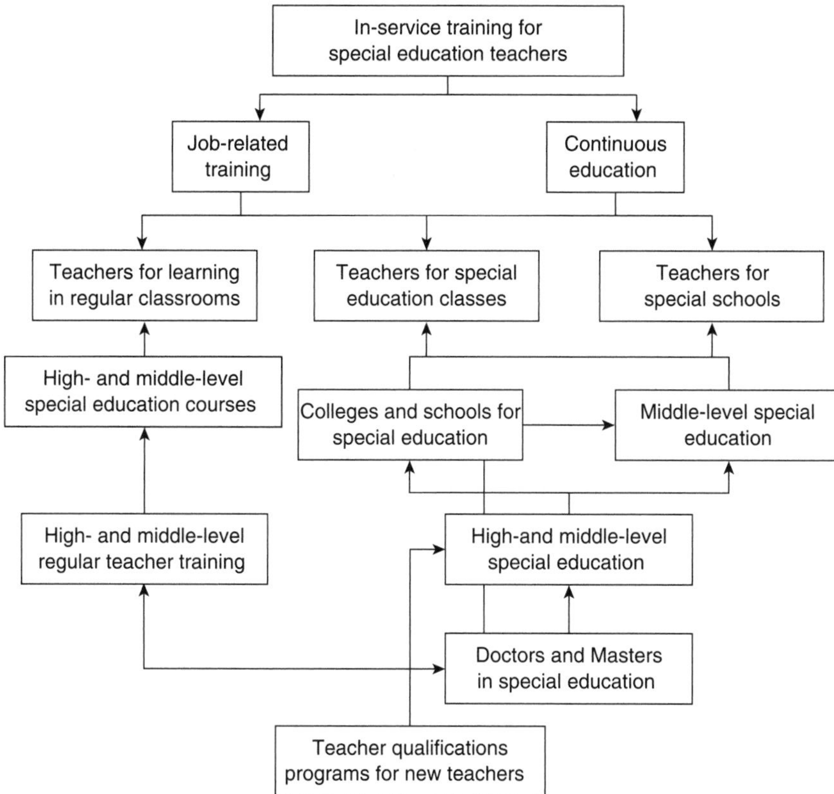

Figure 4.3 The special education teacher training system gradually formed in China from the 1980s onward.

disabilities are returning from special schools to regular schools, and more children with developmental disabilities, such as those with learning difficulties, or language, emotional or behavioral problems, are already studying in regular schools. Thus, teachers in general schools are also in need of further training in special education.

An increase in the provision of special education leads to a demand for the improvement of its quality. Such a process is challenging in three areas. The first challenge is in the area of curriculum development. How can the special education curriculum be oriented towards the individual child with special education needs, and at the same time accommodate the requirements of the new National Curriculum? This is a great challenge for academia in the field of special education, special schools and general schools in China today.

The second challenge comes from the need for effective teaching strategies. On one hand, the degree of disability of students in special schools is now much more severe, so that structured lesson plans based on traditional subject and teaching hours have become less relevant. On the other hand, more and more students with special needs are learning in regular classrooms, which challenges the effectiveness of lesson plans in general education. It then becomes necessary to explore effective teaching approaches for students with disabilities in the regular classrooms.

Education assessment of learning outcomes poses the third challenge. Apart from preparing students for further education, what are the other outcomes of special education? How can the performance of students in integrated education be assessed other than by measuring their academic achievements? These questions invite reflection on the assessment of the teaching achievements in the integrated education.

Modern special education not only cultivates students' skills in subject learning and social adaptation but also integrates support from modern rehabilitation sciences such as physiotherapy, occupational therapy, speech and language therapy, art therapy, play therapy and psychological services. The acute shortage of resources in these areas leads to an insufficient provision of qualified professionals and challenges special education in its professional division and integration.

In contemporary society, barrier-free access to community facilities, communication, information and learning environments is a common goal. Special education not only needs the support of low-end assistive technology, but that of high-end assistive technology served by equipment such as computers. The combination of special education and modern assistive technology has brought new opportunities to teacher specialization. Methods of constructing barrier-free environments in an integrated context and effectively developing and using assistive technologies is another new challenge that modern special education poses to specialized teachers in China.

New ideas to address the challenge

One of the important factors driving the rapid development of special education in China is the change from isolated education to integrated education and the new dilemmas arising from this. The question then is whether special education in China will move further from integrated education to inclusive education and in the end be absorbed completely into the general education system. The author holds the view that inclusive education in this sense will encounter difficulties in China. From a macro perspective, it is suggested that special education in twenty-first-century China will find itself in a multi-dimensional pattern with special schools, special classes and LRC coexisting, and that this pattern will remain for a long time. New ideas are, therefore, needed to meet the new challenges.

From integrated education to supported education

This chapter suggests that the new direction for future development of special education in China is to move from integrated education to supported education, which is oriented towards an improved quality of life. Quality of life recognizes the holistic functions of inclusive education and stresses the personal hopes or dreams of students with intellectual and other disabilities. It is concerned with the inner feelings of these students, including their personal development, sources of satisfaction and happiness. It stresses parents' participation, community involvement and active interpersonal relationships. Supported education aims to enhance independence, productivity, community involvement and satisfaction so that quality of life is improved. Instead of emphasizing the integration of special education into general education, supported education highlights the deployment of educational and professional resources in order to deliver an intrinsically rich education to children with the support of these resources. By circumventing the problems and dilemmas caused by inclusive education, this concept of supported education with its orientation and outcomes rooted in an improved quality of life, should break new ground for the modernization of special education in China.

Theoretical basis and characteristics of supported education

The idea of supported education is based on theories regarding quality of life. An exploratory cross-cultural study indicates that quality of life has the same connotations to all people, able or disabled, in a community of the same social, cultural and economical background, and can be judged on the same standards (Schalock *et al.*, 2005). While participating in this multinational cross-cultural study of the quality of life, the author conducted a survey on people with intellectual disabilities in China and found that seven out of the eight core indicators of quality of life were identified in their participants' responses. Further investigation disclosed that participants differed in their selection of core domains. People with intellectual disabilities believed that they needed to be fulfilled in all seven domains, while their parents and special education professionals suggested that the fulfillment of five and three domains, respectively, would be sufficient to create an adequate quality of life for them. This finding indicates that the views of persons with disabilities need to be particularly addressed if their quality of life is to be enhanced. It is also necessary to consider issues of quality of life in the context of provision of rehabilitation services for people with disabilities and adopt a facilitating approach in the provision of support for aspects of general life, education and employment, with the ultimate goal of enhancing quality of life. Hence, it is essential to provide quality of life oriented supported education for children with special education needs (Xu, 2005).

The following characteristics have emerged in the implementation of supported education in China:

1 The involvement of communities in provision of special education has gradually increased.
2 Resources are being integrated around the core mission of support. Support is a strategy and an approach; it also includes the provision of material

resources. The key to support is to help people with disabilities and people in need to increase their independence in order to provide them with an autonomous life, learning and employment. One important approach to support is to help people with disabilities to obtain effective education by taking advantage of all available resources, including natural and professional resources in the community and effective integration of other resources of the society.

3 Support systems are being created that consist of a dominant natural support and supplementary professional support. In China, supported education needs to fully utilize the natural resources that consists of the non-specialist, low cost and continuous support from parents, as well as relatives, friends, neighbors and fellow students. This natural support plays an important role in the system, particularly at a time when rehabilitation resources in China are scarce.

The implementation of supported education

Based on the theory of supported education and the different social and economic backgrounds of cities and villages in mainland China, several implementation projects in supported education in the city of Beijing and rural districts of five counties have been launched. In the Beijing project, over 40 resource classrooms for supported education were set up in general primary and secondary schools, mainly using existing resources of the schools, community resources and parent resources, and supplemented by local specialist resources such as physiotherapy, occupational therapy and psychological counseling. With the support system made up of natural resources and specialist resources, the practice of learning in regular classrooms gradually moved towards a supported education model and the quality and quantity of education was significantly elevated.

To understand the demand from rural districts, a joint project between the Federation of Disabled People in China and the Government of Sweden on *The Prevention and Rehabilitation of Intellectual Disabilities* was conducted from 2005 to 2007 to study the implementation of supported education in counties such as Huichun in Jilin Province (吉林省琿春縣), Jingyuan in Gansu Province (甘肅省靖遠縣), and Yuanping in Shanxi Province (山西省原平縣). The numbers of cases studied are shown in Table 4.3.

Based on the concept of supported education, children with disabilities were placed in the local communities, with supported services being provided by children's families and resources of the respective communities. Training was first given to the rehabilitation personnel and parents of the community, explaining to them the concept of supported education and setting individual support programs for every child. Most of the programs had relatively set rehabilitation training areas; a few were designed to match the environment of the local community and the special needs of the children. According to the current resources of the community, children were placed in special schools, general schools, nurseries or families and given individualized rehabilitation programs that were

Table 4.3 The implementation of supported education in three counties in China from 2005 to 2007

Name of counties	*No. of children*	*No. of towns*	*Age 0–3*			*Age 3–6*		
			M	*F*	*Sub-total*	*M*	*F*	*Sub-total*
Jingyuan, Gansu	25	2	3	3	6	8	11	19
Huichun, Jilin	19	3	2	2	4	11	4	15
Yuanping, Shanxi	53	3	5	3	8	20	14	34
Total	97	8	10	8	18	39	29	68

mainly supported by natural resources (parents, relatives, neighbors, etc.). Local teachers, medical personnel and social rehabilitation personnel also contributed to these individual support programs. Through such means of support many of these children experienced the same learning opportunities as local children. After two years of implementation, the data collected from school-based assessment procedures in three counties all indicate that these children have made obvious progress (see Figure 4.4).

The results demonstrated that supported education can be an effective concept and approach in specialization training for teachers and allied professionals. Such a concept enables teachers, in the process of multi-dimensional development, to make use of natural and specialist resources in order to carry out rehabilitation training and supported service for children with disabilities.

Directions of specialized teacher education under the new concept

Supported education emphasizes that at the beginning of teacher specialization, teachers should regard a child (whether disabled or not) as a whole person; understand all of his/her disabling conditions, potentials, strengths, and the relationship between the potential and the environment; create for them an actively supporting and integrative environment; and treat him/her with a fully inclusive mind. In this sense, there is no great division between special education and regular education. This understanding of human beings is the joint cornerstone for teacher specialization for both special and regular education.

Possessing the skills to develop multi-dimensional curriculum resources from a new perspective

Curriculum is a key issue in teacher specialization. When developing curriculum from a supported education perspective, teachers need to be concerned with children's needs (visions), happiness and other inner qualities. In the curriculum, teachers should meet not only the individualized needs of general children but also the needs of those with special and diverse conditions. Teachers should be

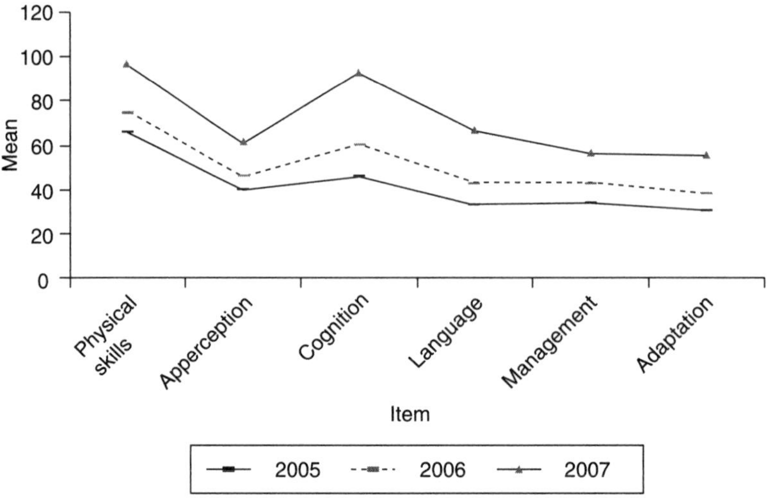

Figure 4.4 Progress of children during the implementation of supported education in rural districts of China.

able to utilize multiple curricular resources and obtain rich input from subject-specific courses, comprehensive courses and individualized courses (such as developmental, functional, environmental and ecological courses), as well as from many other course modalities, in order to meet children's special education needs.

Possessing skills in devising life-energized individualized educational plans

The essence of supported education is to have an insight into children's rapidly changing inner development, so that the individualized education plans match closely with children's life experiences. Thus, professional training should enable teachers to understand, master and apply diagnostic and appraisal technologies in educational psychology to measure children's intellectual development, personality development and psychological profile. It is also necessary to help teachers adopt a dynamic, ecological and career perspective, follow the children's life and socialization process and respect their wishes and interests. In short, teachers need the capability to make individualized education plans that truly meet children's needs by involving them and their parents in the process.

Possessing professional skills in developing open and student-centered teaching approaches

In teachers' specialized training, it is important for them to transform their teaching ideology, understand learning theories, grasp skills involved in guiding study and apply assistive technologies to support students' learning. A highly professional teacher can take the initiative in moving from a dominant to a facilitating position and attaching more importance to developing students' learning strategies, providing learning resources and creating a learning environment. They focus more on increasing students' learning motivation, making learning plans, providing a learning framework, offering behavioral support and applying assistive technologies to help students learn how to learn and become good at learning.

Possessing skills in collaborating with allied professionals on a multidisciplinary team

Students with disabilities require comprehensive support from such disciplines as rehabilitation, psychology, computer science and sociology. Therapy sciences such as physiotherapy, occupational therapy, speech and language therapy, psychotherapy, music therapy, art therapy, drama therapy, computer-assisted technologies and social work are all important resources in modern special education. In this respect, teachers need not only an expertise in special education but also a knowledge of related areas and the capability to consolidate multiple and related disciplines in a multidisciplinary team. Therefore, specialized teacher education should train teachers in having not only their own professional specialities, but also the capacity to understand the relationship between related disciplines and their specialities in order to develop an ability for professional collaboration.

Possessing skills in establishing support systems

Supported education needs to build corresponding support systems composed of natural support and social support. Specialized training in this context should instruct teachers how to use and develop natural support and establish supportive systems that are mainly based on natural supports and supplemented with professional support. Specialized training should develop teachers' capacities and methods to work with communities and families to develop natural support systems and build support systems that integrate natural and social resources.

Basic approaches to training for teacher specialization

School-based training for front line teachers

Teacher specialization in supported education in China starts at special schools, special education classes and integrated classes in regular schools. Different types and levels of schools design their own school-based training to match the specialization needs for their front line teachers. Based on these needs, they conduct curriculum reforms, action research and short-term training programs. These basic approaches to teacher specialization will become the basis for future specialized training. Such school-based training will also produce a cohort of specialized teachers equipped with rich experiences, skilled in putting theories into practice and in multidisciplinary team collaboration. These teachers will become the backbone of supported education.

Resource centers as the platforms for specialized training

School-based training focuses on the characteristics and needs of the school, but lacks emphasis on the integration of related professional resources. Such a gap can be filled by the creation of resource centers. These centers will serve as platforms for specialized training and may facilitate the professional integration and collaboration between special and regular schools, between schools of the same type, and between related professional institutions. In the next five to ten years, resource centers (classrooms) in China, as well as general schools with students learning in regular classrooms, will be important models for the integration of special and general schools. Therefore, resource centers and resource classrooms will be an important platform for teachers' professional training. Resource centers can provide systematic training, specialist training and continuous education to both special schools and schools practicing integrated education. This is an important way to effectively introduce the latest professional resources and apply them in real-life practice in order to promote the growth of teachers' professionalism.

Multi-level and multi-faceted teacher specialization

Professional training for new special education teachers in China will involve a multi-level and multi-faceted system. Multi-level indicates that new teachers will mainly come from special education majors in colleges and undergraduate schools in universities. Graduate education for special education teachers in China will continue to develop, but the secondary level teacher training schools, which have played an important role in China's special education, will decrease in importance. Thus, professional training for special education teachers will move to a higher level. The regular teacher training colleges and the education schools within universities should all offer courses and credits in special education, so that all newly trained teachers have an exposure to special education and can grasp the basic theories and methodology involved in special education. Training will be multifaceted, in that teacher training institutions will not be the only training providers of new teachers for special education. Medical rehabilitation specialists, psychologists, social workers, information technology technicians and other allied professionals will all become important resources for training special education professionals. Multiple sources of teachers will definitely lead to labor division and resource integration in teacher specialization in China and contribute to the formation of teaching teams consisting of multidisciplinary professionals.

Conclusion

The open and reform policy has infused vigor into special education in China after 100 years of sluggish growth. Under the influence of emerging international awareness, special education in China has adopted an integrated approach. The rapidly developing special education field challenges teachers' professionalization from the perspectives of quantity, quality, curriculum, methodology, multidisciplinary cooperation, assistive technology and resources. Coupled with the challenges are new development opportunities. The concept of quality of life oriented supported education opens up a new route for specialized teacher education. The new ideas will make teachers' professionalization more natural, simplified, applicable and convenient by involving relevant resources in education. Therefore, it is proposed that specialized teacher education will become more effective and fruitful.

References

Chen, Y. (2004) *Basis for China's Special Education Study,* Beijing: Education Science Press (in Chinese).

Li, H. and Zhou, G. (1999) *50 Years of Special Education in Beijing,* Beijing: Huaxia Press (in Chinese).

National Bureau of Statistics of China (2006) Data release of the Second National Sample Survey of Disabled Persons in 2006 (2006年第二次全國殘疾人抽樣調查主要數據公報). Accessed 16 October 2007 from http://big5.gov.cn/gate/big5/www.gov.cn/ztzl/gacjr/content_459223.htm

Piao, Y. X. (1996) *Special Education Dictionary,* Beijing: Huaxia Press (in Chinese).

Schalock, R., Verdugo A. M., Jenaro, C., Wang, M., Xu, J., Wehmeyer, M. and Lachapelle, Y. (2005) "Crosscultural study of core quality of life indicators", *American Journal on Mental Retardation*, 110(4): 298–311.

Xu, J. C. (1998) *Additional Provision for Special Education Courses and Teacher Training in High-Level Normal Colleges.* Sponsored by the Normal Education Department of the Ministry of Education of the PRC and the World Bank, Chengdu: Electronic Technology University Press (in Chinese).

Xu, J. C. (2005) "Quality of life for people with intellectual disabilities in China: A cross-cultural study", *Journal of Intellectual Disability Research,* 49(10): 745–9.

Support materials and activities: Section 1

The following support materials and activities provide additional useful information about education reform for special and inclusive education both internationally and in the Asia-Pacific region. The activities are designed to provide authentic approaches to learning that can be contextualized to meet the needs of learners in any given environment.

These websites provide good starting places for further information about education reform

- The revised international *Convention on the Rights of Persons with Disabilities* (December 2006) is available at: http://www.un.org/disabilities/ together with the protocol.
- The *Salamanca Statement and Framework for Action on Special Needs* may be downloaded at the following site: http://www.unesco.org/education/pdf/SALAMA_E.PDF
- The *Inclusion International* website (http://www.inclusion-international.org/) aims to advance inclusive education on a global basis. The site has strategies and interventions that promote the inclusion of children with a disability in order to make basic education available to all children, through the EFA approach and other initiatives. It provides an area to view the progress of Inclusion International, and of others who are advocating for inclusive education globally.
- The 1992 *Disability Discrimination Act* (Australia) is available from: http://www.hreoc.gov.au/disability_rights/dda_guide/dda_guide.htm
- The website of the *Enabling Education Network* (http://www.eenet.org.uk) provides additional information on the progress of inclusive education practice in developing countries, including China and India.
- The *Global Campaign for Education* site (http://www.campaignforeducation.org/) promotes education as a basic human right, and mobilizes public pressure on governments and the international community to fulfill their promises to provide free, compulsory public basic education for all people. It contains a range of references to issues associated with many disenfranchised groups including those with disabilities.

- This special and inclusive education site (http://www.rnld.co.uk/ie.html) contains links to other useful smaller sites providing information about different aspects of inclusion and children with specific learning disabilities.
- The *Disability Equality in Education* (DEE) site (http://www.diseed.org.uk/) is a charity that promotes educational inclusion while celebrating and embracing the differences of individuals.
- The practice of education reform in England may be obtained from: http://www.equals.co.uk
- The *Disabled Parents Network* (DPN) is a national organization of and for people with disabilities and their supporters (http://www.disabledparentsnetwork.org.uk/about/history.htm).
- The UNESCO education toolkits are available from: http://portal.unesco.org/education/en/ev.php-URL_ID=49335&URL_DO=DO_TOPIC&URL_SECTION=201.html
- The UNESCO website (http://www.unesco.org) contains an enormous range of supplementary support materials in addition to the following:
    - The latest *Education For All Global Monitoring Report* (2007).
    - Report on *The Right to Education of Persons with Disabilities* (February, 2007).
    - *Guidelines for the Asia and Pacific EFA Mid-Decade Assessment: Identifying and Reaching the Unreached (Draft)*
    - *Guidelines for Inclusion: Ensuring Access to Education For All* (2005).
    - EFA *Handbook for Decentralised Planning* (2005).
    - *Changing Teaching Practices Using Curriculum Differentiation to Respond to Students' Diversity* (2004).
    - T*owards Inclusive Practices in Secondary Education* (2003).
    - *Understanding and Responding to Children's Needs in Inclusive Classrooms* (2001).
- The *Whole Schooling Consortium* website: http://www.wholeschooling.net is an international network for supporting schools, teachers, parents, administrators, and university faculty and community members.

Professional development activities for special education reform towards inclusive education

1 Discuss inclusion as a philosophy. Trace its origins. Respond to the question: Is an inclusive society a desirable goal?

2 Examine the *Salamanca Statement and Framework for Action on Special Needs Education*. What are the implications for your region?

3 Study how people with disabilities have been treated throughout history in different cultures.

4 Discuss the main features that distinguish integration from inclusion. Make a list of the features of each and compare and clarify the differences.

5 List the challenges for educating children of all abilities (and disabilities) in the same school. Discuss in reference to two students of 13–14 years of age, one being on course for a university education and the other who will always require care to live at home.
6 What human rights do you feel should underpin the provision of schooling for ALL students?
7 What are the differences in schooling provision between a psycho-medical and socio-curricular model? Which model do you think functions in your country and which one would you prefer?
8 Discuss the possible origins of resistance to special education reform towards inclusive education in the Asian-Pacific educational systems. Who is involved in this resistance? Why? How can it be overcome?
9 The transition to inclusive education in the Asia-Pacific region is a highly complex task. Identify some of the complexities and discuss ways of overcoming them.

These texts provide a wealth of ideas about education reform for special and inclusive education

Allan J. (ed.) (2003) *Inclusion, Participation and Democracy: What is the Purpose*? Dordrecht: Kluwer.

Armstrong, F., Armstrong, D. and Barton, L. (eds) (2000) *Inclusive Education, Policy, Contexts and Comparative Perspectives*, London: David Fulton.

Bateman, D. F., Bright, K. L., O'Shea, D. J. and Algozzine, B. (2007) *The Special Education Program Administrator's Handbook*, Boston, MA: Pearson Allyn & Bacon.

Florian, L. (ed.) (2007) *The SAGE Handbook of Special Education*, London: SAGE.

Friend, M. (2008) *Special Education: Contemporary Perspectives for School Professionals*, 2nd edn, Boston, MA: Pearson.

Murdick, N. L., Gartin, B. C. and Crabtree, T. (2007) *Special Education Law*, Upper Saddle River, NJ: Pearson/Merrill Prentice Hall.

Obiakor, F. E. (2007) *Multicultural Special Education: Culturally Responsive Teaching*, Upper Saddle River, NJ: Pearson/Merrill/Prentice Hall.

Reynolds, C. R. and Fletcher-Janzen, E. (eds) (2007) *Encyclopedia of Special Education: A Reference for the Education of Children, Adolescents, and Adults with Disabilities and Other Exceptional Individuals*, 3rd edn, Hoboken, NJ: John Wiley and Sons.

Sheehy, K., Nind, M., Rix, J. and Simmons, K. (eds) (2005) *Ethics and Research in Inclusive Education: Values into Practice*, London: Routledge/Falmer.

Smith, D. D. (2007) *Introduction to Special Education: Making a Difference*, 6th edn, Boston, MA/Hong Kong: Pearson/Allyn & Bacon.

Section 2

Preparing teachers to work in inclusive classrooms

5 Education reform for inclusion in the Asia-Pacific region

What about teacher education?

Chris Forlin

Chapter objectives

- To consider current reforms in teacher education for inclusion.
- The development of a curriculum framework for preservice teacher education for inclusion in the Asia-Pacific region.
- Discussion of appropriate pedagogies for preparing teachers for inclusion.

Focus questions

1. What is the direction of international reform for teacher education?
2. What impact does the Confucian approach have for preparing teachers for inclusive education?
3. What considerations need to be taken when developing a curriculum for teacher education for inclusion in the Asia-Pacific region?
4. What will a curriculum for preparing teachers need to include?
5. What appropriate pedagogies can be employed?
6. What support structures need to be implemented to further the inclusive paradigm in the Asia-Pacific region?

Introduction

With the continual and sometimes dramatic education reforms that occur in various systems and countries, there comes a need to reflect upon the appropriateness of current teacher courses in preparation for such changes. One of the most far-reaching education reforms in recent years in the Asia-Pacific region, similar to other countries, has been the move towards inclusive education (Forlin, 2006). Teacher training institutions, however, have been somewhat slower to make the necessary adjustments to their courses in order to prepare teachers for this change. Without a clearly defined goal for teachers, embedded within a carefully articulated philosophy of teaching, it is not possible to determine a realistic and appropriate teacher education program to enable teachers to cope with this new ideology of inclusive education practice.

Prior to the 1990s, the customary approach to teacher education focused on the teaching and learning process as a means of gaining content knowledge during preservice training, that could then be transmitted to students in their role as a teacher. In more recent years the focus in the West has changed to a constructivist approach that has aimed to prepare teachers to act as facilitators of a child's learning by scaffolding the child through a guided learning approach (Sailor and Skrtic, 1996). This approach has been much more conducive to catering for diverse student populations within the same classroom. In much of the Asia-Pacific region, nonetheless, while endeavoring to establish more inclusive classrooms the pedagogies employed by teachers have remained very didactic, which has not been so favorable towards catering for different learning needs.

Acceptance into teacher training regrettably tends to pay little attention to the conviction of preservice teachers towards their anticipated role, giving more credence to the need to fill places to ensure the maintenance of university courses. In many institutions preservice teachers are accepted into courses based solely on a graduation score without any opportunity to meet and discuss their personal belief systems or their anticipated role as a future teacher. In much of the Asia-Pacific region teachers are in such high demand that benchmarks for being selected into a course are constantly being lowered. It is not surprising then, that for many teachers who have a narrowly defined perspective of their own role that usually reflects their own school experiences, if faced with an alternative viewpoint they find it very difficult and are very reluctant to adjust. This is particularly pertinent in the Asian culture where teachers who have been educated in their own countries have not experienced any form of inclusive education. Such a philosophy is only just starting to permeate the schooling systems in this region.

Clearly, teaching is not simply to impart knowledge. Adopting a Freirean pedagogy, teaching and learning should be the development of mutual understanding through a process of shared enquiry. In order to enable this, Bakken *et al.* (2002, p. 84) posit that: "A teacher cannot be expected to facilitate learning and the construction of meaning around units of knowledge in the absence of his or her belief system." Without an appropriate disposition, how then can a teacher engage fully in supporting all students within an inclusive school environment? This is a critical issue that must be presented as an important aspect of teacher preparation, in addition to the more traditional approach of focusing simply on theoretical and practical knowledge. In particular, the impact that personal beliefs have on a teacher's willingness to engage in inclusive practices is vital to its implementation (Forlin *et al.*, 2007). Although the Confucian approach supports the treatment of people with disabilities with tolerance and acceptance (Pang and Richey, 2006), this does not always translate into education practice. In systems that still consider a high examination result as the most important outcome of education, parents are uncompromising when they perceive that their own child's education may be held back if teachers have to spend time addressing the needs of other students.

Teacher education for inclusion

The expectation that teachers will engage fully and immediately in an inclusive approach to catering for diversity is at best, rather naïve. While most teachers have generally been reported as being supportive of the ideology of inclusive education, they tend to raise many concerns about their ability to be able to execute it effectively (Forlin, 1998). Even in Western countries where more inclusive education philosophies have been promoted for more than two decades not all teachers are supportive of this movement. According to Yeun *et al.* (2004), citing Hong Kong as an example, it would seem that there is a long way to go before appropriate inclusive settings can be expected in the Asia-Pacific region as they posit that:

> it is unwise at this time to expect mainstream primary teachers in Hong Kong to be able to meet these special needs fully, particularly when class sizes are large (35+ students) and teachers appear to lack the necessary expertise or motivation for implementing appropriate in-class remedial interventions.
>
> (Yeun *et al.*, 2004, p. 74)

There are a number of particular issues that have been identified as inhibiting the move towards inclusive education in the Asia-Pacific region. According to Forlin (2007a) such issues include the following key concerns that seem most pertinent to the region:

- large class sizes
- examination oriented curriculum
- school banding systems
- top down approach for decision making
- didactic pedagogy
- autocratic leadership
- teachers have little input in decision making
- lack of appropriate training or upskilling
- trying to move too fast
- insufficient time for collaborative planning and reflection
- cultural diversity
- no strategic long-term plan
- excessive homework.

Large class size is a major issue existing across much of the Asia-Pacific region and it makes catering for the individual and diverse needs of all students extremely demanding (Pearson *et al.*, 2003; Poon-McBrayer, 2005). In these instances, including students with disabilities further increases the complexities of a progressively more difficult and challenging profession and requires thoughtful and considered inspection if teachers are to be competent, confident managers and able to provide a meaningful educational experience for all students (Loreman *et al.*, 2005). For mainstream teachers, large class sizes clearly restrict the time they can spend with individual students. Teachers reportedly find this even more taxing when students with intellectual disabilities, who require a comparatively increased amount of instructional time, are also included (Arbeiter and Hartley, 2002).

Similarly, an inflexible focus on an examination oriented system, which in many instances is paralleled by a school banding system that restricts access depending upon academic achievement, also hinders the successful implementation of inclusive schooling (Forlin, 2007b; Poon-McBrayer, 2005). Other classroom-based issues that have been found elsewhere to cause further concern for teachers include: managing difficult behaviors; a lack of appropriate resources and support; and inadequate funding (Arbeiter and Hartley, 2002).

There have been only a limited number of investigations of the strategies used by teachers to enable inclusion across the Asia-Pacific region. For example, in Hong Kong it has been reported that teachers in primary schools generally make relatively few adaptations, relying mainly on class peers to provide assistance (Chan *et al.*, 2002). Clearly, if teachers are to be able to meet the needs of diverse student populations and cater for the distinctive challenges faced in Asian classrooms, teacher education needs to be re-conceptualized to ensure that all teachers at both pre- and in-service levels have the necessary skills, willingness and ability to accommodate the needs of all students.

Regardless of the situation in which teachers find themselves or the policies or legislation that is enacted within a system, it has been argued that teachers are the ones who are pivotal to the success or otherwise of an inclusive model of education (Forlin, 2005). It would seem decidedly pertinent that, this being the case, teacher preparation for inclusion should be given a very high status of importance and be extremely well conceived to ensure that teachers are given the best possible support. Yet to date, the preparation of teachers to work in inclusive classrooms has been considered to be far less than satisfactory (Loreman *et al.*, 2005). Even when there is legislation that stipulates that teachers must ensure all students' needs are met and they are able to make progress, there is no similar legislation that mandates the training needs of teachers to prepare them for this role. Furthermore, being prepared to accept more diverse classrooms is quite challenging for teachers, particularly where diversity is not reflected in society. In situations where teacher registration does not specify the training curriculum, the emphasis on preparing teachers for inclusion has relied upon individual universities or colleges to determine their own courses and consequently varies enormously between them.

Developing a curriculum for teacher education

Preparing teachers to cater for students with increasingly diverse learning needs in mainstream classrooms is an important facet of teacher education courses for all jurisdictions in the new millennium (Forlin, 2007b). Teachers need to have not only the theoretical and practical knowledge but must also have the capacity to bring about optimal levels of learning for all students (Bakken *et al.*, 2002). To be able to give their best to their work they need to have a detailed understanding of their role as a teacher, requiring what Cruickshank (1987, cited in

Bakken *et al.*, 2002) described as a self-critical perspective that involves a constant engagement in a process of reflection and introspection. Effective inclusive teaching also requires a high level of ethics and morals, an understanding that a teacher's role is not only to inform and facilitate learning but also to act as a role model for guiding the development of their students, and a commitment to enable inclusion to happen.

There have been many myths that surround the challenge to produce a good teacher. One of the most dominant ones has been that good teachers are born and not made. According to Darling-Hammond:

> This superstition has given rise to a set of policies that rely far too much on some kind of prenatal alchemy to produce a cadre of teachers ... and far too little on systematic, sustained, initiatives to ensure that all teachers have the opportunity to become well prepared.
>
> (Darling-Hammond, 2006, p. ix)

For all the criticisms about the poor quality of various teacher education programs, there is increasing evidence that teacher education does matter for teacher effectiveness (Darling-Hammond, 2006). In particular, it has been shown that significant and positive difference in attitudes and instructional competences can be obtained from undertaking just one course in preparation for inclusive education (Turner, 2003; Chong *et al.*, 2007; Forlin *et al.*, 2007; Sharma *et al.*, 2006).

Training institutions throughout the Asia-Pacific region are now embarking on the transformation needed to enable teachers to deliver an appropriate curriculum while catering for the needs of a much broader range of students with progressively more diverse abilities. To enable teachers to be effective, Darling-Hammond also posits that:

> Successful teachers link what students already know and understand to new information, correcting misimpressions, guiding learners' understanding through a variety of activities, providing opportunities for application of knowledge, giving useful feedback that shapes performance and individualizing for students' individual needs.
>
> (Darling-Hammond, 2006, p. 8)

In addition, one of the biggest challenges in the Asia-Pacific region is the conflicting epistemologies for teachers. Most schools still employ a traditionalist approach to teaching that involves the transmission of knowledge from an autonomous teacher through rote learning, memorizing, lecturing and didactic methods with students seen as recipients of knowledge. By contrast, the implementation of an inclusive education approach requires a more progressive or constructivist perspective that involves discovery learning, problem-solving and the teacher acting as a facilitator in order that individual students can make sense of their learning at their own level.

Not only are teachers being asked to cater for students with disabilities in their mainstream classes, but their philosophy of teaching is being challenged as they try to cope with an inclusive classroom. In many instances this is hampered by systems that are inflexible and unprepared to allow teachers to change the existing status quo in classrooms. The conflict between providing a developmental learning approach that is required for an inclusive philosophy while still being expected to meet examinations and standards using a traditionalist approach is fraught with almost impenetrable challenges for mainstream teachers.

With such a demanding challenge it is essential that any curriculum designed to prepare teachers should commence with an opportunity for them to explore their own beliefs and values in an attempt to ensure that they at least start in a positive way. In addition, such considerations must include an in-depth exploration of cultural differences and an understanding of what is possible within an Asian rather than a Western tradition. By the end of their training they must have a strong belief in their role as a teacher, having acquired the appropriate knowledge, dispositions, values and performances required to succeed (Turner, 2003), and a hope that education systems will also change to allow them to implement the new-found strategies they have learned.

The following curriculum is designed for use in preparing teachers to work in inclusive school communities. The development of a vision statement, the identification of the expected outcomes, together with an understanding of the key competencies or standards expected, should be part of the discussion about the proposed teacher preparation course. Whether it is aimed to develop teachers who are knowledgeable, caring, sympathetic, and supportive or professional, should be clearly articulated at the onset of the course development. Having established a strong vision for the course, this should form the foundation for its further development.

Developing an appropriate course for enabling inclusive education for students with disabilities and other challenging needs requires deliberation on two fronts: (i) the curriculum to be offered and (ii) the pedagogy to be employed (see Figure 5.1).

The proposed curriculum

The following curriculum is proffered for preparing teachers to work in inclusive school communities and can be adjusted to accommodate teachers of all levels of students from early childhood through primary to secondary.

It is proposed that the curriculum should consist of three aspects, which focus on: (1) the philosophy of inclusive education; (2) disability, diversity, etiology and education implications; and (3) strategies for implementing an inclusive curriculum. Underpinning all of these will be the need for the development of knowledge, appropriate dispositions towards inclusion and performance practice. It is assumed that teachers will have an understanding of developmental, behavioral and attribution theories, mastery learning, the use of assistive technologies and direct instructional approaches, which all impact directly on preparation for inclusive education. The model orientation can be selected as appropriate to the context and would usually

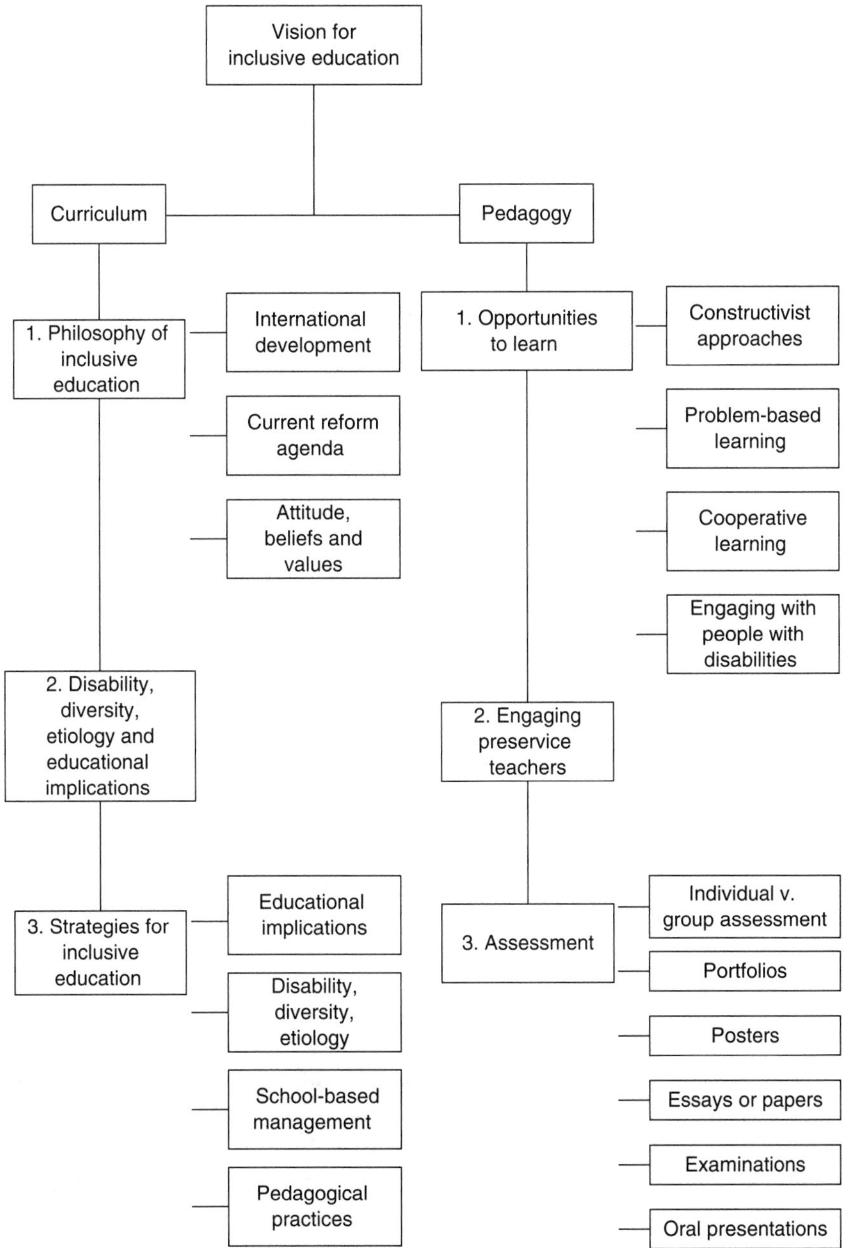

Figure 5.1 Curriculum framework for preparing teachers for inclusive education.

involve a humanistic, pedagogical (skills) or developmental psychological approach as the key focus, with some aspects of all orientations being included at various stages.

1 Philosophy of inclusive education

Discussion of the goals and theoretical background will help teachers to analyze and develop their own understandings while making personal sense of the philosophy. The ability to appreciate diversity from cognitive, cultural and behavioral perspectives and the development of a language of inclusion will enable further dialogue to occur within a common framework of understanding.

Current reform agendas within the jurisdiction in which the teachers will work should also include information about legislation, policy, practice and societal issues pertinent to the context. In particular, careful consideration should be given to the support that is available and how to access this. The importance of accountability and the development of a framework to enable this should occur in a collaborative manner. The roles of all stakeholders, including teachers, families, schools, peripatetic providers, community, society and government, need to be explored from the perspective of understanding and contributing to the concept of a fully inclusive school community.

Once teachers have an appreciation of the philosophy of inclusive education, a language with which to discuss it, and knowledge about their own jurisdiction's proposed directions, they are then in a position to start reflecting upon their own beliefs about inclusion. Their developing background knowledge will provide them with a context for debate about inclusion, their attitudes, myths, beliefs and assumptions. Consideration of the specific cultural issues, equity problems and discrimination issues will help to identify the challenges to be faced by inclusive education within their specific context. Acceptance, personal commitment and knowledge of how they can make a difference will enable the commencement of a moral and ethical stance about the individual roles they will need to play. This will also help them to become critical self-reflectors, a skill that will enhance their capacity to cope with future education change.

2 Disability, diversity, etiology and educational implications

Teachers will need the content knowledge about major types of disabilities and their etiologies. This should consider a medical model of disability, which was the traditional approach used to identify a student's need, and the more recent and generally more accepted social model approach. Information about disabilities that result in physical, intellectual or sensory impairments and other special needs that their students may have is important from the perspective of discussing ways in which they may support these students. A focus on student need and access issues taking a socio-ecological perspective will ensure attention to curriculum adaptation rather than attempting to 'fix' the child.

The most critical aspect of learning about disability is the need to consider the educational implications for systems, schools and teachers. This should involve a review of educational implications at a systemic and school level, such as the need for potential restructuring, provision of specific physical adaptations, and the initiation of curricula and instructional changes to support inclusion. The use of acceptable alternative and adaptive assessments and examination accommodations and the issue of peer acceptance across whole school communities and society at large are pertinent aspects to explore.

3 Strategies for inclusive education

With this background knowledge teachers can now explore the strategies that they can employ to enable them to help develop more inclusive school communities. School-based management strategies include an examination of whole school approaches and methods of identifying students with disabilities. The development of networks to support inclusion and the establishment of school-based support services in collaboration with other stakeholders and ways of developing school community links are all important aspects to consider, as many of these teachers will be the change agents of the future and called upon to help schools in transitioning towards inclusive school communities. Consideration of assessment practices for identifying levels of need and measuring achievement of students with disabilities, together with discussions about time management, are critical to ensure that as teachers they are able to manage all aspects of their work without undue stress or depression. Particular attention must be given to ways of differentiating homework so that students are only required to complete work at an appropriate level of difficulty (Westwood, 2004).

The final section of the teacher education curriculum should focus on the pedagogical practices that teachers employ to cater for the needs of all students in their classes. In the Asia-Pacific region, in countries such as Hong Kong, there is an education system where, according to Law *et al.* (2007), conflicting pedagogical orientation can be encountered at all levels. Curricula adaptation and modification across all learning areas, therefore, must involve both generic strategies and more specific skills related to students with targeted disabilities and in particular curricula areas. The application of cognitive and metacognitive approaches should be explored and strategies for addressing education, social, emotional and behavioral classroom issues identified. Procedures for identifying and monitoring student learning, recognizing and responding to different learning styles, and methods for utilizing peer support in classrooms should all be covered. Lesson planning for diversity and the use of Individual Education Plans where necessary should be explicitly taught.

The proposed pedagogy

Providing an appropriate pedagogy to engage teachers in their learning to become inclusive is vital. It will not only direct their own development but will also have the potential to allow them to engage in the type of pedagogical approaches that they can use in their own classrooms. Three aspects need to be considered, namely: (1) opportunities to learn, (2) engaging teachers, and (3) assessment.

There are numerous ways in which teachers can be provided with opportunities to learn about inclusive education and a multiple cross-disciplinary approach is highly desirable. Utilizing constructivist pedagogy, teachers can be expected to be actively involved in their own learning. By constructing their own knowledge base they are better able to consider the application to the local context and by sharing with colleagues to develop their own inclusive teaching philosophy. A problem-based learning (PBL) approach will require teachers to engage in working in collaborative groups to seek solutions to authentic problems. The problems should be related directly to the implementation of inclusive education in the local context and should stimulate their curiosity and help to initiate learning. Problem-based learning will encourage a realistic, critical and analytical approach to teaching and learning.

Cooperative learning will provide another opportunity to learn, by involving teachers working together to accomplish shared goals, resulting in positive interdependence. The teaming approach also establishes the idea of network support, which is an important aspect of inclusive education.

Access to people with disabilities is another important aspect of preparation as many teachers in the Asia-Pacific region will have had no prior opportunities to learn directly from involvement with people with disabilities. Visiting local schools where students with disabilities are educated and involving guest speakers as personal advocates for people with disabilities and parents of students with disabilities will help them to see the person first and not the disability. Involving students with disabilities from local schools in on-campus activities is another valuable opportunity to learn (see Forlin, 2003).

Engaging teachers in their own learning can take a number of different forms, which support constructivist, problem-based and cooperative learning philosophies. These include, but are not limited to, activities and strategies such as the use of case studies, videos, interviews with teachers, administrators, parents or students with disabilities, and action research.

If teachers are to be involved in constructing their own knowledge in preparation for teaching in inclusive classrooms, then it is important to review how best this learning can be assessed on completion of their course of study. This is particularly pertinent if they are engaging in a range of different pedagogies that will by their nature require alternative methods of assessment. Many of the proposed pedagogies involve group collaboration; therefore, consideration should be given to some assessment that requires group work while also retaining some individual assessment practices. Portfolios are particularly useful for allowing teachers to demonstrate learning over a period of time. They can include journal entries, lesson planning and information gleaned about different types of disability and educational implications for including students with disabilities. Examples of how lessons can be modified or ways of differentiating the curriculum to meet the needs of different groups of students are very useful.

Conclusion

The paradigm shift towards the education of students with disabilities in mainstream schools has been slowly increasing over the past two decades in the Asia-Pacific region. The normalization principle initiated in the early 1970s (Wolfensberger, 1972) established the move towards more inclusive societies, which was then furthered in education by the highly influential Salamanca Statement (UNESCO, 1994). Teacher education to support this changing philosophy has, however, tended to lag behind the practice in the Asia-Pacific region. While education systems have been relatively supportive of the inclusion movement by encouraging inclusive schools, teacher training institutions have been somewhat slower to make the necessary adjustments to preparation courses to prepare teachers for this change. Enacting the philosophy of inclusion necessitates not only theoretical and practical knowledge but also requires teachers to have the appropriate values, ideals, moral principles and ethical understandings to enable inclusion to happen. A teacher's belief system must be in agreement with the philosophy if they are going to be willing supporters of the development of really inclusive school communities.

Developing an appropriate curriculum for teachers across the Asia-Pacific region, while fraught with challenges, does provide the opportunity to ensure that they are better prepared to act as inclusive advocates. A suitable teacher curriculum requires attention to the framework to be adopted, the pedagogy to be used to access the curriculum, cultural sensitivities and the means of assessing learning. Underlying all aspects is the importance of developing critical thinkers who are problem-solvers and reflective practitioners who can work collegially so that they can adapt to the ever changing education school systems. Teachers need to gain the knowledge and appropriate dispositions and have had sufficient practice to be able to feel confident in becoming inclusive teachers.

Concomitantly, education systems in the Asia-Pacific region need to consider other education reforms such as smaller class sizes, more flexible pedagogies, alternative assessments and appropriate support mechanisms to sustain the growth of inclusion. There are many challenges to developing an inclusive approach to education and support for these needs to be considered across a range of circumstances (Forlin, 2007c). By developing a statewide equitable system for identifying and processing applications for accessing additional support from governments, schools are likely to feel more comfortable in accepting students with disabilities. By organizing the systematic upskilling of existing teachers, better training of new teachers, and encouraging collaboration and the development of localized support networks, school communities can begin to help each other in moving this model forward. With the introduction of school-based curriculum advisers and district consultants with specialized knowledge in specific disabilities and the development of inclusive schools, a hierarchical system of support will be ensured. Above all, education systems in the Asia-Pacific region need to support schools as they aim to build a new inclusive culture within their communities and to be prepared to provide the degree of support needed together with appropriate teacher training to enable inclusion to occur in a positive and productive mode.

References

Arbeiter, S. and Hartley, S. (2002) "Teachers' and pupils' experiences of integrated education in Uganda", *International Journal of Disability, Development and Education*, 49(1): 62–78.

Bakken, J. P., Aloia, G. F. and Aloia, S. F. (2002) "Preparing teachers for all students", in F. E. Obiakor, P. A. Grant and E. A. Dooley (eds), *Educating All Learners: Refocusing on the Comprehensive Support Model*, Springfield, IL: Charles C. Thomas, pp. 84–98.

Chan, C. W. M., Chang, R. M. L., Westwood P. and Yuen, M. (2002) "Teaching adaptively: How easy is it in practice? A perspective from Hong Kong", *Asia-Pacific Educational Researcher*, 11(1): 27–58.

Chong, S., Forlin, C. and Au, M. L. (2007) "The influence of an inclusive education course on attitude change of preservice secondary teachers in Hong Kong", *Asia-Pacific Journal of Teacher Education*, 35(2): 161–79.

Darling-Hammond, L. (2006) *Powerful Teacher Education: Lessons from Exemplary Programs*, San Francisco, CA: Jossey-Bass.

Forlin, C. (1998) "Teachers' personal concerns about including children with a disability in regular classrooms", *Journal of Developmental and Physical Disabilities*, 10(1): 87–110.

Forlin, C. (2003) "Preservice teacher education: Involvement of students with intellectual disabilities", *International Journal of Learning*, 10: 183–200.

Forlin, C. (2005) "Implementing an outcomes-focussed approach to learning: Implications for inclusive education", *Centre for Advancement of Special Education*, 1(2): 3–6.

Forlin, C. (2006) "Inclusive education in Australia ten years after Salamanca", *European Journal of Psychology of Education*, XXI(3): 265–77.

Forlin, C. (2007a) "Classroom diversity: towards a whole school approach", in S. N. Phillipson (ed.), *Learning Diversity in the Chinese Classroom: Contexts and Practice for Students with Special Needs*, Hong Kong: Hong Kong University Press, pp. 95–123.

Forlin, C. (2007b) "Inclusive educational practices: A way forward for Hong Kong", *Chinese Education and Society*, 39(5): 79–95.

Forlin, C. (2007c) "A collaborative, collegial and more cohesive approach to supporting educational reform for inclusion in Hong Kong", *Asia Pacific Education Review*, 8(2): 1–11.

Forlin, C., Loreman, T., Sharma, U. and Earle, C. (2007) "Demographic differences in changing preservice teachers' attitudes, sentiments and concerns about inclusive education", *International Journal of Inclusive Education*, 1–15.

Law, E. H-F., Joughin, G., Kennedy, K. J., Tse, H. and Yu, W. M. (2007) "Teacher educators' pedagogical principles and practices: Hong Kong perspectives", *Teaching in Higher Education*, 12(2): 247–61.

Loreman, T., Deppeler, J. M. and Harvey, D. H. P. (2005) *Inclusive Education: A Practical Guide to Supporting Diversity in the Classroom*, Sydney: Allen and Unwin.

Pang, Y. and Richey, D. (2006) "The development of special education in China", *International Journal of Special Education*, 21(1): 77–86.

Pearson, V., Lo, E., Chui, E. and Wong, D. (2003) "A heart to learn and care? Teachers' responses toward special needs children in mainstream schools in Hong Kong", *Disability & Society,* 18(4): 489–508.

Poon-McBrayer, K. F. (2005) "Full inclusion for children with severe learning difficulties: Ideology and reality", *Journal of International Special Needs Education,* 8: 19–26.

Sailor, W. and Skrtic, T. M. (1996) "School/community partnerships and educational reform", *Remedial and Special Education,* 17: 267–70.

Sharma, U., Forlin, C., Loreman, T. and Earle, C. (2006) "Preservice teachers' attitudes, concerns and sentiments about inclusive education: An international comparison of the novice preservice teacher", *International Journal of Special Education,* 21(2): 80–93.

Turner, N. D. (2003) "Preparing preservice teachers for inclusion in secondary classrooms", *Education,* 123(3): 491–5.

United Nations Educational, Scientific and Cultural Organization (1994) *The Salamanca Statement and Framework for Action on Special Needs Education*, Spain.

Westwood, P. S. (2004) *Learning and Learning Difficulties: Approaches to Teaching and Assessment,* London: David Fulton.

Wolfensberger, W. (1972) *Normalisation*, Toronto: National Institute on Mental Retardation.

Yeun, M., Westwood P. and Wong, G. (2004) "Meeting the needs of students with specific learning difficulties in the mainstream education system: Data from primary school teachers in Hong Kong", *The International Journal of Special Education,* 20(1): 67–76.

6 Preparing teachers to work with young children with disabilities

Hsin-Yi Wang

Chapter objectives

- To consider the importance of increasing the willingness of regular early childhood teachers in the Asia-Pacific region to work with children with disabilities.
- To provide an overview of how field experiences influence prospective regular early childhood teachers' attitudes about inclusive education.
- To offer an Industrial Collaboration model to provide special education training to regular early childhood educators.

Focus questions

1. How could a regular early childhood training program improve participants' willingness to work with children with disabilities?
2. How could a regular early childhood training program provide meaningful and practical training?
3. What models could be practically and efficiently applied in existing teacher training programs in the Asia-Pacific region to support inclusion?
4. What are the attitudes, concerns and perceptions of prospective early childhood teachers about inclusive education after interacting with children with disabilities?

Introduction

In order to meet the demands of inclusive education in the Asia-Pacific region, educational personnel must attain the necessary knowledge and skills required to work with children with disabilities. Insufficient training for early childhood educators working with children with disabilities, however, is often reported in the literature (e.g. Garner, 2000).

Practitioners in Taiwan, like those in other parts of the world and, in particular, the Asia-Pacific region, have been overwhelmed by the shift towards inclusive education. This movement encourages parents to enable their children with disabilities to receive education in regular classrooms; regular early childhood teachers, therefore, face a new challenge in assuming new roles and responsibilities. In Taiwan, the prevalence of children with a developmental delay is about 10 per cent (Simeonsson and Sharp, 1992). As there were 1,733,790 children under the age of six years in Taiwan in 2005 [Children's Bureau Ministry of the Interior (CBMI), 2006], this means there is likely to be at least 173,379 children with a developmental delay in Taiwan. There were, however, only 17,997 children receiving services in 2005 (CBMI, 2006). In other words, one hundred thousand children with developmental delays are either still unidentified or are placed in regular classrooms without receiving any special education services. Given this, the importance for early childhood personnel to have knowledge of young children with disabilities is apparent. Unfortunately, insufficient training in working with young children with disabilities is often reported in the literature (e.g. Garner, 2000).

In order to improve early childhood teachers' capabilities in working in inclusive environments in Taiwan, the Chia Nan University of Pharmacy and Science has launched an Early Intervention Program (EIP), in which an Industrial Collaboration model was utilized to provide practical knowledge and skills, as well as opportunities for field experience in early intervention institutions. Most of the preparation programs for early childhood teachers provide only two or four credit classes related to special education, which would seem to be insufficient to equip early childhood teachers to provide adequate inclusive education. The Industrial Collaboration model has emerged to help solve this problem. In Taiwan, universities can apply to the government for funding to seek partnerships with private industries/enterprises. Through these partnerships, professionals from partner institutions are invited to co-teach with university professors, and provide placements for field experience. While students attend these courses, they receive not only theory and practical information, but also field experience. There are many benefits of applying this model in existing programs. First, universities do not need to modify their course requirements, but simply add a few elective courses. Second, universities do not need to pay for this program, as government funding does. Third, professionals from the field are happy to be associated with universities because much of this funding is used to pay for their instruction and field supervision. Fourth, the training courses are less than a minor requirement and students can receive a certificate issued by the government. In addition, students get more hands-on experience.

The reason the Taiwan Government offers this funding is to increase college graduates' competitiveness in obtaining a teaching position upon completion of the course. This fund was initially given to business-related majors. The Chia Nan University of Pharmacy and Science is the first to employ this model for education-related courses. The aim of this program is twofold. First, it reflects the trend towards inclusion. Second, it encourages early childhood teachers to work with children with disabilities in regular classrooms after graduating.

Early childhood education for inclusion

Preschools or daycare centers are often the first place for a child's special needs to be recognized. When children receive a diagnosis, early childhood teachers are responsible for providing services to them as well as the rest of the class. Preschools and daycare centers are the places that will give children and parents their initial exposure to inclusion (Smith and Dlugosh, 1999). As a result, early childhood teachers' beliefs and attitudes towards children with disabilities will affect children's initial school experiences and further influence their outcomes and performance. Bricker (1995) suggests that attitude is one important factor of successful inclusion. In order for inclusion to be successful, regular early childhood teachers need to have a positive attitude towards young children with disabilities, as their beliefs and attitudes towards inclusion will influence their classroom behaviors, students' classroom behaviors, and students' learning outcomes.

Dinnebell *et al.* (1998) reported that early childhood teachers are willing to work with children with special needs; however, they are concerned about their capabilities to serve this group of students. Scruggs and Mastropieri (1996) reviewed 28 investigations that identified teachers' perceptions of inclusion from 1958 to 1995. The respondents included 10,560 teachers and other school staff from rural, urban, suburban, or combined school districts in the United States, New South Wales, Australia, and Canada. Of these, 6,459 respondents were identified as general education classroom teachers, two thirds of whom supported the concept of mainstreaming/inclusion, but only one third or less believed they had sufficient skills and training for inclusion. Lack of knowledge is clearly a barrier to catering for children with disabilities in regular environments (Pivik *et al.*, 2002). According to a survey conducted by Tang *et al.* (2005), most early intervention teachers have little training specializing in children with disabilities. Dew-Hughes and Brayton (1997) also indicated that over half of the participants they interviewed indicated that their college training had not prepared them to teach students with disabilities in regular classrooms.

The professional background of teachers and caregivers, including their training and experience in working with students with disabilities, has been found to influence their attitudes, beliefs, and expectations for children with disabilities (Sadler, 2005). Hastings and Oakford (2003), on the contrary argued that these effects are limited. In particular, Hastings *et al.* (1996) reported that the attitudes of prospective teachers were not affected by completion of special education courses but only by their previous experience with students with disabilities. Tait and Purdie (2000) similarly agreed that changes in prospective teachers' attitudes towards disability over a one-year general teacher training course were found to be minimal. However, Bender *et al.* (1995) found that attitudes towards including children with disabilities in regular classrooms did correlate positively with the number of courses taken on special education. Campbell and Gilmore (2003) investigated whether formal instruction with structured fieldwork experiences could foster a favorable change in attitudes towards disabilities and inclusion. Their results demonstrated that participants had a much more positive view of the benefits of inclusion, and nominated a regular classroom as the best educational settings for children with disabilities after appropriate experience.

Training and previous experiences with students with disabilities, as well as positive attitudes towards inclusion, may interact with each other to influence regular early childhood teachers' willingness to teach children with special needs.

Employing an Industrial Collaboration model

In order to improve graduates' prospects in the market as well as reflect the trend of inclusion, the Department of Childhood and Infancy in Chia Nan University of Pharmacy and Science launched an EIP in September 2005. The program was designed to increase prospective early childhood teachers' skills and awareness when working with young children with disabilities. In order to finish the EIP, students had to complete ten courses related to young children, comprising of: (1) child development; (2) observation; (3) health care; (4) body evaluation; (5) developmental evaluation; (6) problem behavior; (7) introduction to special education; (8) individualized education program (9) behavioral management; and (10) health care of young children with disabilities. The first seven courses are major requirements with the latter three being electives. These courses are taught using a co-teaching model involving university professors and professionals from one child center serving children with developmental delays. Participants receive lessons in the classroom and attend at least 36 hours of field experience.

The design of the EIP is grounded in the work of John Dewey (1904, 1959) in that teacher preparation should not be limited to a theoretical basis but should also include relevant practical experience. Combining both campus-based training and field experience has been found to be one of the most effective training methods. The purpose of the EIP training program is to increase prospective early childhood teachers' willingness and skills when working with young children with disabilities in inclusive environments.

A review of the program was undertaken to establish its success in achieving these aims and in order to identify how to make changes in the program to increase its efficiency and effectiveness. A survey was developed to collect the opinions and suggestions of the 82 students participating in the EIP. After collecting data, the researcher found some interesting contradictory opinions expressed by the participants. As a result, 20 participants were randomly drawn for an informal interview.

Instrument

A total of nine questions were presented in the survey. In the first section, the participants were asked if they would be willing to work with young children with disabilities in the future. The response option was a dichotomous yes/no. If the participants answered yes, they were invited to indicate which listed resources and supports (i.e., more information on children with disabilities, behavioral management skills, etc.) were needed in order to care for a young child with disabilities. Participants were then asked to identify all that applied to their own situation. If the participants answered no, they were asked to indicate the potential reasons (not having sufficient information on children with disabilities, not having patience, etc.) for not wanting to work with young children with disabilities in the future.

In the second section, opinions were sought regarding the EIP. First, participants were asked if their attitude changed after participating in the EIP. Next, they were asked what they had learned from field experiences. In addition, they were also asked how they felt about instruction from outside professionals using the co-teaching style. An anonymous survey was distributed at the end of the training program with a return rate of 100 per cent. Interviews focused on how useful the participants believed the content provided from the outside instructors was.

Changing attitudes towards children with disabilities

Fifty-eight participants (70 per cent) stated that their attitude towards young children with disabilities had changed after participating in the EIP, while 56 participants (68 per cent) indicated that their attitude had changed from fearfulness to acceptance and care. The remaining participants either continued to hold the same attitudes or in the case of two participants they indicated a change from acceptance and care to fearfulness.

Being willing to work with children with disabilities

Of the cohort 32 participants (39 per cent) indicated a willingness to become special educators or work in special education institutions after graduating; while 48 participants (59 per cent) were unwilling to do this. Sixty-five participants (80 per cent) were welcoming of young children with disabilities into their regular classrooms, although 17 participants (20 per cent) did not agree with inclusive environments.

Supports and barriers to serving children with disabilities

Students who indicated a willingness to work with children with disabilities were asked to state the supports they would need in order to provide quality of care. The need for knowledge of teaching strategies was reported most frequently; then more information on disabilities, environmental adaptations, behavioral management skills, more adult assistance, and funds for special equipment were listed, in that order.

While investigating why they were unwilling to become a special educator or work in special education institutions, most participants stated that they believed that they did not have sufficient knowledge and skills to take care of young children with disabilities. The second reason cited was that they were worried that they could not take good care of them and might hurt the children in some way. Participants witnessed the need for additional health care and assistive technology for young children with disabilities during their field placements and they expressed their concerns about this in their reflective journals. The third reason was that they were concerned that they might not have patience with young children with disabilities. Other reasons reported included being unable to provide needed assistive technology, worrying about the legal issues of taking care of young children with disabilities, insufficient experience, and fearfulness.

Learned knowledge

Students were asked to identify what they had learned from the EIP. The most reported item was the realization of the job description for special education teachers. The second was that field experience provided a practical opportunity to understand inclusion and to become familiar with special education environments. In addition, the field experience gave them an opportunity to consider whether or not they would like to work in early intervention institutions and, finally, to practice what they had learned in school.

Co-teaching

Fifty-four participants (66 per cent) expressed their appreciation of the co-teaching mode of instruction, although 17 participants (21 per cent) did not like this style. The participants were asked to tick all benefits that resulted from using outside instructors. The most reported benefit was learning useful practical information (80 per cent). The second most reported benefit was the opportunity to combine theory and practice (62 per cent). Only 34 participants (41 per cent), however, believed the content provided by the outside instructors would be useful for them in the future, with 12 participants (15 per cent) indicating that they did not think it would be useful. Individual interviews were conducted to find out more about this apparent contradiction. Three out of 20 interviewees stated that while outside instructors gave much practical information, without fully understanding the theoretical aspects, it was hard for them to make the most of the information.

Discussion

Training and experiences appear to influence prospective early childhood teachers in a positive direction. First, these increased their positive attitudes towards young children and helped to change their stereotypical impressions of children with disabilities. During the field placements participants used terms such as "adorable", "handsome", "cute", and "charming" to describe children with disabilities. Unfortunately, a few students witnessed the arduous work of taking care of young children with profound needs, and this made them more negative towards young children with disabilities. It is, however, important for prospective early childhood teachers to examine their motivation for working with children with disabilities as early as possible. Higher internal motivation is correlated with a higher level of commitment to work; a higher commitment to work will subsequently result in greater performance and better student outcomes.

Second, 80 per cent of participants expressed a willingness to welcome young children with disabilities into their regular classrooms in the future. This was very encouraging, as successful inclusive education depends on collaboration among special educators, regular educators, and other school teachers. Third, it came as a surprise that 39 per cent of participants would like to work in special education schools in the future. The EIP was designed to increase prospective early childhood teachers' abilities and willingness to work with young children with disabilities in regular classrooms instead of preparing them as special education teachers. The exposure to young children with disabilities gave participants opportunities to see how special education services influence a child and also made them more willing to work as a special educator.

Although there are encouraging results arising from the EIP, a lack of confidence is still noticeable in the participants. Those who were willing to work with children with disabilities have now received training in behavioral management skills, special education, and planning individualized education programs, as well as other related courses; yet they still reflect the need for increased training in teaching methods, more practical information, greater knowledge of environmental adaptations, and behavioral management skills. For those who expressed an unwillingness to work in a special education environment, the major reason was insufficient confidence in working with young children with disabilities. Moreover, it was interesting that participants also considered that having too much practical information without supporting theoretical knowledge might not be valuable.

In order for training to be beneficial, some suggestions might be considered. These ideas, while applicable to the Taiwanese situation, would also be relevant for most of the Asia-Pacific region. First, the theoretical background of teaching knowledge should be introduced and completed before participants are involved in too much practical work. Next, the duration of field experience could be extended. Participants reflected that they still did not have sufficient time to interact with young children in the field placements and to stay in the special education classrooms in order to involve themselves in the children's daily life. One possibility may be to offer internships during the summer vacation. Third, there is a need to provide more knowledge regarding the use of assistive technologies and special equipment for young children with disabilities.

Conclusion

The aim of the EIP in Taiwan is to improve prospective early childhood teachers' capabilities of working in inclusive environments and to develop more positive attitudes towards young children with disabilities. This is critical across the whole of the Asia-Pacific region, where the movement towards greater inclusion of children is being embraced in many early childhood settings. Although a positive influence could be observed from the EIP training, it is undeniable that some modification needs to be made. For example, both university professors and outside professionals may need to adjust their co-teaching style, and the time spent in field placements should be extended. The EIP offered in Chia Nan University of Pharmacy and Science does, however, present some encouraging results. It is hoped that other early childhood teacher preparation programs in Taiwan and elsewhere in the Asia-Pacific region could also develop similar programs to promote prospective early childhood teachers' enthusiasm in working with children with disabilities. It is important if inclusion is to be employed well in early childhood settings throughout the Asia-Pacific region that more and more regular early childhood teachers are ready to welcome young children with disabilities into their classrooms and are adequately prepared to provide an appropriate inclusive environment.

References

Bender, W. N., Vail, C. O. and Scott, K. (1995) "Teachers' attitudes toward increased mainstreaming: Implementing effective instruction for students with learning disabilities", *Journal of Learning Disabilities*, 28(2): 87–94.

Bricker, D. (1995) "The challenge of inclusion", *Journal of Early Intervention*, 19: 179–94.

Campbell, J. and Gilmore, L. (2003) "Changing students' attitudes toward disability and inclusion", *Journal of Intellectual and Developmental Disability*, 28: 369–79.

Children's Bureau Ministry of the Interior (2006) Online. Available at: http://www.cbi.gov.tw/welcome.jsp (accessed 15 March 2007).

Dewey, J. (1904) "The relation of theory to practice in the education of teachers", in C. A. McMurry (ed.), *The Third Yearbook of the National Society for the Scientific Study of Education*, Chicago: University of Chicago Press, pp. 9–30.

Dewey, J. (1959) *Experience and Education*, New York: MacMillan.

Dew-Hughes, D. and Brayton, H. (1997) "Initial teacher training and pupils with special education needs", *Support for Learning*, 12: 175–9.

Dinnebell, L. A., McInerney, W., Fox, C. and Juchartz-Pendry, K. (1998) "An analysis of the perceptions and characteristics of childcare teachers regarding inclusion of young children with special needs in community-based programs", *Topics in Early Childhood Special Education*, 18: 118–28.

Garner, P. (2000) "Pretzel only policy? Inclusion and the real world of initial teacher education", *British Journal of Special Education*, 27: 111–16.

Hastings, R. P. and Oakford, S. (2003) "Student teachers' attitude toward the inclusion of children with special needs", *Educational Psychology*, 23: 87–94.

Hastings, R. P., Hewes, A., Lock, S. and Witting, A. (1996) "Do special educational needs courses have any impact on student teachers' perceptions of children with severe learning difficulties?", *British Journal of Special Education*, 23: 139–44.

Pivik, J., McComas, J. and LaFlamme, M. (2002) "Barriers and facilitators to inclusive education", *Exceptional Children*, 69: 97–107.

Sadler, J. (2005) "Knowledge, attitudes and beliefs of the mainstream teachers of children with a preschool diagnosis of speech/language impairment", *Child Language Teaching and Therapy*, 21: 147–63.

Scruggs, T. E. and Mastropieri, M. A. (1996) "Teacher perceptions of mainstreaming/inclusion, 1958–1995: A research synthesis", *Exceptional Children*, 63: 59–74.

Simeonsson, R. J. and Sharp, M. C. (1992) "Developmental delays", in R. A. Hoekelman, S. B. Friedman, N. M. Nelson and H. M. Seidel (eds), *Primary Pediatric Care*, 2nd edn, St. Louis, MO: Mosby-Year Book, pp. 867–70.

Smith, M. K. and Dlugosh, L. L. (1999) "Early childhood classroom teachers' perceptions of successful inclusion: a multiple case study", Paper presented at the Annual Conference of the American Educational Research Association, April, Quebec, Canada.

Tait, K. and Purdie, N. (2000) "Attitude toward disability: Teacher education for inclusive environments in an Australian university", *International Journal of Disability, Development and Education*, 47: 25–38.

Tang, C., Ling, J., Kung, J., Wu, S., Jean, Y. and Lin, M. (2005) "The study of role and competence of the early intervention professionals of the institutions for the young children with special needs in Taiwan", *Journal of Disability Research (Taiwan)*, 3: 141–58.

7 Training of Special Needs Officers in Singapore to support inclusion

Kaili Chen and Kenneth Poon

Chapter objectives

- To examine Special Needs Officers' (SNOs) perspectives on including students with disabilities in general education classes in Singapore.
- To identify the expectation of the training needs of SNOs.
- To look into the feasibility of successful inclusion in Singapore and the concerns of SNOs.

Focus questions

1. What are the SNOs' expectations of the Diploma of Special Education training program?
2. How can the mainstream schools and different levels of the society provide support for the special needs personnel?
3. What are the SNOs' concerns, hopes and needs of having students with special needs in the general education setting?
4. How can education systems in the Asia-Pacific region provide suitable programs for training special needs personnel in mainstream schools?

Introduction

To support students with dyslexia and autism spectrum disorder in regular education schools in Singapore, Special Needs Officers (SNOs) have been introduced in primary and secondary schools. This chapter examines the SNOs' perspectives on including students with special needs in general education classes, and thereby considers the feasibility of successful inclusion in Singapore. Issues addressed include the SNOs' expectations of the training program, how mainstream schools and different levels of the society can provide support for them, and their concerns, hopes and needs for having students with disabilities in the general education setting.

An inclusive education system is one that strives to produce the best outcomes for all students (National Association of State Boards of Education, 1992). More than merely referring to physical placement, inclusion has to do with how schools respond to individual differences and needs by developing environments that promote the social and educational success of students with disabilities. When implementing transformation in the climate of support for students with disabilities in schools, professional training for inclusive education plays an essential role.

Although the inclusion of students with disabilities in general education settings has been written into the US legislation since the 1960s, guaranteeing the right to a free, appropriate public education and merging general and special education into one system adequate for all students, this has not been realized in many countries of the Asia-Pacific region, including Singapore. Currently, the majority of students with moderate to severe physical or intellectual disabilities in Singapore are educated in special schools. In 2004, only about 730 students with physical and sensory disabilities attended mainstream schools (Tan and Yap, 2004), compared to the 3–5 per cent of the student population with dyslexia and the 0.5 per cent with autism who are not identified and supported within the mainstream schools (Lee, 2004).

In Singapore, special education schools are mainly run by voluntary welfare organizations that are responsible for the school curriculum and management rather than the Ministry of Education (Chen and Tan, 2006). Nevertheless, the government has taken on a central, coordinating and monitoring role in special education. In August 2004, the Ministry of Education proposed measures to improve special education in the mainstream setting. This involved the training of SNOs to support students with autism spectrum disorder and dyslexia in particular in general education schools (Lee, 2004). These SNOs are to provide structured and systematic support to enable these students to cope with the academic, social, physical and emotional demands of school life in selected schools. The main responsibilities of SNOs include: (a) provision of withdrawal and in-class support, specialized remediation and implementation of Individual Education Plans; (b) consultation with teachers and parents to facilitate better understanding of the students' needs and how to support them; (c) set up and maintenance of special needs friendly classroom/school environments; and (d) collaboration with external professionals/agencies supporting the special needs students.

Training for the Special Needs Officers

The stated aim was that by 2010, 236 SNOs would be recruited and trained at diploma level (Lee, 2004). From July 2005 to May 2007, 32 SNOs were trained in the Diploma of Special Education (DISE) program at the National Institute of Education (NIE). The program is highly practice oriented to ensure a direct linkage with the real issues and problems encountered by the teachers. The major courses offered in the DISE include: introduction to special education, educational psychology I and II, information and communications technologies (ICT) for engaged learning and practice and intervention techniques. The SNOs are required to select two of the following courses: (a) sensory and physical disabilities; (b) intellectual disabilities; (c) multiple disabilities; and (d) emotional/behavioral disorders; and to select additional courses either from the Autism Resource Center or the

Dyslexia Association of Singapore. Field experience is also required at the end of the training.

This first batch of SNOs has been receiving training part-time while they are working in the mainstream schools. However, from the academic year 2006–7 onward, the DISE will be offered as a one-year full-time program. Beninghof (1996) posits that to maximize the success of training programs for educational personnel, staff development activities must be shaped in such a way that take staff's attitudes, perceptions, readiness and knowledge of inclusion into consideration. To this end, a summary was administered to examine the SNOs' (*N*=30) perspectives on including students with disabilities in mainstream settings, and, thereby, consider the feasibility of successful inclusion in Singapore.

Data on the SNOs perspectives regarding inclusion were collected during a class period of their first course, "Introduction to Special Education and Understanding Disabilities", in the DISE program in July 2005. The SNOs were asked to fill out a survey developed by the authors focused on their perspectives on special education and the inclusion of students with disabilities in the general education setting in Singapore. Only one out of the 30 had more than five years of teaching experience. The rest of the participants had previously worked in different professions, including social work, business, the military and nursing. About 73 per cent were aged between 21–30 years. The others were older than 30.

The data accrued from the surveys were analyzed through a descriptive format that identifies the small narrative units of the meaning within it and the themes of the information they provide (Bogdan and Biklen, 2003). The following sections present and interpret these qualitative data.

Perceptions of the Special Needs Officers

Four overarching themes were revealed in the data: (a) SNOs' expectations of the DISE training program, the mainstream schools, and the community in terms of support for their role as SNOs in the general education setting during the training; (b) the SNOs' concerns of having students with special needs in the general education school setting; (c) the SNOs' perceptions of hopes (i.e. what they hope to see happen after the child with special needs has been integrated into the general education system) of having students with special needs in the general education school setting; and (d) the SNOs' perceptions of their needs (i.e. what can be done on their part to help them obtain their hopes) of having students with special needs in the general education school setting.

SNOs' expectations of the DISE training program, the mainstream schools and the community

The SNOs gave a variety of responses to the first question, which asked them about their expectations of the DISE training program, the mainstream schools and societal support. All of them were able to give reasons in terms of what they expected. Some of their expectations of the DISE program included having a website designed specially for them, so that they could have a forum page for discussion and sharing. A few of them hoped that they would be equipped with skills, experiences, tools and knowledge (both theoretical and practical) so that they could confidently help students and assist regular education teachers. Some of them expressed an interest in learning more about the different types of support given by associations from Singapore and other countries. Some expected the DISE to provide extra programs such as counseling, and useful training and workshops. Many hoped that the courses provided would be relevant and applicable to their work and that at the end of the training they would be able to meet the expectations of the schools and the Ministry of Education. Some came to the program expecting that their perceptions of special needs education would be broadened and that they would understand the challenges of students with disabilities better. Quite a few of the participants also indicated that they would like to gain more practical knowledge that would enable them to work effectively with students with disabilities, prepare them for the society, and eventually to make an impact on the children's lives.

Some SNOs suggested that the DISE program should: (a) be amended to allow specialization in more than one area; (b) provide more field trips; (c) have a full-time DISE course so that the SNOs could have the option to complete it part-time or full-time; (d) raise the standard in terms of subjects and topics taught; and (e) provide a clear and standardized identification of students with special needs.

Regarding their expectations of the mainstream schools, the majority of the SNOs hoped that schools would provide ongoing, proactive support for them and for the students with disabilities. With regards to the expectations of the community and society at large, SNOs hoped to have increased interaction with social services in the community. They would like the community to organize talks and workshops on different disabilities and to make members in the community more aware of their roles. Some mentioned that there should be increased publicity of efforts on special education in Singapore.

There was some overlap in the expectations of the DISE training program, schools and society at large. Generally speaking, the SNOs responses provided valuable information. They made positive and hopeful comments about inclusion. This information should be taken into consideration as the NIE and the Ministry of Education continue to improve the training program and the general welfare of students with disabilities in Singapore.

SNOs' concerns of having students with special needs in the mainstream school setting

In general, the SNOs were concerned about the lack of support from schools and that students with disabilities were not accepted and may be discriminated against in the schools. They were worried that the teachers may not be aware of the needs of students with disabilities in a general education setting and, therefore, might not be tolerant and patient towards the students, or be unwilling to cooperate.

Another theme that emerged from responses to this question was the SNOs' concerns about their own competency. Some were worried because they felt that they would have to learn by trial and error in order to find something effective for a particular child, as they were not yet fully trained while they were working. A few commented that at this stage they were not sure how to support students with disabilities and help them adapt and blend better into the mainstream setting. Some were concerned that even with the support from the SNOs, students with disabilities might still be unable to cope with the mainstream curriculum.

Some of the concerns regarding inclusion that the SNOs voiced revolved around the lack of parental support, peer support and environmental support for the students with disabilities. They felt that schools should be more flexible and proactive about receiving students with disabilities, as the students will need people's understanding and willingness to adjust and allow them to integrate. Some were afraid that these students might be isolated because of their disabilities. Another concern raised was that some of these children might not have any place to go to after their secondary school education.

Some SNOs were concerned about their roles and responsibilities in schools. One example given was that schools will look to them alone to provide all the support when it actually involves parents, teachers and other professionals. One SNO commented that since they have to go through the training part-time while they are working in the schools, it would be challenging for them to cope with assignments, examinations and work. Other concerns raised included the impact of students with disabilities on learning, their medical status and low socio-economic status, as well as the procedures involved to identify and include these children in the regular education schools.

SNOs' perceptions of hope

This question was about their aspirations after the students with disabilities were included into the general education system. The majority hoped to see more support from other stakeholders. They would like to work closely with the classroom teachers to improve strategies to help the students. They also hoped that that school principals and other professionals would give full support to programs for students with disabilities; and that parents and school staff could come together for a collaborative effort to understand the children with special needs better and to create a support group for these children.

The SNOs' hopes for the students with disabilities were fivefold: academic, existential, independence, society and social. Many commented that they would like to see these students lead relatively normal lives and survive in society on their own or with minimal assistance from others. It was also hoped that students with disabilities would have to study fewer subjects in school so that they could cope with their learning disabilities better. Last but not least, some SNOs would like to see students with disabilities accepted better by society; their desire being that people would recognize them as unique individuals who have the potential to learn and grow despite their disabilities.

SNOs' perceptions of their own needs

Regarding attitude and commitment, the participants mentioned that they would need to accept the children for who they were; they also needed to have the right attitude, a lot of patience, perseverance, love and compassion, and passion and enthusiasm to learn and find out more.

With regards to skills and knowledge needed, the participants perceived that they would require the skills and techniques to gather information and resources and to have a good working knowledge of students with disabilities in order to be able to create awareness programs when needed. Some mentioned that they needed to gain greater awareness of how to support students with disabilities and to seek external help from more experienced people.

The need for collaboration with others included the opportunity to work with parents and teachers closely and to provide school staff with the correct information so as to create a conductive environment for students with disabilities. Communication with the special needs students and their peers, families and general education teachers was also considered important.

Conclusion and implications for practice

The results of the present investigation demonstrate the SNOs' perspectives on including students with disabilities in regular education schools in Singapore. In summary, their expectations for the different stakeholders involved in the training as well as the wider society are reasonable. They also had a positive outlook on inclusion, and, in general, their comments about having special needs students in the regular classroom were optimistic and hopeful. They believed that, with the right attitude and commitment, sufficient knowledge and skills, and effective collaboration with others, students with special needs will be successfully integrated into the general education system.

However the SNOs did have a number of areas of concern regarding their own roles and responsibilities in supporting these students in mainstream schools. Many mentioned that school staff and society at large should be more aware of the SNO scheme and should give them sufficient respect and recognition. The findings also highlight concerns about the lack of support from schools, parents and the community. The data suggest that the situation can be improved if there is a shared understanding between the schools and the community about the SNOs' roles and responsibilities. Better awareness programs of special education services (e.g. support provided by the SNOs) and information sharing on disabilities and interventions are needed. Many of these issues are likely to be reflected across the Asia-Pacific region as all systems investigate a range of options for supporting students with disabilities in mainstream schools. We also suggest that in order to strengthen paraprofessional support, the local government, the training institute and schools should work together more closely and collaborate effectively to provide appropriate training and supervision for paraprofessionals.

The perspectives of the SNOs regarding having students with disabilities in the general education setting provide invaluable information for planning appropriate training. These perceptions should be taken into consideration as the NIE and the Ministry of Education continue to improve the DISE training program and the general welfare of students with disabilities in Singapore. We also suggest that future policy development and training programs for special education paraprofessionals should consider the expectations, concerns, hopes and needs of the SNOs in order to improve the SNO scheme, as well as other professional development opportunities.

More research is needed to determine how special education professional development programs can be improved and how to effectively support and utilize paraprofessionals in inclusive schools. We hope that by raising the issues presented here, we can extend the discussion in Singapore concerning the best practices to support special needs students in general education settings to other Asia-Pacific regions.

References

Beninghof, A. M. (1996) "Using a spectrum of staff development activities to support inclusion", *Journal of Staff Development*, 17(3): 12–5.

Bogdan, R. and Biklen, S. (2003) *Qualitative Research for Education: An Introduction to Theory and Methods*, 4th edn, Boston, MA: Allyn & Bacon.

Chen, K. and Tan, C. S. (2006) "Education and services for children and youth with emotional/behavioral problems in Singapore", *Preventing School Failure*, 50(2): 37–42.

Lee, L. (2004) "Teachers get special needs training", *The Straits Times*, 24 September, p.1.

National Association of State Boards of Education (1992) *Winners All: A Call for Inclusive Schools*, Alexandria, VA: Author.

Tan, T. and Yap, S. (2004) "Specials kids coping in mainstream", *The Straits Times*, 24 September, p. 1.

8 Teachers' attitudes, perceptions and concerns about inclusive education in the Asia-Pacific region

Chris Forlin, Mei-Lan Au and Stella Chong

Chapter objectives

- To consider current school reform in Hong Kong for inclusive education.
- To provide an overview of teachers' beliefs and concerns about inclusive education.
- To forward the discussion about relevant teacher education for inclusion in the Asia-Pacific region.

Focus questions

1. What is the direction of special education reform in Hong Kong for children with special education needs in mainstream schools?
2. What are the attitudes, concerns and perceptions of teachers about inclusive education at the start of their teacher training?
3. What considerations need to be given to the training needs of teachers to prepare them for working in inclusive schools in the Asia-Pacific region?

Introduction

The movement towards inclusive education has become a major focus in recent education reform across the Asia-Pacific region. This is particularly noticeable in Hong Kong. As teachers are being expected to cater for students with diverse abilities in their classes, there is an urgent need to reconsider current teacher preparation courses by identifying and responding to the concerns of teachers in training and those already in the workforce. This chapter discusses the major changes for Hong Kong regarding special education in relation to the reform process for mainstream schools and considers the implications for preparing teachers for inclusion across the Asia-Pacific region. An investigation of the beliefs, attitudes and concerns of teachers as they participate in a teacher training course was conducted to enable a discussion about how best to address these in order to support the inclusive movement.

The inclusion movement

Increasingly, both in the West and throughout the Asia-Pacific region, regular class teachers are being asked to cater for the needs of students with disabilities and diverse abilities in their mainstream classrooms (Loreman *et al.*, 2005). Many teachers, though, hesitate about including students with disabilities since they feel that they lack the specialized skills to cater for this group of students. A teacher's willingness to include specific students is also strongly influenced by factors such as their attributes (Sachs, 2004), the nature and severity of the disabling conditions of the learners (Elkins and Porter, 2005), availability of physical and human resources (Bradshaw and Mundia, 2006), and their teacher training (Chong *et al.*, 2007). A teacher's support and positive attitude towards inclusive education is, however, essential for its successful implementation as they are the ones who work closely with students on a daily basis (Forlin, 2007a).

Special education reform in Hong Kong

Education reform in Hong Kong has, particularly in recent years, focused on the need to develop more inclusive schools that can cater for students with special education needs (Forlin, 2007b). There is clearly a new direction for special education with the expectation that regular schools should all work towards adopting a whole school integrated approach. The idea of including students with disabilities in mainstream schools is not new to Hong Kong, as the government first proposed integration in the mid-1970s (Hong Kong Government, 1977, 4.2c), but it is only in recent years that, following the declaration of the Salamanca Statement (UNESCO, 1994), the *Disability Discrimination Ordinance* (DDO) was enacted in Hong Kong (1996), making it unlawful to discriminate against a person in education provision on the grounds of disability [Equal Opportunities Commission (EOC), 2007]. The government initially implemented a pilot project on integration in 1997. At that time only children with five types of disabilities – mild grade intellectual disability, visual impairment, hearing impairment, physical disability and autistic disorder with average intelligences – were officially recommended to study in mainstream schools [Education Bureau (EDB), 2007a], and only then if they could participate in the mainstream curriculum with little adaptation. Their learning progress was measured by the existing assessment system.

Following the later enactment of the DDO *Code of Practice on Education* (EOC, 2001), the EDB required all schools to adopt a whole school integrated approach to cater for the special needs of students (Education Department, 2002). This policy is regarded as equivalent to inclusion and requires schools to make full use of all available resources within the school including peer support, adopt differentiated teaching strategies and accommodations in assessments, and make curriculum adaptation to meet students' diverse learning needs (EDB, 2007a).

Though this new policy seems to be driving special education reform towards the implementation of inclusion in schools, the practice continues to be stalled by the fundamental structure of the Hong Kong schooling system. Such foundational problems are also occurring in many other Asia-Pacific regions. In this highly academic oriented and selective education system, each student is allocated to a secondary school with reference to their academic achievement in the last two years of primary schooling (Luk, 2005). A three-tier banding system exists (with Band 1 for the superior performers and Band 3 for the poor performers). Thus, children who have low academic performance are only eligible for a place in less demanding primary schools and then in Band 3 secondary schools. Children with autism, sensory impairments and other disabilities will be placed depending upon their academic ability. As a result, a dual system of special and mainstream schooling continues.

Despite these constraints, the EDB is still fully supportive of establishing a whole school approach. Schools that elect to take on this approach must develop an "...integration policy, create(s) an inclusive environment and mobilize school personnel to support students with special educational needs" to accommodate all students needs (EDB, 2007a). In the 2007–8 school year 39 primary and 38 secondary schools in Hong Kong have adopted this *Whole School Approach to Integrated Education*. In addition, there are 282 schools participating in the new funding mode pilot scheme entitled the *Whole School Approach to Cater for Students' Diverse Learning Needs* (EDB, 2007b). Schools participating in this new mode are given greater autonomy and flexibility in resource usage. These schools are required to adopt five strategies of school-based support, including (1) early identification, (2) early intervention, (3) an whole school approach, (4) home–school cooperation, and (5) cross-sector collaboration. The government is supporting teachers by providing a range of professional development (PD) training days and funding short PD training courses at universities.

Teacher training for inclusion

Since the 2004–5 school year in Hong Kong all graduates of preservice primary and secondary teacher education programs have to be degree holders. It is also the government's long-term policy to require all existing teachers at sub-degree status to upskill to degree level. In the 2006–7 school year, there were approximately 540 public sector primary schools and 410 secondary schools that accepted students with special education needs (including those identified as low academic achievers). In these schools 7 per cent ($n = 1300$) of primary teachers and 5 per cent ($n = 930$) of secondary teachers had received some type of special education training (EDB, 2007c). Clearly the vast majority of mainstream teachers have received no relevant training at this time.

If inclusive education is to become a reality in Hong Kong then it is essential that all teachers are not only sufficiently trained but also willing to support this reform (Forlin, 2007b). Preservice training is frequently promoted as being the best time to address teachers' concerns, and possibly modify their negative attitudes towards students with disabilities and their perceptions about inclusive education (Chong *et al.*, 2007; Loreman *et al.*, 2005). The initial attitudes of preservice teachers can be crucial to the success of inclusion (Wilczenski, 1992). To this, Loreman *et al.* (2007) found in their study with Australian and Canadian preservice teachers that there was a positive trend in attitudes, less concerns and increased levels of comfort associated with greater knowledge of disability, either through a better understanding of disability discrimination or education acts.

Furthermore, many researchers have also found that preservice teachers who have had contact with siblings or a range of different people with disabilities indicate the lowest levels of discomfort during interactions and indicate more positive sentiments about and less concern towards inclusive practices (Chong *et al.*, 2007; Loreman *et al.*, 2007).

Preparing teachers to cater for diversity in schools in Hong Kong has undergone a number of meaningful changes in recent years. In the past, training about children with disabilities or special needs was mainly given to special school teachers. Apart from organizing in-service courses for mainstream teachers, teacher training institutions now aim to ensure that preservice teachers are better equipped with the basic knowledge and skills to cater for the needs of an increasing range of diverse learners in mainstream settings. Many of these training courses, though, are only 30 hours, which barely cover the basic knowledge and skills; others are one-off thematic talks and seminars organized by various organizations. Such courses have been criticized as being similar to an instant noodles approach (Lo, 2003), which does nothing to address the fundamental shift necessary in attitudes and beliefs to bring about real change.

Formal training has been recognized as a critical time to address teachers' concerns and to develop more positive attitudes towards students with disabilities and inclusive education (Sharma *et al.*, 2006). The next section of this chapter discusses a study that aims to identify the attitudes, perceptions and concerns about inclusive education of a group of students who were undertaking a postgraduate degree course to qualify as teachers in regular primary or secondary schools. The cohort included some participants who were already working as teachers in schools and were using this course to gain more specific skills.

Attitudes, perceptions and concerns about inclusion

All participants in the study were enrolled in a one-year full-time or two-year part-time Postgraduate Diploma in Education (PGDE) course. While this would enable them to become qualified teachers, some had already been working in schools as uncertificated teachers, as they already had an undergraduate degree in a range of curriculum areas. The cohort of 86, included approximately equal numbers of male and female participants. Of these, 55 per cent were studying to teach in a secondary school and 45 per cent were preparing to teach in a primary school. All were enrolled in the same institution in Hong Kong and most were planning to teach locally when qualified.

A self-reporting questionnaire that had been used in Australia and Canada for similar purposes was employed (Sharma *et al.*, 2006). The questionnaire was translated into Chinese, through which data were collected prior to the commencement of their course about inclusive education (Chong *et al.*, 2007). The survey included four main parts.

Part 1 requested general demographic information from participants, including gender, age, highest level of education, prior contact with people with a disability, previous training about disability, knowledge of the local DDO and level of confidence in teaching students with disabilities.

Part 2 of the questionnaire included the Attitudes Towards Inclusive Education Scale (ATIES) (Wilczenski, 1992), with 16 items measuring attitudes towards students with social, physical, academic and behavioral challenges. Participants were asked to record their attitude towards inclusion by rating the items using a 6-point Likert scale ranging from (1) strongly disagree to (6) strongly agree. The scale yielded a total score ranging from 16 to 96, indicating the higher the scores, the more positive the attitudes.

Part 3 of the questionnaire was modified from the original version of the Interaction with Disabled Persons Scale (IDP) (Forlin *et al.*, 2001). This section included 20 items measuring the level of comfort or discomfort of participants upon interacting with people with disabilities. Each item was measured using a similar 6-point Likert scale. The scale yielded a total score ranging from 20 to 120, indicating the higher the scores, the greater the discomfort.

Part 4 involved the Concerns about Inclusive Education Scale (CIES) (Sharma and Desai, 2002), which included 21 items measuring the degree of concern of participants about implementing inclusive education. Each item was measured by a 4-point scale rating level of concern from (1) not at all concerned to (4) extremely concerned. The scale yielded a total score ranging from 21 to 84, with higher scores indicating that the respondents were more concerned about their abilities to implement inclusion.

Data indicated that the majority of the participants (80 per cent) were in the 19–29 age group, with only 20 per cent being older, suggesting that they had enrolled in the PGDE either immediately or within a few years following the completion of their undergraduate course. Of the cohort, 90 per cent indicated that they had not undertaken any training focusing on the education of students with a disability, while 22 per cent reported that they had previously taught a student with a disability. Nine people had a family member, six had a close friend, and one had other acquaintances with a person with a disability.

The participants were asked to consider how good their knowledge was about the local DDO. With the exception of two people who indicated a good knowledge and three who reported average knowledge, the rest of the participants surveyed rated their DDO related knowledge to be either poor ($n = 24$) or nil ($n = 57$), indicating overall very limited knowledge about their requirements under the DDO. (*Note*: Not all numbers total 86 because of missing data.)

Regarding their confidence levels in teaching students with disabilities, their responses ranged from very high ($n = 2$), high ($n = 13$), average ($n = 54$), low ($n = 15$), and very low ($n = 1$), indicating an overall average confidence in teaching students with disabilities.

The overall means of the scales indicated that participants' attitudes towards including students with different special education needs was slightly lower than average with a mean of 55.4 ($SD = 11.22$). Overall, they were very concerned about all aspects of inclusion, with a mean of 54.6 ($SD = 9.43$). In respect of their interactions with people with disabilities, they reported slightly less than average levels of comfort on interaction with a mean of 67.8 ($SD = 8.80$).

Table 8.1 Postgraduate preservice teachers' attitudes towards inclusive education

Item no.	*Item*	*Responses (n = 86)*	
		M	*SD*
	Most positive attitudes		
A04	Students who are shy and withdrawn should be in regular classes.	4.57	1.27
A16	Students who are frequently absent from schools should be in regular classes.	4.10	1.23
A15	Students who do not follow school rules for conduct should be in regular classes.	4.03	1.24
A08	Students who are verbally aggressive toward their peers should be in regular classes.	3.86	1.13
A09	Students who have difficulty expressing their thoughts verbally should be in regular classes.	3.80	1.10
	Least positive attitudes		
A01	Students whose academic achievement is two or more years below the other students in the grade should be in regular classes.	2.84	1.04
A14	Students who cannot hear conversational speech should be in regular classes.	2.84	1.15
A02	Students who are physically aggressive toward their peers should be in regular classes.	2.91	1.05
A07	Students who cannot read standard print and need to use Braille should be in regular classes.	2.99	1.31

Note: Mean responses range from 1 (strongly disagree), 2 (disagree), 3 (disagree somewhat), to 4 (agree somewhat), 5 (agree) and 6 (strongly agree).

Whereas the participants were more supportive of including children with only minor problems, they were not very positive about including those who were either academically below their peers or physically abusive (Table 8.1). They also considered that students who were deaf or blind should not be included in regular classes.

Regarding confidence level when interacting with people with disabilities, given that only 20 per cent of the cohort had any previous contact with a person with a disability, they were not too concerned about interacting with them. From Table 8.2 it can be seen that they expressed little concern about physical contact with people with a disability and were not bothered by their own lack of disability. Although they were apparently grateful that they did not have a disability themselves, they admired the ability of those with a disability to cope with their challenges. They felt that it was personally rewarding when they were able to help and were empathetic when they could see that a person with a disability was unable to do something that they wanted to.

Their major concerns about inclusive education revolved around a lack of suitable resources, such as specialized equipment, specialist staff, or administrative support to effectively implement an inclusive education program (Table 8.3).

Table 8.2 Postgraduate preservice teachers' confidence levels when interacting with people with disabilities

Item no.	*Item*	*Responses (n = 86)*	
		M	*SD*
	Less agreement		
B16	I feel overwhelmed with discomfort about my lack of disability.	2.28	1.11
B17	I am afraid to look at the person straight in the face.	2.50	1.11
B11	I can't help staring at them.	2.79	1.10
B18	I tend to make contacts only brief and finish them as quickly as possible.	2.86	1.08
	More agreement		
B01	It is rewarding when I am able to help.	5.12	0.91
B13	I admire their ability to cope.	4.95	0.93
B07	I am grateful that I do not have such a burden.	4.66	1.24
B02	It hurts me when they want to do something and can't.	4.53	1.04

Note: Mean responses range from 1 (strongly disagree), 2 (disagree), 3 (disagree somewhat), to 4 (agree somewhat), 5 (agree) and 6 (strongly agree).

They were also very concerned about being unable to cope with students who had limited self-help skills and were worried that students with disabilities would not be accepted by their peers. They were less concerned about maintaining the academic standard of the school or of individual students and were not overly worried by a lack of personal incentives. They were, however, concerned about their own performance as a classroom teacher.

Consideration was given for any differences due to a range of demographics. Table 8.4 reports the differences for gender, course, family member, close friend, training and previous teaching experience. While there are some differences in mean responses between these, none are statistically significant ($p > .05$). Of particular note is that it did not matter whether the participants were training to work in primary or secondary schools, as their perceptions and concerns were similar regarding inclusion. In addition, those with the lowest levels of confidence were also the least willing to include students with the more challenging disabilities in their classes.

Discussion

The participants were all studying to qualify as a teacher in a postgraduate mode, having previously obtained an undergraduate degree. In Hong Kong, most teachers are newly qualified graduates and this was clearly evidenced by the 80 per cent majority being younger than 30 years. Consequently, they would have had limited exposure to broader community issues, with many also having had little opportunity to travel or to explore alternative education systems. Thus, it is

Table 8.3 Postgraduate preservice teachers' concerns about inclusive education

Item no.	*Item*	*Responses (n = 86)*	
		M	*SD*
	More concerned		
C14	My school will not have adequate special education instructional materials and teaching aids (e.g. Braille).	3.02	0.81
C08	There will be inadequate paraprofessional staff available to support students with disabilities (e.g. speech pathologist, physiotherapist, occupational therapist).	2.97	0.83
C19	I will not be able to cope with students with a disability who do not have adequate self-care skills (e.g. students who are not toilet trained).	2.90	0.75
C05	Students with disabilities will not be accepted by students without disabilities.	2.88	0.79
C13	There will be inadequate resources/special teacher staff available to support inclusion.	2.88	0.83
C20	There will be inadequate administrative support to implement the inclusive education program.	2.87	0.78
	Less Concerned		
C15	The overall academic standard of the school will suffer.	1.97	0.86
C16	My performance as a classroom teacher will decline.	2.08	0.79
C07	The academic achievement of students without disabilities will be affected.	2.14	0.90
C09	I will not receive enough incentives (e.g. additional remuneration or allowance) to teach students with disabilities.	2.30	0.87

Note: Mean responses range from 1 (not at all concerned), 2 (a little concerned), 3 (very concerned), to 4 (extremely concerned).

not surprising that only 9 per cent had been in contact with a person who had a disability either as a close friend or other acquaintance, while a further 11 per cent had a family member with a disability. The lack of contact with a person with a disability has been found previously to lead to much greater discomfort for teachers when interacting with people with disabilities. Although all these participants reported slightly less than average levels of comfort when interacting with people with disabilities and little concern about potential physical contact, there were no significant differences dependent upon previous contact. Such conclusions, however, need to be considered with caution because of the small overall percentage (20 per cent) that had had any previous contact.

Similarly, because of their age, it is most unlikely that any of these participants would have undertaken their own schooling in an inclusive setting, since the first integration trial in Hong Kong only began in 1997 and was limited to a few schools with a small number of students. In the same way, this cohort would have most likely attended a more academically oriented school that catered for

Table 8.4 Analysis of variance for the ATIES, IDP and CIE for a range of independent variables (n = 86)

Independent variable		*ATIES*			*IDP*		*CIE*	
		n	*M*	*SD*	*M*	*SD*	*M*	*SD*
Gender	Male	42	56.29	10.55	66.62	9.10	54.71	9.20
	Female	42	54.98	11.92	68.55	8.50	54.45	9.98
Course	PGDE(S)	47	55.02	10.80	66.98	9.76	55.34	9.08
	PGDE(P)	39	55.92	11.82	68.74	7.48	53.62	9.87
Family member	Yes	9	56.67	9.08	68.89	7.87	49.00	9.85
	No	75	55.43	11.44	67.67	9.03	55.49	9.15
Close friend	Yes	6	54.00	6.32	65.33	9.18	51.33	11.43
	No	77	55.42	11.31	67.83	8.84	55.06	9.31
Training	Yes	9	58.22	13.25	70.44	6.11	54.67	10.76
	No	77	55.10	11.01	67.47	9.04	54.55	9.34
Taught	Yes	19	58.21	12.34	68.74	7.92	56.21	10.00
	No	67	54.64	10.84	67.51	9.07	54.09	9.29

Notes
ATIES: Attitudes Towards Inclusive Education Scale.
IDP: Interaction with Disabled Persons Scale.
CIE: Concerns about Inclusive Education Scale.

university entrance students and would, therefore, not have had any personal exposure to learning alongside students with learning or intellectual disabilities. It is perhaps not unexpected that they appeared very concerned about all aspects of inclusion.

Their attitudes towards accepting students with disabilities in mainstream classes were not very positive. While they were supportive of including students with very minor special education needs, they were not at all positive about including those who were unable to work at the academic class level or who were physically abusive. They were also not accepting of those who were blind or deaf; yet in many systems it is these students who are usually fully included in all mainstream classes as a matter of course. They were most concerned about the adequacy of support in their schools to enable inclusion, suggesting that there would be inadequate materials or administrative support and insufficient support staff to sustain their teaching. While it has previously been found that there has been less support for inclusion in secondary schools (Loreman *et al.*, 2005; Pearce and Forlin, 2005), there was no difference found in these participants as their concerns were similar regardless of whether they were training to teach in primary or secondary schools.

These participants had all completed a three-year undergraduate degree in a chosen curriculum area and were just embarking on a formal teacher training course. Although a small percentage of them indicated that they had received some training (10.5 per cent) and some of them had taught students with disabilities (22 per cent), this had made no significant difference to their rather negative attitudes towards inclusion or their concerns about it.

As this experience and training was most likely to have occurred in private tutoring schools where many of them worked in a part-time or casual role, the emphasis would have been on working with individuals or small groups of children. These participants, though, were preparing to teach in large classes of 30–40+ students where opportunities for working with individuals were almost non-existent. Such large classes are common in many schools throughout the Asia-Pacific region with limited emphasis being placed on any major class size reduction in the immediate future. It is, therefore, foreseeable that this made little difference to their concerns about inclusion in mainstream schools.

The respondents' knowledge of the DDO (EOC, 2007) or the *Code of Practice on Education* (EOC, 2001) in Hong Kong, which has directed that regular schools should accept students with disabilities (Forlin, 2007b), was minimal upon entering the course. Almost all participants indicated very poor or no knowledge about the Acts. As postgraduate students they are only required to complete one year of study in education. During this condensed course, while there is no core module on inclusive education, they are offered one 30-hour elective module to equip them with a wide range of content knowledge about disability and adapting the curriculum, while also endeavoring to address their concerns about inclusive education and increase their willingness to engage in it. This cohort of participants represented those who had enrolled in this elective module. This signifies 26 per cent of all participants enrolled in the PGDE secondary course and 11 per cent of those in the primary course. Plainly, this suggests that a very small number of participants have chosen to upskill in this area. The difficulty in preparing teachers for working in inclusive schools is further heightened by their limited personal exposure to inclusive practices in schools and the little emphasis on social justice and rights for people with disabilities in the broader community where the DDO seems to have made narrow impact to date. A positive note from this investigation, nevertheless, is that those who felt more confident about teaching students with disabilities expressed significantly more positive attitudes towards inclusive education.

Conclusion

The findings that the participants training to become qualified teachers had little previous contact with people with disabilities, were relatively young, and had not experienced inclusive education themselves are not unanticipated. Their rather poor attitude towards the inclusion of students with anything more than a mild support need and their generally high level of concern regarding all aspects of inclusion, however, indicate that if they are to be prepared to teach effectively in inclusive schools, much has to be addressed.

They are undoubtedly commencing their teacher training course with very limited background information or understanding about the rights of students with disabilities and an ingrained belief that only students with the mildest form of disability should be included in regular school settings. Unless this is attended to during training this is unlikely to change, as the lack of adequate professional knowledge and no relevant training about teaching students with special needs has already been cited by more than 60 per cent of current teachers in Hong Kong as being a concern (Tsui *et al.*, 2006).

Research has demonstrated that teachers become less concerned and more willing participants in inclusive education after having undertaken more studies about disability (Elkins and Porter, 2005; Sharma *et al.*, 2006) and that professional teacher training is the best time to address their concerns about inclusion (Loreman *et al.*, 2005). The development of appropriate courses, therefore, needs to consider all of these findings. More compulsory training is required that must address the rather negative attitudes, and very poor prior knowledge about the legal requirements regarding inclusion and not focus simply on factual knowledge about disability, which has tended to be the norm previously in most teacher training courses.

As both school and societal reform for a more inclusive community occurs across the whole Asia-Pacific region, teacher training institutions must also transform existing courses to ensure that the real needs of teachers as identified here are fully addressed. It is critical that for special education reform to be effective in the Asia-Pacific region and inclusive school communities to develop appropriately, teachers must begin their teaching with much more positive attitudes towards inclusive education practices than those with which they have commenced their formal training.

Teacher training institutions could do a lot to fill this knowledge gap. For example, during their courses they could increase opportunities for contact with people with a disability through voluntary community service, allow participants to undertake supported practice in different types of special schools, and establish opportunities to observe good role models from special education teachers in handling children with special education needs. Throughout the Asia-Pacific region it is widely accepted that students who want to learn English effectively learn better through an immersion program. Offering a similar immersion opportunity to teachers who want to learn how to cater for the needs of students with disabilities in their classes would seem a logical and authentic approach.

While the government should continue to support the upskilling of teachers to cater for students with a broad range of needs in mainstream schools, the teacher training institutions must also ensure that concomitant with the education reform process in place throughout the region there is a similar refinement of teacher training courses to support these changes. It is essential that all new teachers are given appropriate training to enable them to cater for a wide range of student abilities. Such training needs to move from an elective approach to a compulsory one where the attitudes and concerns of teachers are fully addressed. Without appropriate adjustments to teacher preparation and continued support by the government, the ideal of developing fully inclusive schools is likely to be no more than rhetoric.

References

Bradshaw, L. and Mundia, L. (2006) "Attitudes and concerns about inclusive education: Bruneian inservice and preservice teachers", *International Journal of Special Education,* 21(1): 35–41.

Chong, S., Forlin, C. and Au, M. L. (2007) "The influence of an inclusive education course on attitude change of preservice secondary teachers in Hong Kong", *Asia Pacific Journal of Teacher Education,* 35(2): 161–79.

Education Bureau (2007a) *Whole-School Approach to Integrated Education.* Online. Available at: http://www.edb.gov.hk/index.aspx?nodeID=185&langno=1 (accessed 18 September 2007).

Education Bureau (2007b) *Whole School Approach to Cater for Students' Diverse Learning Needs.* Online. Available at: http://www.edb.gov.hk/index.aspx?node ID=181&langno=1 (accessed 18 September 2007).

Education Bureau (2007c) *An Evaluation of 2007-2008 Education Expenditure* [Response number: EDB082 circular, Question number: 1411], Hong Kong: Hong Kong Special Administration Region Government.

Education Department (2002) *Implementation Guidelines on Whole School Approach to Integrated Education,* Hong Kong: Hong Kong Special Administration Region Government.

Elkins, J. and Porter, J. (2005) "Departmental differences in attitudes to special educational needs in the secondary school", *British Journal of Special Education,* 32(4): 188–95.

Equal Opportunities Commission (2001) *Disability Discrimination Ordinance, Code of Practice on Education,* Hong Kong.

Equal Opportunities Commission (2007) *Disability Discrimination Ordinance.* Online. Available at: http://www.eoc.org.hk/EOC/GraphicsFolder/ddo.aspx (accessed 8 October 2007).

Forlin, C. (2007a) "A collaborative, collegial and more cohesive approach to supporting educational reform for inclusion in Hong Kong", *Asia Pacific Education Review,* 8(2): 1–11.

Forlin, C. (2007b) "Classroom diversity: Towards a whole school approach", in S. N. Phillipson (ed.), *Learning Diversity in the Chinese Classroom: Contexts and Practice for Students with Special Needs,* Hong Kong: University of Hong Kong Press, pp. 95–123.

Forlin, C., Jobling, A. and Carroll, A. (2001) "Preservice teachers' discomfort levels toward people with disabilities", *Journal of International Special Needs Education,* 4: 32–8.

Hong Kong Government (1977) *Integrating the Disabled into the Community: A United Effort* [s4.2c Specific objectives for future development], Hong Kong: Government Printer.

Lo, L. (2003) "The continuous development of integration", *Hong Kong Special Education Forum,* 6(1): 97–113.

Loreman, T., Deppeler, J. M. and Harvey, D. H. P. (2005) *Inclusive Education: A Practical Guide to Supporting Diversity in the Classroom,* Sydney: Allen & Unwin.

Loreman, T., Forlin, C. and Sharma, U. (2007) "An international comparison of preservice teacher attitudes towards inclusive education", *Disability Studies Quarterly,* 27(4). Online. Available at: http://www.dsq-sds.org/_articles_html/2007/fall/dsq_v27_04_2007_fall_fs_loreman.htm

Luk, F. Y. Y. P. (2005) "Managing change in an integrated school, a Hong Kong hybrid experience", *International Journal of Inclusive Education,* 9(1): 89–103.

Pearce, M. and Forlin, C. (2005) "Challenges and potential solutions for enabling inclusion in secondary schools", *Australasian Journal of Special Education*, 29(2): 93–105.

Sachs, S. K. (2004) "Evaluation of teacher attributes as predictors of success in urban schools", *Journal of Teacher Education,* 55(2): 177–87.

Sharma, U. and Desai, I. (2002) "Measuring concerns about integrated education in India", *Asia and Pacific Journal on Disability,* 5(1): 2–14.

Sharma, U., Forlin, C., Loreman, T. and Earle, C. (2006) "Preservice teachers' attitudes, concerns and sentiments about inclusive education: An international comparison of the novice preservice teacher", *International Journal of Special Education,* 21(2): 80–93.

Tsui, K. T., Tse, C. Y., Yue, H., Sin, K. F., Wong, Y. P. and Yung, K. K. (2006) *The Implementation of Integrated Education in Hong Kong Primary Schools,* Hong Kong: Hong Kong Elementary Education Research Association and Special Education Society of Hong Kong.

United Nations Educational, Scientific and Cultural Organization (1994) *The Salamanca Statement and Framework for Action on Special Needs Education,* Salamanca, Spain.

Wilczenski, F. L. (1992) "Measuring attitudes toward inclusive education", *Psychology in the Schools,* 29(1): 306–12.

Support materials and activities: Section 2

The following support materials and activities provide additional useful information about preparing teachers to work in inclusive classrooms in the Asia-Pacific region. The activities are designed to provide authentic approaches to learning that can be contextualized to meet the needs of learners in any given environment. They are intended to support teacher educators in preparing teachers for special and inclusive education.

These websites provide good starting places for further information to support teacher preparation for inclusion

- The *Disabling Imagery* site was developed by the British Film Institute and is particularly interesting as it provides a wealth of information on how disability has been represented in moving image from the earliest days (http://www.bfi.org.uk/education/teaching/disability/). The approach is from a disability equality and human rights perspective, which draws on the Disabled People's Movement.
- A range of short video clips of Australian films that include people with disabilities can be accessed via: http://australianscreen.com.au/titles/
- The http://www.teachers.tv/ website provides literally thousands of education programs available on television in the United Kingdom and also available online. Many of them relate to special and inclusive education.
- The *Behavior 4 Learning* website (http://www.behaviour4learning.ac.uk/) provides high quality relevant resources that allow trainers and trainees to investigate the principles of behavior for learning to improve the management of classroom behavior, to ensure that all students can learn.
- The *Federation In Community Support* website: http://www2.ied.edu.hk/fpece/fics/ is a central hub for obtaining information about support services for students with special needs in Hong Kong. It also has extensive links to international websites about special and inclusive education.
- The following website has extensive information about special education in Singapore: http://www.moe.gov.sg/specialeducation/Introductionpercent202003.htm
- Information and job description on the special needs officer in Singapore can be obtained from here: http://www.moe.gov.sg/eas/SNOindex.htm

- Council for Exceptional Children USA: http://www.cec.sped.org
- Centre for Studies on Inclusive Education, United Kingdom http://inclusion.uwe.ac.uk/csie/csiehome.htm
- This short streamed video provides a brilliant way to finish any course of study on special and inclusive education. Just watch it yourself first! http://www.makeadifferencemovie.com/

Professional development activities for teacher training for inclusion

The activities suggested below may preferably be carried out in small groups, encouraging participants to engage in collective reflection and analysis. Where possible, it is recommended that these activities involve people with a disability as resource persons. Many of these activities may be presented in the form of oral presentations, posters, written reflections or general class discussions.

1 In small groups, design a simulation game using various props that provide a multi-sensory experience of what it feels like to have an autism spectrum disorder. Each group may then lead the class in the simulation game. Conclude with a discussion reflecting on the experience.
2 Take a field trip to a public playground where typically developing children of diverse ages are engaged in play. To gain practice in formal and informal assessment techniques, record observations in the form of field notes and using the Integrated Play Groups (IPG) observation tool (Wolfberg, 2003). Reflect on patterns of peer socialization and play.
3 Working from videotapes of children with ASD struggling in peer play, record observations using the IPG observation tool. In small groups, compare findings with that of the field trip observations of typically developing children (see previous activity).
4 Invite parents of children with disabilities and self-advocates for people with disabilities to talk about their educational experiences.
5 A teacher has just learned that a student with a disability is enrolling in the class. Develop a resource that the teacher could use which explains how to teach the student. The resource could be a pamphlet, a booklet, a CD, or a video clip.
6 Watch a film featuring a person with a disability (see recommended websites in this section). How is the character portrayed? What impact does this have on peoples' attitudes to people with disabilities?
7 Use case studies to consider how a teacher could include a student academically. For example, Alison is a student with a mild intellectual disability in her first year of high school. She has just learned to write and read simple sentences and can count to ten. The rest of the class is studying a novel. How can Alison be included in the activities? John is aged eight and is having trouble making friends. He sits alone in the playground. Brainstorm ways of helping John make friends.

8 Discuss the following statement: "I have a learning problem not a problem learning". What does this statement mean for students with learning difficulties?
9 Think back to something that was difficult for you to solve/learn. (It could be, for example, a mathematical problem, driving a car, learning to swim, meeting new friends, or studying for an examination.) Write a personal reflection on what you did (strategies) that enabled you to learn or solve the problem.
10 In a small group of six, read out loud a text which has unfamiliar language and is difficult to interpret (e.g. a law document) and give a verbal summary of it. What is happening when you read the text? What are you concentrating on? How much of the text is understood? Is any part of the process automatic? How do you feel doing this activity in front of your peers?
11 Arrange to interview persons with a disability who are achievers in their own right, to understand their success, struggles and aspirations. Keep in mind that the objective of this exercise is to see the person rather than the disability. In order to do so, it may be useful to first come up with a list of their own needs, wants and aspirations as individuals. This list would serve as a guideline that could direct the information-gathering process. A plenary session of discussion will help consolidate the group's findings and address their misconceptions.
12 Prepare a webliography of websites that explain the medical and the social models of disability. Try to ensure that at least half of these readings are authored by persons with a disability. Post the list on an e-discussion board, and explain insights gained from this search. Trainees should also respond to two other postings, encouraging a good discussion.
13 Select a curriculum framework of another country from the web and study its policy on inclusion of children with a disability, specifically looking at the provisions for accommodations, the use of assistive technology, curricular modifications and alternative assessment. How does this compare with the provisions of the present policy in their own country? Consolidate this with a mock group exercise to draft an ideal curriculum framework for the inclusion of children with a disability at the school level.
14 In small groups investigate special education and inclusive practices as well as related services (e.g. rehabilitation services, mental health services) in various Asia-Pacific regions. Regions to be selected may be allocated randomly and include: Hong Kong, China, Indonesia, Japan, Malaysia, South Korea, Thailand, Taiwan and Vietnam. A 15-minute presentation should cover: (a) the overall structure of the special education system, which will include legislation, policies and inclusive practices in that country; (b) how disabilities/exceptionalities are viewed; (c) how children/youth are identified as having special needs; (d) unique features of the service delivery system(s) (e.g. school systems, agencies); (d) types of services available (including school-age and post-secondary practices); (e) other considerations; and (f) implications.
15 Document an actual case study on a child with a special education need. In groups present the study and an action plan with intervention/adaptation

strategies by using the APIE model (Assess student performance and learning needs, Plan teaching and learning activities, Implement program, and Evaluate progress).

16 Reflect upon one's own experiences by discussing previous contacts with people with disabilities, raising issues of concern. A range of myths about people with disabilities could be tabled as true or false and explanations provided as to the reasons.

17 Using a digital or video camera to record progress, arrange in small groups to travel between two places (e.g. university and a shopping center) while one of the group experiences life as person with a disability. If possible provide a wheelchair or eye patches or hearing muffs to experience being physically disabled, blind or deaf. Record how to access public transport and basic facilities such as public toilets and the problems encountered.

18 Access the Federation In Community Support website (www2. ied.edu.hk/fpece/fics) or other local regional websites and select a support agency to visit. Make arrangements to visit the agency and find out exactly what they provide, the children or adults they support and what the major challenges are.

19 Individually or in pairs, select a specific disability and undertake research to find out the etiology, characteristics and educational implications for including a student with these needs in a mainstream classroom. Additional information could be sought on: (a) the support that is available; (b) the educational opportunities that are offered; and (c) strategies for differentiating the curriculum to meet the needs of these students in local schools.

20 In teams prepare to debate on relevant topics e.g. "All students with special needs should be included in mainstream classes"; "All included students should have an educational assistant to support them".

These texts provide a wealth of practical ideas about preparing teachers to work in inclusive classrooms and have been written with teacher educators in mind

Bondy, E. and Ross, D. D. (eds) (2005) *Preparing For Inclusive Teaching: Meeting the Challenges of Teacher Education Reform*, Albany, NY: State University of New York Press.

Conrad, C. F. and Serlin, R. C. (eds) (2006) *The Sage Handbook for Research in Education: Engaging Ideas and Enriching Inquiry*, Thousand Oaks, CA: Sage.

Denicolo, P. M. and Michael Kompf, M. (eds) (2005) *Teacher Thinking and Professional Action*, London: Routledge Falmer.

Jorgensen, C. M., Schuh, M. C. and Nisbet, J. (2006) *The Inclusion Facilitator's Guide*, Baltimore, MD: Paul H. Brookes.

Lenski, S. D. and Black, W. L. (eds) (2004) *Transforming Teacher Education Through Partnerships*, Lewiston, NY: E. Mellen Press.

Pierangelo, R. (2007) *Special Education Eligibility: A Step-By-Step Guide For Educators*, Thousand Oaks CA: Corwin/Sage.

Punter, A. (ed.) (2007) *Mentor Development for Teacher Training: A Scenario-Based Approach,* University of Hertfordshire School of Education, Hatfield: University of Hertfordshire Press.

Puri, M. and Abraham, G. (eds) (2004) *Handbook of Inclusive Education for Educators, Administrators, and Planners: Within Walls, Without Boundaries,* Thousand Oaks, CA: Sage.

Ravitch, D. (ed.) (2006) *Forgotten Heroes of American Education: The Great Tradition of Teaching Teachers,* Greenwich, CT: Information Age.

Wade, S. E. (2000) *Inclusive Education: A Casebook and Readings for Prospective and Practicing Teachers,* Hillsdale, NJ: Lawrence Erlbaum.

Wade, S. E. (ed.) (2000a) *Preparing Teachers for Inclusive Education: Case Pedagogies and Curricula for Teacher Educators,* Hillsdale, NJ: Lawrence Erlbaum.

Weishaar, M. K. and Scott, V.G. (2006) *Practical Cases in Special Education for All Educators,* Boston, MA: Houghton Mifflin.

Section 3

Effective special and inclusive practices

9 The challenge of raising student levels of achievement in an inclusive national curriculum

Keith Humphreys

Chapter objectives

- To identify how students in special schools can access the same curriculum as their able-bodied peers in mainstream schools.
- To assert the right of every child no matter what their level of ability to an equal opportunity to reach the highest level of educational attainment of which they are capable.
- To indicate with pragmatic examples how teachers in England have successfully attempted to do this.
- To identify the implications for teachers in special schools in the Asia-Pacific region of the culture changes that will occur in their practice as they shift paradigms from a psycho-medical to a socio-curricular model of education.

Focus questions

1 What is the current paradigm that influences special school curriculum in your country?
2 What principles do you feel should underpin the education that is offered to students in special schools?
3 Why are special schools an important part of the inclusive education system of curriculum provision?
4 In what ways would the proposed new culture for special schools impact upon your own teaching practice abilities?

Introduction

In the European climate of educational change there is a concern that special school education should remain within the domain of the State curriculum for all students. This desire is not only based on the sound principles of equality of educational opportunity, but also on the need to ensure that the raising of education standards of student attainment is a concern and a human right for all areas of schooling. Many of the Asia-Pacific regions are just commencing this process and are working towards making the State curriculum available for students in special schools as this has not hitherto been the case. This chapter explores the paradigm shift involved, and then identifies a pragmatic approach to achieve this goal – an approach that has led to significant improvements in professional practice in special school education in England. The chapter draws on the English example to discuss a way forward for the Asia-Pacific region.

The purpose of this chapter is to demonstrate how a State curriculum can be adapted so that all students, including those with disabilities, can have equal opportunity to access the same subjects. The students are those who may be otherwise described as having severe and profound multiple disabilities. This work is based on the ideas developed by a national organization for teachers in special education in England called EQUALS. This is a voluntary group of teachers from special schools who are working within a legislative context, that demands one equal access to a national curriculum for all students whether they are located within mainstream or special schools.

Curriculum development for special education

Within the global economic perspective, many European states see education as a major resource that makes a significant contribution to national wealth (Hargreaves, 2003). In attempting to maximize this resource the UK Government is adopting a free market, competitive economy approach to schooling, thus moving to a position whereby each school has its own autonomy with the goal of raising education standards. This goal not only applies to high achievers, but across Europe there is a concern for some 25 per cent of the school population that is forming a disaffected underclass of underachievement, which in turn is leading to significant social problems.

As a consequence, the challenge to raise the standards of achievement for all in education is a major political goal (Mander and Goldsmith, 2003). Within this context, the social principles of inclusive education demand that all students are expected to achieve at higher levels (Forlin, 2005), and of course, this includes those with severe and profound multiple disabilities. To achieve this goal special school educators have had to work in a parallel context to the education developments in mainstream schools.

According to Barton (1988), equal opportunities for all are a fundamental human right the enactment of which embodies three key principles:

1 The first principle is that all students should have access to a common state curriculum. In doing so there is a requirement that the subject material is identified in a way that covers access for a wide range of ability.
2 The second principle is that every student has the right to become an educated person (Cole, 2000). This means that skills competency is only a part of the education goal. A more significant demand is to enhance each student's curiosity of the world around them, within the context of the state's curriculum, at the cognitive level at which each student is capable of understanding.

3 The third principle is that every student has the right to a higher standard of education (UNESCO, 1999). In the case of students with severe and profound multiple disabilities, this clearly implies that love is not enough, and that good care is not necessarily synonymous with good education. To raise the standards of education achievement of these students, schools must be able to measure objectively the qualitative improvement that takes place.

Opportunities in special schooling for students with differing learning abilities

A breakthrough in the United Kingdom was to recognize the existence of a curriculum continuum that identified a set of levels of achievement for each curriculum subject from the least able to the most able. Initially eight levels were identified to cover the achievement of all students in mainstream education [Qualification and Curriculum Authority (QCA), 2006]. Subsequently, another eight levels that covered all students with severe and profound multiple disabilities were devised. Together these 16 levels provided a continuum that covered all students within schools, while recognizing that there existed a common curriculum to which all students could have equality of opportunity to access.

Based on these levels, appropriate subject content was developed that encouraged rich and stimulating learning environments. One problem that exists in the special schools is that, whilst the teachers have to teach all of the subjects in the State curriculum, they do not possess the appropriate knowledge in each of those subjects. A second problem is the tradition in special schools of focusing on the individual needs of a child at the expense of the quality of the subject material (Carpenter *et al.*, 1997). A third problem is the need for mainstream-trained teachers to appreciate the barriers to learning created by disability (Lewis, 2003). The production of appropriate schemes of work is a breakthrough in allowing teachers the confidence to deliver exciting subject matter that encourages each student's enjoyment, curiosity and achievement. Furthermore, by referring to the levels, teachers can become more aware of how to differentiate their responses according to the level of each child's ability.

Clarifying differentiated performance levels

For each subject that is to be taught a number of levels of student performance can be identified that cater from the most challenged students with differing abilities in special schools through to those who may be educated within a mainstream setting. The performance levels, or P scales as they are called, are different for every curriculum subject (QCA, 2005).

In addition, the P scales are written in such a way as to distinguish between those students who are at an early developmental level of learning and those who are more able. This structure is influenced by the work of Piaget (1955) and Dunst (1980), amongst others. As a consequence, the first performance levels P1–P3 relate to Piaget's notion of sensori-motor development and imply that a child at this level thinks very differently from a child who has developed beyond this stage across the performance levels P4–P8.

It is important to note that the child development stages (Layton *et al.*, 2003), seen throughout the P levels of the national curriculum subjects, are matched by a further eight national curriculum (NC) levels for students in mainstream schools, so that a student at NC8 level is likely to be a high achiever in the State examination system. This continuity from P levels to NC levels is an important factor in inhibiting the glass ceiling effect, which can reduce teacher expectation of student attainment in special schools.

Applying performance (P) levels to inform teaching and learning

In order to understand how to develop curiosity in students who are functioning between levels P1–P3, an approach based loosely around a sensori-motor perspective on cognitive development from zero to two years of age (Piaget, 1955) was employed. The six strands of development identified by Piaget allows the teacher to appreciate a developmental sequence of student learning, which may be used as the basis for a guide to explore a developmental curriculum. These form the developmental levels of progression in learning that became the basis of the performance (P) scales 1–3.

1 The development of visual pursuit and the permanence of objects.
2 Means of obtaining desired environmental events.
3 The development of a) vocal and b) gestural imitation.
4 The development of operational causality.
5 Construction of object relations in space.
6 The development of objects in relation to schemes.

The performance descriptions for P1–P3 are common across all subjects. They outline the types and range of general performance that some students with disabilities might characteristically demonstrate. Subject focused examples are included to illustrate some of the ways in which teachers might identify attainment in different subject contexts.

Performance description exemplars for P1–P3

P1 (i) Students encounter activities and experiences. They may be passive or resistant. They may show simple reflex responses; for example, startling at sudden noises or movements. Any participation is fully prompted.

P2 (i) Students begin to respond consistently to familiar people, events and objects. They react to new activities and experiences; for example, withdrawing from a person who is new to them. They begin to show interest in people, events and objects; for example, watching as they bring their own hands together. They accept and engage in coactive exploration; for example, sharing a hand massage with an adult.

P3 (i) Students begin to communicate intentionally. They seek attention through eye contact, gesture or action. They request events or activities; for example, prompting a peer or adult to continue an interaction. They participate in shared activities with less support. They sustain concentration for short periods. They explore materials in increasingly complex ways; for example, reaching out to touch the hair or face of another person during an interactive sequence. They observe the results of their own actions with interest; for example, listening as an adult imitates their own vocalizations. They remember learned responses over more extended periods; for example, cooperating with support for frequently repeated personal care procedures from day to day.

At the P1–P3 levels these performance scales are common across all of the subjects, for in these cases the subjects are vehicles for the development of sensori-motor thinking, and are the context for learning, not the focus for learning. In taking this approach it allows the teacher to teach the same subject to all students as long as the teacher has different expectations of each student's style of learning.

Developing curiosity in teaching and learning from P4 to P8

Once students have a sufficiently developed level of symbolic understanding, exploring the subject itself as the vehicle for learning can encourage their curiosity. In these cases the teacher needs to be aware of a range of responses that are appropriate at different levels within the subject. The performance level descriptors from P4 to P8 are specific to each subject. So, in the following example for Science, a number of statements that indicate progression are included. These statements are independent from the detail of the curriculum that is being taught; they are generic statements where each phrase within that statement is indicative of a level of understanding.

P4 Students explore objects and materials provided, changing some materials by physical means and observing the outcomes; for example, when mixing flour and water. Students communicate their awareness of changes in light, sound or movement. They imitate actions involving main body parts; for example, clapping or stamping. They make sounds using their own bodies; for example, tapping, singing or vocalizing, and imitating or copying sounds. They cause movement by a pushing or pulling action.

P5 Students take part in activities focused on the anticipation of and enquiry into specific environments; for example, finding a hamster under straw, or a CD or video in a pile. They match objects and materials in terms of single features or properties; for example, temperature or colour. They indicate the before and after of material changes. They try out a range of equipment in familiar and relevant situations; for example, initiating the activation of a range of light sources. They respond to simple scientific questions; for example, "Show me the flower." "Is this wet/dry?".

P6 Students recognize distinctive features of objects; for example, the features of living things in their environment, and know where they belong; for example, feathers on a bird, leaves on a tree. They begin to make generalizations, connections and predictions from regular experience; for example, expecting that ice cream will melt, or making wheeled objects move faster by pushing on a smooth surface or releasing them down a slope. Students sort materials according to a single criterion when the contrast is obvious. They closely observe the changes that occur, for example, when materials are heated, cooled or mixed. Students identify some appliances that use electricity. They show they know some sources of sound and light; for example, remembering the location of the source.

P7 Students understand the scientific use of some simple vocabulary, such as "before", "after", "bumpy", "grow", "eat", "move", and can communicate related ideas and observations using simple phrases; for example, which food to give which animal. Students can demonstrate simple properties of light, sound and movement; for example, bright, noisy/quiet, fast/slow. They make simple records of their findings; for example, by putting pictures of an activity in sequence. They begin to make suggestions for planning and evaluating their work; for example, responding to the question "Was that right or wrong?".

P8 Students show they have observed patterns or regular changes in features of objects, living things and events; for example, chrysalis/butterfly, day/night. They make some contribution to planning and evaluation and to recording their findings. They identify a range of common materials and know about some of their properties. They sort materials using simple criteria and communicate their observations of materials in terms of these properties. Students make their own observations of changes of light, sound or movement that result from actions; for example, using a volume control or a dimmer switch, and can describe the changes when questioned directly.

The purpose of the scales is not to influence week-by-week progression for the teacher; they are primarily meant to be used once a year as a marker of general student progression. However, they may also be used to help the teacher to appreciate different levels of understanding students may show within a lesson.

Practical implications for students with severe and profound multiple learning disabilities

Identifying schemes of work at appropriate levels of subject knowledge

It is important that schemes of work are written as an inclusive part of a State's national curriculum for all students (Tilstone and Rose, 2003). In order to be able to measure the amount of time needed to deliver such a balanced curriculum, the subject content should be unitized into discrete blocks of knowledge that can be succinctly applied to a school's timetable of delivery for each class. In

Science, for example, the units for students aged 11–13 years are as follows (Humphreys, 2003):

Science –Schemes of work Key Stage 3 (11-13 years) summary of units

1 Scientific enquiry
(This unit permeates all units and reference to it is within each subsequent unit.)

2 Life processes and living things

2.2a Green plants
2.2b Keep healthy
2.2c Living things and their environment
2.2d Variation and classification

3 Materials and their properties

3.3a Grouping and classifying materials and their properties
3.3b Changing materials and their properties
3.3c Separating materials and their properties

4. Physical processes

4.4a Forces and motion
4.4b The earth and beyond
4.4c Electricity and magnetism
4.4d Light and sound.

It is then possible to take any one of these units and to identify key components that will support the teachers in delivering the content. To begin with, the emphasis is on the objectives for the delivery of that lesson or series of lessons. The teacher is asked to be very clear about the purpose of the lessons so that they can be inspired in their delivery. The teachers are also given a summary of the key language that they may use, the range of resources that they may use and a general idea about the range of responses that they might expect for students of this age and ability range. In doing so, this encourages the teacher to deliver varied rich learning environments that are exciting and which seek to maximize the stimulation of the students' enjoyment and curiosity.

An important point to note is that the content of the lessons and the range of differentiated learning outcomes may be modified and developed as the use of the units increases over the years of schooling and as the abilities of the students in a school changes. Each unit within a scheme of work (see Table 9.1) can be modified. For example, the column on "Possible experiences and teaching activities" can be rewritten to suit a teacher's own subject knowledge. Also the column "Differentiated outcomes of learning difficulty" can be modified to suit the ability of students in a class. Some things within a unit cannot be changed, however, such as the objectives "About the unit" (see Table 9.2).

Table 9.1 Science materials and their properties: Unit detail

Key Stage 3 Unit: 3.3b

***Scientific enquiry**: This unit permeates all other units and reference to it is within each subsequent unit. In all units in scientific enquiry students will: (a) predict the results of simple investigations; (b) obtain and present evidence; (c) consider evidence and evaluate.*

Learning objectives	*Possible experiences and teaching activities*	*Differentiated outcomes of learning difficulty*
Students should experience, explore, and investigate, record and communicate what they discover and learn about: Heating and cooling.	Encourage the class to experience materials that exist as both solid and liquid, e.g. ice melting in their hand, chocolate melting on their tongue, butter melting on toast, ice cream melting in their mouth, liquid chocolate being cooled in the fridge or making chocolate crispy cakes, freezing ice. Investigate which materials can exist as both solid and liquid, using the following methods: warmth of their body, heating in warm water, freezing in the freezer, or cooling in the fridge.	Students will: • cooperate with shared exploration and supported participation; • explore materials provided, changing them by physical means and observing the outcome; • closely observe changes that occur when materials are heated; • describe their observations using scientific vocabulary and record them using simple tables.
Students should experience, explore, and investigate, record and communicate what they discover and learn about: Reversible changes.	Encourage the class to watch an ice cream which will melt and then refreeze (use hairdryer or place on radiator to speed up process; prepare refrozen one earlier). Explore a variety of different materials to mix together. Then see if they can extract the original materials once they have mixed them.	Students will: • actively explore materials for extended periods; • engage in experimentation and answer simple scientific questions; • make their own observations of changes that result from their actions on materials; • observe and compare objects and record the differences.

Note. If using candles and wax, ensure that students are aware of the dangers of hot wax.

Table 9.2 Science materials and their properties: Unit outline

Key Stage 3 Unit: 3.3b

About the unit

Through this unit students will be introduced to:

- solids, liquids and gases
- changes are reversible and irreversible
- changes that occur when solids and liquids are mixed
- separating solids from their solutions

Scientific enquiry covers: predicting and testing predictions, making observations and measurements, and presenting these and grouping according to results.

Expectations

At the end of this unit:

- All students will have encountered changes that occur when solids are added to water and will have experienced solids to different temperatures.
- Most students will: ask questions in relation to physical changes and draw appropriate conclusions.
- A few students will: investigate and interpret their ideas and findings and begin to apply their knowledge and understanding of scientific ideas to everyday things.

Identifying the whole-year curriculum plan and weekly timetables for a class

Once the value of working to the guidance in each of the units is recognized, it is then possible to appreciate the significance of seeing all of the units within a whole-year curriculum plan. The range of the subjects to be offered and the amount of time spent on each set of subject units needs to be carefully balanced to meet the needs and interests of the students. By referring to the unit titles, a plan can be worked out for each class that gives a picture of all of the subjects to be taught for the whole year.

This is a very useful overview for senior school managers because it allows class teachers and senior managers to ensure that an appropriate and differentiated balance of curriculum is being offered, given the age level and different abilities of the students. It also enables the senior managers to be able to monitor progression in the delivery of all the subjects that are on offer to each specific cohort of students in all of their classes. From the whole-year plan (see Table 9.3), a teacher only needs to draw out one vertical column and then it is easily converted into a timetable for that half term (see Table 9.4).

This approach also allows the school to effectively manage the curriculum that they intend to offer and then to evaluate whether that curriculum has been delivered. When this data is analyzed together with student attainment and achievement it allows the school to reflect on the implications for the allocation of future resources.

Table 9.3 Yearly planner for all subject units being taught to one class

	Autumn 1st half term	*Autumn 2nd half term*	*Spring 1st half term*
Maths	Reasoning about numbers or shapes (Unit 1.1b) Shape and space (Unit 1.3b) Number (Unit 1.2b) Shape and space (Unit 1.3b) Number and the number system (Unit 1.2b)	Reasoning about numbers or shapes (Unit 1.1b) Shape and space (Unit 1.3b) Number (Unit 1.2b) Shape and space (Unit 1.3b) Number and the number system (Unit 1.2b)	Responding (Unit 1.4a) Length, size and height (Unit 1.3d) Number and the number system (Unit 1.2b)
Language and literacy	Sentence level (Unit 3a/b)	Sentence level (Unit 5a/b)	Text level (Unit 4 a/b)
PSHE and citizenship	Being aware in the community (Unit 1.1b)	The people around me (Unit 1.4b)	Looking after our environment (Unit 1.2b)
Science	Ourselves (Unit 1.2b)	Ourselves (Unit 1.2b)	Sorting and using materials (Unit1.3a)
ICT	Looking at information (Unit 1.1b)	Looking at information (Unit 1.1b)	Control: Moving pictures (Unit 1.2b)
DT	Masks (Unit 1.2.5) Picnics (Unit 1.2.7)	Puppets (Unit 1.2.2) Picnics (Unit 1.2.7)	Winding up (Unit 1.2.3) Picnics (Unit 1.2.7)
Geography	Improving our school environment (Unit 1.6) Changing our school playground (Unit 1.7)		
History		Anniversaries and celebrations: Divali (Unit 1.6)	Toys and games: From long ago (Unit 1.4)
PE	Dance (Unit 4b)	Dance (Unit 4b)	Gymnastics (Unit 4a)
Art	Flexibility of median (Unit 2a)	Changing textures (Unit 2b)	Manipulation of materials (Unit 2c)
Drama	Relaxation (Unit 2a)	Relaxation (Unit 2a)	Body awareness (Unit 2b)
RE	Spiritual places (Unit 2c)	Spiritual places (Unit 2c)	Sharing (Unit 2d)
Ideas for visits/visitor	Local area; grandparent/parent	Church/mosque/police	Local area

Table 9.4 Timetable for one week taken from the whole-year plan

Time	*Monday*	*Tuesday*	*Wednesday*	*Thursday*	*Friday*
8:50–9:00	Play Register, Calendar	Play Register, Calendar	Play Register, Calendar	Play Register, Calendar	Play Register, Calendar
9:00–9:30	PSHE & C Personal responsibility (Unit 1.5b) Circle Time – News	Assembly	English Sentence level (Unit 3a/b) Library	English Sentence level (Unit 3a/b)	Assembly
9:30–9:40	PE Dance Unit 2 Ground Hall	PSHE & C play Personal responsibility (Unit 1.5b)	PSHE & C play Personal responsibility (Unit 1.5b)	PSHE & C play Personal responsibility (Unit 1.5b)	PSHE & C play Personal responsibility (Unit 1.5b)
9:40–10:10		Maths Exploration (Unit 1.3a) Searching (Unit 1.1a)	English Sentence level (Unit 3a/b)	English Word level 'Peggy Lego' Handwriting scheme	Maths Exploration (Unit 1.3a) Searching (Unit 1.1a)
10:10–10:20	Toilet, wash hands				
10:20–10:40	BREAK				
10:40–10:50	Maths Encountering permanence (Unit 1.2a) (Fruit)				
10:50–11:50	Design technology Masks (Unit 1.2.5) *Alternate weeks* PSHE – Moberley Centre	ICT Looking at information (Unit 1.1b)	Music	Science Ourselves (Unit 1.2b)	Science Ourselves (Unit 1.2b)
11:50–11:55	Toilet, wash hands				
12:00–1:00	LUNCH				

(Continued)

Table 9.4 (Continued)

Time	*Monday*	*Tuesday*	*Wednesday*	*Thursday*	*Friday*
1:00–1:15	RE Spiritual places (Unit 2c) Relaxation	RE Spiritual places (Unit 2c) Relaxation	RE Spiritual places (Unit 2c) Relaxation	PE Swimming	RE Spiritual places (Unit 2c) Relaxation
1:15–2:15	PSHE & C Being aware in the community (Unit 1.1b)	Geography Improving our school environment (Unit 1.6) Changing our school playground (Unit 1.7)	PSHE & C play Personal responsibility (Unit 1.5b) 1:15–1:45		Design technology Picnics (Unit 1.2.7) (Cooking)
2.15–2.30	Drama Relaxation (Unit 2a)	Drama Relaxation (Unit 2a)	Art Flexibility of media (Unit 2a) Ball pool	Drama Relaxation (Unit 2a)	Drama Relaxation (Unit 2a)
2:30–2:40	Toilet, wash hands	Music Drumming		Toilet, wash hands	

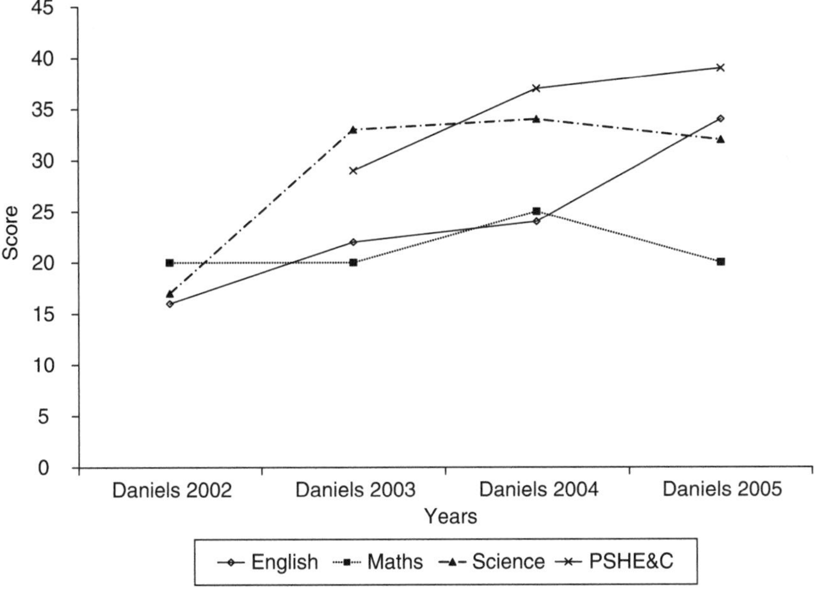

Figure 9.1 Tracking student progress: P scales for 2002/2003/2004/2005.

Confirming student levels of attainment and achievement year on year

Using the P scales as a form of assessment for annual review purposes, all students in a school can be assessed once a year to see whether or not they have progressed in their learning. When this data is fed into a computer, patterns in progression in each subject for individual students across the school can be identified.

The data give information about the current level of attainment for each student in each of the subject areas assessed, thereby enabling schools to look at attainment profiles of individual students as well as profiles of cohorts across the school (Ayres, 2006). Figure 9.1 shows how one school tracked the attainment progress of one student over several years using the data from the scheme.

The school can see that attainment in the subject of English has shown a steady improvement for this student over the years but that progress in Mathematics is less satisfactory. The data does not give any answers in this case but it does prompt the right sort of questions and promotes good professional dialogue based on quantitative data.

The school is also in a position to look at cohort achievement progress as well as individual progress. By looking at the collective data from all the schools, cohorts of pupils can be formed who are the same age and have the same attainment scores. In doing so we can arrive at an average score for the cohort and look at whether individual pupils have made above or below average progress

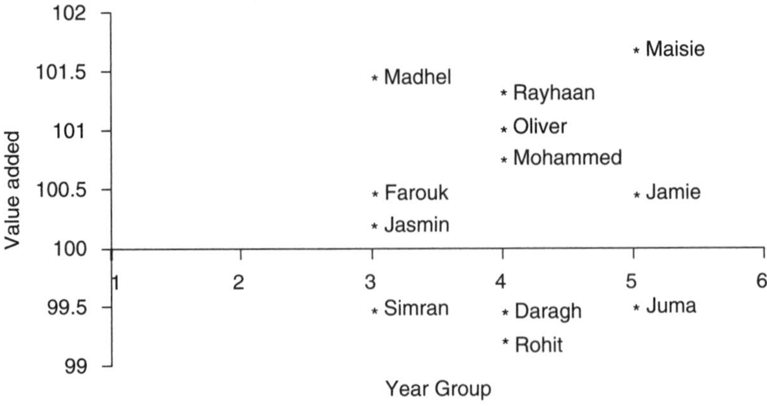

Figure 9.2 Achievement data from P scales in Science for one year

against that cohort. This is expressed as a score of above or below 100. Figure 9.2 demonstrates this.

The figure shows achievement scores for a group of pupils in the area of Science. Maisie's score of over 101 indicates she has made very good progress in this subject area in comparison to her peers. Rohit's score of below 99.5 indicates relatively poor progress.

Creating a new professional culture

The importance of school cultures in education reform has long been recognized (Lieberman, 2005). In giving teachers access to a new curriculum orientated paradigm there are clear issues that will become a part of a new professional culture in special school education. They involve the acquisition of six additional professional skills that need to be highlighted for teachers in special schools if the standards of education for all are to be raised.

First, all class teachers should see themselves as curriculum managers at a whole school and classroom level (Dean, 2005). They need to see their daily teaching and learning activities in the context of a progression in the year-on-year school career of their students. This requires curriculum-planning skills that allow them to easily prepare and evaluate whole-year planning in the context of their daily timetable.

Second, there is a need to respect and promote opportunities for skilled professional conversation within the normal working day (Durrant and Holden, 2005). Teaching is an oral culture (Taubert, 2006). Teachers like to talk about their work and they are at their best when they are exchanging their views in informal settings, such as during staffroom breaks or spontaneously at the end of the day. Evaluation procedures are important if standards are to be raised, but this does not mean that paperwork needs to be excessive. Clearly developing their basic computer skills will allow them to work quickly and flexibly (Mohanty and Vohra, 2006), keeping their writing time to a minimum and at the same time presenting subject timetables and student learning data that can be used as the basis for critical professional conversations.

Third, if teachers are to develop their skills in encouraging curiosity in their students, they need to access two vital elements. The first is to understand the nature of all of the subjects they have to teach and to appreciate exciting and stimulating ways to prepare their lessons with clear objectives (Harlen and Qualter, 2004). The second is the essential need to appreciate good timing in interaction, so that students are not taught at, but rather are allowed time to feel the learning tension of curiosity. When teachers are not confident in some of the subjects that they have to teach, or feel threatened by the challenging behaviors of the students in their classes (Levin and Nolan, 2006), they tend to keep talking and controlling whole-class lessons, to the significant detriment of the students' freedom to learn at their own individual levels.

Fourth, teachers need to develop their skills in creating large-scale curriculum experiences that reflect real-life situations. The range of learning abilities that students in special schools have produces many barriers to learning. The challenge is how to overcome these barriers. There is a need for teachers to think of education as a series of holistic learning experiences.

Fifth, teachers need to be able to assess their student's attainment across the Central Curriculum subjects of mainstream education in order to ascertain the effectiveness of the learning that has taken place (Gross and White, 2003). This information can then be used to inform school developmental planning on such issues as resource needs to teach subjects better or professional training programs for teachers who need to develop their knowledge in certain subjects.

Sixth, if these five skills are developed well, this will enable teachers to create one common professional community. Standards in special school education will rise if the teachers who work with students of similar abilities start to share their emerging innovative practices. In particular, there is a need to develop teacher knowledge of each subject that they teach (Turner-Bisset, 2006). The special school community should see itself as part of the whole schooling community. In this way, the raising of education standards becomes an inevitable dynamic of professional practice.

There are many already recognized skills required of the teacher in special schools but the six additional skills raised have an important contribution to make if teachers are to stimulate enjoyment and raise education standards of achievement for students with different learning abilities in special schools.

Acknowledging the impact of culture on educational reform

Clearly, there are cultural issues that need to be considered when contemplating the application of a similar program in the Asia-Pacific region.

The first cultural issue relates to the educational culture of the country (UNESCO, 1999). For some national systems such a rigorous approach based on objective accountability would be untenable. Even where such an approach is acceptable there may be different schooling systems for mainstream and special schools. This is even more important to respect when talking about an inclusive education approach where special school systems of education will need to be in harmony with those in the mainstream schools.

The second cultural issue relates to the obvious fact that the schemes of work are embedded within the requirements of the mainstream curriculum. So, for example, in Geography the notion of glaciers would receive far more attention in an Icelandic culture and far less attention in an Asian context. This clearly means that any scheme of work, and therefore performance levels, would have to be written anew in whichever country wished to use such a model.

The third cultural issue is that within any one school there will be a culture of professional practice, part of which may be exclusive to special school communities, such as the issues identified in the previous section of this chapter, and part of which will be independently unique to each school (Fullan, 2001). Special schools in particular are subjected to differences such as the perceived balance between care and education, the professional paradigms that dominate the thinking of the teachers and the way the curriculum is, or is not, managed. These differences also add to the micro-cultural perception of what is feasible in an inclusive setting.

It is clear that the challenge of redefining special school education is not merely one of conceptual concern, of agreeing sound education principles. It is also one of recognizing cultural identities, which at several levels can undermine attempts at reform. Such are the dangers that can lead to innovation without change.

Conclusion

Notwithstanding the challenge of cultural identities, the approach discussed in this chapter allows for the following to occur:

1. It provides an opportunity to excite the student's desire to be educated, providing rich, meaningful and enjoyable learning opportunities that are inclusive within a limited variety of ability ranges and where teacher responses are appropriate to the student's level of curiosity.
2. It enhances the teacher's enthusiasm by offering clear guidance on providing a balanced curriculum of opportunity, by ensuring that timetables efficiently match the school's culture of education, by giving fundamental access to appropriate subject knowledge and by supporting responses to appropriate developmental levels of the student's understanding.
3. It meets the needs of the State by encouraging schools to be efficient and effective, giving clear, objective evidence of the raising of education standards, which in turn provides evidence that within a market-driven economy, schools for these students provide value for money.

As many education systems and independent schools in the Asia-Pacific region similarly grapple with how to provide equal opportunities for all children and particularly those who will continue to receive their education in a special school, the ideas presented in this chapter may provide a useful starting point for discussion.

References

Ayres, J. (2006) "The use of P Scale Analysis to Promote Inclusive Practice", *Centre for Advancement of Special Education (CASE) News*, 3 (May): 3–6.

Barton, L. (1988) *The Politics of Special Education Needs*, London: Falmer Press.

Carpenter, B., Ashdown, R. and Bovair, K. (1997) *Enabling Access*, London: David Fulton.

Cole, M. (2000) *Education, Equality and Human Rights*, London: Taylor & Francis.

Dean, J. (2005) *Subject Leadership in the Primary School*, London: David Fulton.

Dunst, C. (1980) *A Clinical and Educational Manual for Use with Uzgiris and Hunt Scales of Infant Psychological Development*, Austin, TX: Pro-Ed.

Durrant, J. and Holden, G. (2005) *Teachers Leading Change: Doing Research for School Improvement*, London: David Fulton.

Forlin, C. (2005) "Implementing an outcomes-focussed approach to learning: Implications for inclusive education", *Centre for Advancement of Special Education (CASE) News*, 1(2): 3–6.

Fullan, M. (2001) *Leading in a Culture of Change*, San Francisco, CA: Jossey-Bass.

Gross, J. and White, A. (2003) *Special Educational Needs and School Improvement: Practical Strategies for Raising Standards*, London: David Fulton.

Hargreaves, A. (2003) *Teaching in the Knowledge Society: Education in the Age of Insecurity*, New York: Teachers College Press.

Harlen, W. and Qualter, A. (2004) *The Teaching of Science in Primary Schools*, London: David Fulton.

Humphreys, K.A. (ed.) (2003) *Science; Schemes of Work*, Newcastle, UK: EQUALS.

Layton, L., Williams, A., Mason, S., Anderson, A., Morgan, J. and Tilstone, C. (2003) *Child Development and Teaching Students with Special Educational Needs*, London: Taylor & Francis.

Levin, J. and Nolan, J. F. (2006) *Principals of Classroom Management: A Professional Decision Making Model*, London: Allyn & Bacon.

Lewis, V. (2003) *Development and Disability*, London: Blackwell.

Lieberman, A. (2005) *The Roots of Educational Change: International Handbook of Educational Change*, New York: Springer-Verlag.

Mander, J. and Goldsmith, E. (2003) *The Case Against the Global Economy: And for Local Self-Reliance*, San Francisco, CA: Earthscan Publications.

Mohanty, L. and Vohra, N. (2006) *ICT Strategies for Schools*, London: Sage.

Piaget, J. (1955) *The Child's Construction of Reality*, London: Routledge and Keagan Paul.

Qualification and Curriculum Authority (2005) *Using the P Scales*, London.

Qualification and Curriculum Authority (2006) *National Curriculum 5-14*. Online. Available at: http://www.qca.org.uk/qca_7124.aspx (accessed 4 October 2007).

Taubert, C. L. (2006) *Eight Habits of the Heart for Educators*, London: Sage.

Tilstone, C. and Rose, R. (2003) *Strategies to Promote Inclusive Practice*, London: Routledge Falmer.

Turner-Bisset, R. (2006) *Expert Teaching: Knowledge and Pedagogy to Lead the Profession*, London: David Fulton.

United Nations Educational, Scientific and Cultural Organization (1999) *Salamanca Five Years On*, Paris: UNESCO Special Needs Education Division of Basic Education.

10 Promoting inclusion in the primary classroom

Richard Rose

Chapter objectives

- To consider the challenges and opportunities that teachers face in inclusive primary classrooms.
- To discuss effective approaches for developing inclusive primary schools and creating a supportive classroom environment.
- To challenge conventional approaches to assessment and teaching that inhibit the development of inclusion.
- Involving students with disabilities in self-assessment and teaching and learning decisions.
- Promoting the idea of the teacher as an inquiring professional who through interrogation of practice can promote more inclusive learning.

Focus questions

1. What are the attitudes, knowledge skills and understanding apparent in successful teachers in inclusive primary schools?
2. How can teachers develop the attitudes, knowledge, skills and understanding to become inclusive in their practice?
3. What kind of support is necessary in assisting teachers to further their professional development for teaching in inclusive primary classrooms?

Introduction

The primary school years are a critical and formative time for all learners. It is during this period that children are introduced to the culture of schooling, and for many it is their first opportunity to engage in those social processes that help to shape attitudes and beliefs about the societies in which we live. During this period of schooling most children develop the foundations upon which all later learning is built. This is also a time during which children begin to identify their own learning strengths and weaknesses, which are likely to influence their attitudes, choices and behaviors throughout their school years and beyond. The relationship between any teacher and student is critical and at the heart of effective learning, and it is often in the primary classroom that a child first encounters an adult outside of their immediate family who takes responsibility and makes demands of them. Most children manage the transition into school without too much trauma. For some, however, this formative period may be one of distress and challenge, which, if inappropriately managed, can have a lasting damaging effect upon the child's future education.

Establishing the foundations for effective learning

Students who enter school at a disadvantage as a result of developmental difficulties, learning difficulties or with limited local language skills will usually be given additional attention by teachers who are aware of their needs. For some students the early stages of schooling may in fact exacerbate learning difficulties through either a failure to create an adequately supportive learning environment or to recognize individual student needs. The challenge for teachers in the primary years is to provide the type of classroom that encourages all students to feel that they are respected, valued and included in all aspects of social and educational activity.

Education alone cannot provide all of the answers to developing a more inclusive society (Forlin, 2006). The role that teachers and schools can play in ensuring that positive attitudes to difference and an acceptance of individuality become the norm is considerable. Not all students learn or develop at the same rate and it is important that primary school teachers acknowledge this and refrain from making early judgments about the abilities of their students. It is equally important to remember that the age difference in students across a class or year group in school can be up to 12 months. In a class at the beginning of the primary years this difference could be the equivalent of one fifth of a student's life. It is not acceptable, therefore, to expect that all students will be performing at the same level. By creating the conditions that enable students to be fully included in learning, teachers are accepting individuality and recognizing that a professional commitment to teaching demands a flexible approach. It also requires a preparedness to change teaching style to accommodate the needs of students who have difficulties in accessing learning. This is making a considerable demand upon teachers and it is important to recognize that even the most creative and well-organized teachers will still sometimes encounter difficulties in managing some students as a result of their individual learning needs or behaviors.

What is inclusive teaching?

Research exploring the notion that there may be a pedagogy that is particularly favorable to addressing the needs of students with disabilities has proven to be inconclusive. Studies conducted by Davis and Florian (2004), for example, indicated that whilst teachers who were flexible in their approaches and who were prepared to use a broad range of teaching strategies were more likely to be successful in inclusive classrooms, it was not possible to identify a specific pedagogical trait that could be described as uniformly beneficial.

The principles of effective teaching have been discussed over many years and it is possible to identify a number of characteristics of successful teachers upon which most observers are agreed. Attention to planning, good communication with students, high expectations, demonstrating respect for all learners are all characteristics that appear common to effective teachers (Dunne and Wragg, 1994). Even those teachers who demonstrate these traits, though, will confess to having difficulties engaging some students. Effective teaching must begin with an emphasis upon positive attitudes and high expectations of all students.

Barnes (1999) has discussed the impact of positive thinking and attitudes upon the management of all successful primary classrooms. He believes that when teachers are faced by challenges in the classroom they are most successful when they maintain an objectivity that enables them to view the difficulties before them and take a considered approach to addressing these problems. A commitment to a problem-solving approach may be a critical factor in developing inclusive primary school teachers. When considering the conditions that support the development of inclusive schools, Ainscow (1999) has identified a commitment to education reflection and inquiry as essential. Teachers who confront those students who challenge their conventional approaches to teaching without an analytical approach are more likely to see the difficulties before them as "within the student" rather than one of classroom management or teaching approach. Accepting that effective classroom practice can best be developed through the creation of an environment that is conducive to an inquiry-based approach to teaching demands that teachers adopt high expectations of both their students and themselves.

Building upon the notion of the reflective practitioner, Christensen (1991) has proposed that the relationship between the teacher and the learner should be one of reciprocal inquiry. Classrooms, she suggests, function better when they are built upon mutual trust and a genuine interest in each other by all class members, including teachers. Such a relationship lends itself well to the development of inclusive teaching. There are, of course, many challenges that can become obstacles to teachers who want to create such an ethos of learning. When confronted by students who challenge their conventional approaches to teaching, some teachers feel insecure and unless they are provided with additional support and advice they may prefer not to accept this challenge, thereby leaving students to struggle.

A number of attitudinal factors have an influence upon the creation of inclusive teaching. Not least of these is the negative impact that the use of deficit labels can have upon teacher perceptions of what they might expect from students. Educational and psychological assessments continue to follow medical deficit models, which perpetuates stereotypical views and expectations of students. Where students have been given a label, such as Attention Deficit Hyperactivity Disorder (ADHD) or autistic spectrum disorder (ASD), this can serve to increase teacher anxiety with regards to the challenges of the teaching task before them. Such labels can lower expectation and promote the types of stereotypical views that ultimately lead to educational exclusion and failure. Whilst there is an inevitability that the use of labels associated with medically diagnosed 'conditions' will persist, it is essential that such labels are regarded as no more than broad descriptors. Jupp (1992) suggests that teachers need to develop a personal, child-centered philosophy that is founded upon a belief that all students can learn. He believes that it is the skills, knowledge and understanding of effective teachers, who have a commitment to ensuring that all students are included in learning, that will enable them to find the means of making this happen. Other researchers (e.g. Ellins and Porter, 2005) have similarly demonstrated how teacher attitudes can impact upon the learning outcomes of individual students described as having special education needs.

Teacher attitudes are inevitably shaped in part during initial training. Several studies from different parts of the world have been conducted into the attitudes of students in initial teacher training towards learners with special education needs (Avramedis *et al.*, 2000; Chong *et al.*, 2007). Mintz (2007) conducted research into the attitudes towards students with disabilities and inclusion of 127 students who were training to be primary school teachers in England. He concluded that attitudes were generally positive but that many of his respondents expressed concerns for their abilities to address what they saw as "within child" problems. Mintz' research (2007) suggests that a critical factor in ensuring positive attitudes is the provision of appropriate training and support that increases the confidence of teachers in their ability to teach all of the students in their class.

Approaches for supporting students with disabilities

Whilst it may be difficult to identify a specific pedagogy for students with disabilities, it does appear that there are some teaching approaches that enable certain students to engage more effectively with the processes of learning. Many teachers who have experience of working with students with complex needs, including those working in special schools, have devised teaching approaches and adopted techniques that have been seen to promote greater access to learning.

Examples of these approaches include the use of augmentative systems of communication, such as Makaton (a form of signed language), or symbol systems to support the teaching of students who experience difficulties with communication. Similarly, the use of Structured Teaching, which has been used by many teachers of students with autistic spectrum disorders (ASDs), or kinaesthetic approaches for learners with dyslexia have often proven successful. The introduction of social stories (Gray, 2002; Howley and Arnold, 2005) has been a feature of some successful inclusive classrooms that have addressed the needs of students with ASDs. Initial reviews of the development of nurture groups (Cooper, 2004) have indicated that for some students with social, emotional and behavioral difficulties a whole school approach to creating a responsive environment, which structures pastoral and academic support, can prove efficacious.

Teaching methods to support inclusion

In order to succeed in classrooms that have a diverse range of learning needs, teachers must address a number of significant considerations about the teaching methods that they will adopt. Evidence suggests that teachers are more likely to succeed if they are prepared to develop an inquiring approach and to consider varying their teaching in order to address the needs of all the students in their class. In a thorough examination of classroom influences upon learning, Joyce *et al.* (2002) demonstrated how a range of complex learning situations and individual learners benefit from the adoption of flexible teaching approaches. They suggest that whilst some learners, including those with special education needs, will feel most comfortable when working within one model, learning becomes most effective when they can adapt to a range of different models. Similarly, teachers who feel at home with one approach to teaching and are not prepared to move away from this, are unlikely to be successful in addressing the needs of all learners in the primary classroom. The most effective teachers in primary classrooms are those who are able to recognize the preferred learning styles of their students and adjust their teaching accordingly.

In addition, Henley *et al.* (2002) have emphasized the need to link learning experiences, which may often be seen as irrelevant or abstract by students with disabilities, to real-life experiences. Students will certainly respond more readily to teaching if it is seen to be both interesting and relevant to their own situations. Inclusive teachers in primary schools recognize the shortcomings of teaching materials and curriculum content that appear distant from their students. In order to overcome this situation and motivate their students they often have to personalize or adapt resources. Teachers who have been imaginative and constructed, for example, a reading scheme around a student's interest in popular music, or focused the use of graphs in maths on the performance of a favored football team, have often yielded results that the use of conventional materials has failed to achieve. It is often the case that the personalization of teaching materials as described here will also find favor with many students in the class, not just those with disabilities.

What approach to take as a teacher committed to inclusion is one of the most difficult questions that need to be asked. There is a danger that when the majority of students appear to be making progress, those on the periphery who are struggling to learn can be ignored and become marginalized. When most of the class are doing well it is easy to adopt an attitude that says that if this approach to teaching is succeeding for most, it must be the individuals who are not making progress who are at fault. Indeed seeing problems as being "within the child" rather than associated with teaching is a common inhibitor of inclusive practice (Rose and Howley, 2007). Similarly, some primary school teachers are understandably cautious about changing a teaching approach, which seems to be addressing the needs of the majority, in case any new method may be less successful. The key to overcoming these apprehensions lies in the deployment of practical approaches to assessment and the ability to plan for the use of complementary teaching approaches in all lessons.

The uses and abuses of assessment

When referring to students with disabilities, the term assessment is usually associated with the learner. It is often perceived as a first step in identifying either the nature or the cause of a problem. This approach assumes that the difficulties lie with the student and that by assessing them it will be possible to take actions to remediate the problem. Making assumptions that the problems are within the student ignores the fact that the classroom environment or the approaches to teaching being used may be equally or even more significant. Salvia *et al.* (2007) suggest that assessment of the instructional environment and the methods being used by the teacher may be at least as informative as focusing upon student deficits. This requires that teachers are open to suggestions that they, or at least their classroom management, may be a part of the problem and that the solution lies with them. Such an acceptance, I would argue, is an important part of being an inclusive teacher. This is not to apportion blame, but rather to return to the view expressed by Ainscow (1999) cited previously that inclusive teachers are committed to an inquiry into their own practice, which will ultimately enable them to adjust their teaching to meet a diversity of learning needs. Asking critical questions about the efficacy of teaching and of the materials and resources used can be an important starting point for teachers who wish to develop inclusive primary classrooms. Whilst assessing the performance of students at the end of a period of teaching is certainly important and will provide useful information for future planning, to ignore this procedure in respect of pedagogy is to overlook the potential for developing more inclusive teaching practices.

Involving students in learning decisions

Teachers need to ask questions about their own teaching and the learning environments that they create. In order to do this they need to gather evidence and analyze the impact of their teaching upon students. The most obvious place to begin this process is with the students themselves. Asking students about their personal experiences of learning can provide useful insights for teachers, but only if they are prepared to treat student opinions with respect and demonstrate a willingness to take action. Assumptions have sometimes been made that only older or more experienced students have the maturity to make judgments about their own performance or the ways in which teaching experiences have affected them, yet there is evidence (Griffiths and Davies, 1995) that even the youngest of primary school children can provide insights into their own performance and needs. Similar assumptions have been made about the abilities of students with disabilities to make useful observations about their learning experiences. Such students, though, often surprise teachers with the depth of their understanding about what helps them to learn and those factors that inhibit effective participation. Research conducted with students with severe learning difficulties in special and mainstream schools in the United Kingdom revealed that enabling them to interrogate their own learning needs and the ways in which these were addressed by teachers had a number of benefits (Rose, 1999).

Rose and Howley (2007) have argued that the involvement of students in the assessment process is a critical part of creating inclusive primary classrooms. They have, however, identified a number of key issues that need to be addressed if tokenism is to be avoided.

The first of these they describe as a necessity that teachers accept that no matter how great their experience and expertise they cannot know everything about a student. Students who are concerned not to appear to be having difficulties may sometimes adopt strategies that give the appearance of them being full participants in an activity when in fact they are struggling to learn. An over-reliance upon student outputs in respect of the work that they present in their books may provide a far from true indication of performance. Some will be adept at gaining information from other students and passing this off as their own understanding. Likewise, some students may demonstrate a superficial understanding of concepts presented in a lesson, whilst not comprehending the learning that the teacher has in mind. Teachers can assure themselves of learning by involving students and respecting the unique insights that they can provide about their own learning experiences.

Rose and Howley's (2007) second point is that teachers who want to involve students in making accurate and useful assessments must establish a clear focus. Students will only be able to reflect accurately upon their own performance if they are clear about what they are supposed to have achieved. The use of naïve questions such as "how do you feel you are doing in maths?" will not enable students to provide teachers with anything other than superficial information, which will not aid planning. Teachers should involve students in discussions that are about what they have done, why they have done this and what they found easy or difficult. In this way suitable adjustments to teaching may be made. Assessing learning conditions as well as content and outcome is a principle that assists teachers in the development of a suitably inclusive learning environment. This is not to suggest that the assessment of students' work is anything less than essential. However, much is to be gained by focusing attention on the conditions that students find most conducive to learning. Students can be perceptive about their peers with whom they work well and others who may create barriers to their personal performance. Similarly, they will often express a view with respect to which classroom locations they find most conducive to work, and which resources and materials help them to access lessons. The development of strategies to support learning on the basis of information obtained is essential. However, providing feedback to students in order to confirm their views with them and making it clear what actions are to be taken is equally important. Teachers need to encourage students to self-assess in respect of which actions have enabled them to work better. Similarly, if the student is continuing to experience difficulties, such a review can be useful in reselecting strategies or modifying existing teaching approaches in order to make learning more effective.

The training of teachers has for many years placed an emphasis upon new teachers having the skills to assess student learning outcomes, but has seldom considered the self-assessment of teaching or the appraisal of conditions that may support or interfere with learning. This situation is exacerbated by education systems that have become increasingly market driven and competitive. In England, for example, the use of league tables, which exhibit the test results of primary school students, thereby placing schools in competition with each other, has been a hindrance to the progress of inclusion (Booth *et al.*, 1998). Head teachers who perceive that students who under-perform may have a negative impact upon their standing in the league tables and, therefore, in the view of the local community, have become reluctant to receive greater numbers of students with special education needs. The nature of assessment has become focused upon a narrow range of curriculum areas and with an emphasis upon attainment, which fails to recognize the significant progress that some students with special education needs may make. For those who are attaining levels beneath age-related expectation the publication of test results can have a devastating impact upon self-esteem. This is, of course, not a concern that is located only within the English education system, as the strong emphasis on an examination led curriculum is evident throughout the Asia-Pacific region, being frequently cited as a negative influence on the inclusion movement (Forlin, 2007). Morris (1997), for example, writing of the curriculum in Hong Kong demonstrates its exclusive and, therefore, exclusionary emphasis upon a narrow range of academic subjects and outcomes. As he states:

> A curriculum biased strongly towards achievement in high-status subjects is not necessarily appropriate for low achievers, nor for those whose interest and capabilities point them in other directions.
>
> (Morris, 1997, p. 346)

Inclusive teaching in primary schools demands that teachers are sensitive to the additional stresses that assessment of attainment can place upon their students. Furthermore teachers need to take positive actions to address the self-esteem of learners who are inevitably conscious of the fact that their performance is being compared to that of others. Some students who struggle academically may excel in other activities, or display personal attributes that will be equally important in respect of their future development. Inclusive teachers celebrate personal success even when this is unrelated to the curriculum or the academic demands of a formal education system.

Creating a supportive classroom environment

Having written of the need for teachers to assess their own teaching approaches and the learning environments in which they operate, it is necessary to consider how shaping the primary classroom and managing all of the individuals within this might promote inclusion. In so doing, it is important to remember the diversity of contexts and conditions that constitute primary classrooms and the ways in which these may impact upon teaching and learning.

Creating a supportive classroom environment is acknowledged as critical to the promotion of successful inclusion in the primary school years. The management of classroom layout and organization, the provision of class rules and routines, and the organization and accessibility of resources have all been cited as important factors in whether students with disabilities succeed or fail (Newton, 2005). Aspects of classroom environment have also been considered in relation to specific individual needs. Mesibov and Howley (2003) for example consider the importance of providing visual support for students with autistic spectrum disorders, whilst classroom seating arrangements and grouping for students with learning difficulties are discussed by Farrell (1997). Waine and Kime (2005) describe organization and location issues when conducting assessments with students with dyslexia. Cockerill (2005) urges teachers to address the ergonomics of the classroom, suggesting that a focus upon the use of supportive seating is a component of creating a supportive climate in all classrooms and emphasizing the need for specialist seating for some students with disabilities.

When asked about the conditions that are necessary to enable students with special education needs to be educated in inclusive primary school classrooms, teachers often suggest that they need the support of an additional adult (Rose, 2001). In some countries such as England, Teaching Assistants (TAs) have become important professionals within the school workforce and are a common feature of most schools. In much of the Asia-Pacific region, though, the use of paid assistants has been limited to special schools, with parent helpers as volunteers being rarely used. Elsewhere the role of additional classroom support has been clearly focused upon working with students with disabilities, as is the case in Ireland (Logan, 2006). There is evidence to suggest that the effective use of additional adult support in the classroom can be beneficial to teachers working in inclusive classrooms (Groom, 2006). It is also apparent that the poor use of such support can lead to further exclusion of students and in extremes lead to social isolation. Where learning support adults are allocated to an individual student this may actually create dependency in the student who will be reluctant to work without adult intervention. Furthermore, where a student has an adult attached to them in lessons this often discourages other students from wishing to work with him because of the additional attention that they too might receive from this adult. Such a situation can lead to increased isolation from peers and a student with special education needs resenting the very support that was intended to improve access to learning (Rose and Coles, 2002). A much more effective way of using additional adults in classrooms is by allocating this support to the teacher. In this way the teacher may make independent decisions about how to use the support and may vary this from working with groups of students, or individuals as the need arises. In the best models seen in inclusive primary classrooms the teacher will often allocate other adults to work with a group of more able students whilst focusing their own attention on those who are having difficulties with learning.

The development of inclusive classroom teams is also an important aspect of providing support in many European countries where additional adult learning support is common. In much of the Asia-Pacific region the availability of additional adults in the classroom is limited, though there is evidence that some are beginning to explore models of providing such support (Forlin, 2007; Shinohara *et al.*, 2005). Peer support is, however, a much more common feature of many primary schools within the Asia-Pacific region (Yuen *et al.*, 2005). In traditional models of primary school provision, students grouped according to ability have been the norm. This form of grouping students will inevitably persist and indeed there is evidence to suggest that in some situations it is particularly effective.

Teachers in inclusive primary classrooms can do much to provide effective peer support, which has benefits for both students with disabilities and their able peers. Research into classroom grouping shows that with careful planning mixed ability grouping can provide a particularly effective platform for teaching. In particular, in mixed ability groups learners with disabilities benefit from having good role models who assist in scaffolding learning. The more able students also gain from being in a situation where they have to explain concepts and ideas to less able members of the group. Such peer support has become common in many classrooms; however, its management does require teachers who are prepared to be imaginative about the ways in which they organize classrooms and promote student interaction. Simply placing students together in a group without providing adequate structure for learning will often fail to produce positive results (Blumenfeld *et al.*, 1996). Teachers need to provide clear instructions to students and clarify the roles that they are expected to play in group situations. Where able students are expected to support their peers they need to be clear about what the teacher expects to be achieved. Initiating group work of this nature often requires additional interventions by the teacher during the early stages until students have gained confidence and learned the rules of interaction. Once this has been achieved the opportunities for improving both learning and self-esteem become greatly enhanced (Doveston, 2007). Differentiation of outcome is also crucial where teachers are expecting students to work in mixed ability groups and wish to ensure that they recognize that they are being treated fairly, and also to protect the self-esteem of learners with special education needs.

Differentiation is often seen as an important part of ensuring that students with disabilities can access learning in the inclusive primary classroom. At its most effective, differentiated teaching recognizes that students learn at different rates, access meaning in a range of ways and have diverse interests and motivations (Garner and Dwyfor Davies, 2001). This means that the teacher who simply tries to teach every student in a similar way and using the same materials is probably destined to fail and will certainly not be including those students whose needs are significantly different from those of their peers. Teachers providing differentiated access through the use of a range of media or materials – for example, one student writes an account of a school visit to a museum whilst another draws a picture and a third makes a tape recording – has become common practice in many classrooms.

Whilst differentiation can undoubtedly provide an effective means of ensuring participation, if used in an ill-considered manner it can be discriminatory and exclude a student from participation. Differentiation when well managed begins with a consideration of the intended learning outcome and ensures that this is a step forward from where the student was in their learning at the beginning of a task or lesson. Simply giving a student a different task or allowing them to draw a picture because they have difficulty with writing is not an effective way of promoting inclusion. It can be an easy option for teachers to give students work that they know they can do and with which they will be comfortable, but such activity is more often symptomatic of low expectation on the part of the teacher.

In order for differentiation to be effective teachers need to ask a number of critical questions. First, what is the student's current level of skills, knowledge and understanding in relation to the activity we are going to pursue in the lesson? Second, what are the skills, knowledge and understanding that I would like him to gain through the lesson? And finally, how can I plan activities to ensure that the student will move forward in gaining these skills, knowledge and understanding? These questions can form the basis for effective inclusive teaching, particularly when combined with those principles of assessment outlined earlier in this chapter.

One of the factors often discussed in relation to inclusive schooling is that of class size. Certainly there are considerable discrepancies in the numbers of students in primary classes across the world. This can range from fewer than 20 in countries such as Iceland, Denmark or Switzerland to above 60 in some schools in the Asia-Pacific region, such as in China or India. The correlation, however, between academic attainment and class size is weak, and classroom organization in primary schools is not solely a size issue (OECD, 2006). Teachers need to consider how they organize their classrooms in order to promote interaction between peers and support for those students who require specific interventions.

Conclusion

The topics discussed in this chapter leave no room for doubt that becoming an inclusive primary school teacher is far from easy. For those who have a positive attitude and believe that all students can learn, and furthermore have a right to learn, the path becomes easier. High expectations of all students and an organized approach to classroom management and teaching are critical factors in promoting inclusive learning in the primary years. The responsibility upon teachers is great, and the obstacles to success are likely to be many. Yet a failure to accept the challenge to ensure that all students have an opportunity to become effective learners has for many years been one of the most significant factors in denying a large group of learners an opportunity to progress. At the beginning of this chapter I suggested that for even the most accomplished teachers there will be times when students present challenges that appear insurmountable. The inclusive teacher is not necessarily the one who always succeeds but is certainly someone who rises to the challenge, has a commitment to inquiry about their own teaching and the needs of their students, and is prepared to critically review their own performance and make changes where necessary to meet the needs of students with disabilities.

Throughout this chapter I have emphasized the need for teachers to work as reflective practitioners who are prepared to question not only the learning needs of the students in their class, but also their own attitudes, beliefs and practices. Those charged with the responsibility of training teachers, whether in initial training or through continuing professional development, also have a responsibility to look beyond the simplistic provision of knowledge to the development of methods that will encourage inquiry and critique. This requires confidence on the part of all parties but is also an important aspect of being an inclusive teacher.

References

Ainscow, M. (1999) *Understanding the Development of Inclusive Schools*, London: Falmer.

Avramedis, E., Bayliss, P. and Burden, R. (2000) "Student teachers' attitudes towards the inclusion of children with special educational needs in ordinary school", *Teaching and Teacher Education,* 16(3): 129–47.

Barnes, R. (1999) *Positive Teaching, Positive Learning*. London: Routledge.

Blumenfeld, P., Marx, R., Soloway, E. and Krajcik, J. (1996) "Learning with peers: From small group cooperation to collaborative communities", *Educational Researcher,* 25(8): 37–40.

Booth, T., Ainscow, M. and Dyson, A. (1998) "England: Inclusion and exclusion in a competitive system", in T. Booth and M. Ainscow (eds), *From Them to Us: An International Study of Inclusion in Education*, London: Routledge, pp. 193–225.

Chong, S., Forlin, C. and Au, M. L. (2007) "The influence of an inclusive education course on attitude change of pre-service secondary teachers in Hong Kong", *Asia-Pacific Journal of Teacher Education*, 35(2): 161–79.

Christensen, C. R. (1991) "Premises and practices of discussion teaching", in C. R. Christensen, D. Garvin and A. Sweet (eds), *Education for Judgement: The Artistry of Discussion Leadership,* Boston, MA: Harvard Business School.

Cockerill, S. (2005) Are you sitting comfortably? *Special*! Autumn 19–23.

Cooper, P. W. (2004) "Learning from nurture groups", *Education 3-13*, 32(30): 59–64.

Davis, P. and Florian, L. (2004) *Teaching Strategies and Approaches for Students with Special Educational Needs: A Scoping Study*, Nottingham: Department for Education and Skills Research Report 516.

Doveston, M. (2007) "Developing capacity for social and emotional growth: An action research project", *Pastoral Care in Education,* 25(2): 46–54.

Dunne, R. and Wragg, E. C. (1994) *Effective Teaching*, London: Routledge.

Ellins, J. and Porter, J. (2005) "Departmental differences in attitudes to special educational needs in secondary school", *British Journal of Special Education,* 32 (4): 188–95.

Farrell, P. (1997) *Teaching Students with Learning Difficulties: Strategies and Solutions*, London: Cassell.

Forlin, C. (2006) "Inclusive education in Australia ten years after Salamanca", *European Journal of Psychology of Education*, XXI(3): 265–77.

Forlin, C. (2007) "A collaborative, collegial and more cohesive approach to supporting educational reform for inclusion in Hong Kong", *Asia Pacific Education Review*, 8(2): 1–11.

Garner, P. and Davies, J. D. (2001) *Introducing Special Educational Needs: A Companion Guide for Student Teachers*, London: David Fulton.

Gray, C. (2002) *My Social Stories Book*, London: Jessica Kingsley.

Griffiths, M. and Davies, C. (1995) *In Fairness to Children*, London: David Fulton.

Groom, B. (2006) "Enabling inclusion for students with social emotional and behavioral difficulties: The role of teaching assistants", *Proceedings of the Inclusive and Supportive Education Congress*, University of Strathclyde, Scotland 1–4 August.

Henley, M., Ramsey, R. and Algozzine, R. (2002) *Characteristics of and Strategies for Teaching Students with Mild Disabilities*, 4th edn, Boston, MA: Allyn & Bacon.

Howley, M. and Arnold, E. (2005) *Revealing the Hidden Social Code: Social Stories' for People with Autistic Spectrum Disorders*, London: Jessica Kingsley.

Joyce, B., Calhoun, E. and Hopkins, D. (2002) *Models of Learning, Tools for Teaching*, New York: McGraw-Hill.

Jupp, K. (1992) *Everyone Belongs: Mainstream Education for Children with Severe Learning Difficulties*, London: Souvenir Press.

Logan, A. (2006) "The role of the special needs assistant supporting students with special educational needs in Irish mainstream primary schools", *Support for Learning*, 21(2): 92–9.

Mesibov, G. and Howley, M. (2003) *Accessing the Curriculum for Students with Autistic Spectrum Disorders*, London: David Fulton.

Mintz, J. (2007) "Attitudes of primary initial teacher training students to special educational needs and inclusion", *Support for Learning*, 22(1): 3–8.

Morris, P. (1997) "School knowledge, the state and the market: An analysis of the Hong Kong secondary school curriculum", *Journal of Curriculum Studies*, 29(3): 329–49.

Newton, D. (2005) "Teaching and learning in the primary school", in E. English and L. Newton (eds), *Professional Studies in the Primary School: Thinking Beyond the Standards*, London: David Fulton, pp. 35–49.

Organization for Economic Cooperation and Development (2006) *Education at a Glance: OECD Indicators*, Paris.

Rose, R. (1999) "The involvement of students with severe learning difficulties as decision-makers in respect of their own learning needs", *Westminster Studies in Education*, 22(4): 19–29.

Rose, R. (2001) "Primary school teacher perceptions of the conditions required to include students with special educational needs", *Educational Review*, 53(2): 146–57.

Rose, R. and Coles, C. (2002) "Special and mainstream school collaboration for inclusion", *Journal of Research in Special Educational Needs*, 2(2): 58–72.

Rose, R. and Howley, M. (2007) *The Practical Guide to Special Educational Needs in Inclusive Primary Classrooms*, London: Paul Chapman.

Salvia, J., Ysseldyke, I. and Bolt, S. (2007) *Assessment in Special and Inclusive Education*, 10th edn, Boston, MA: Houghton Mifflin.

Shinohara, Y., Ebihara, K. and Ono, S. (2005) "Special educational provision for children with mild developmental disabilities in mainstream schools in Japan", *Proceedings of the Inclusive and Supportive Education Congress*, University of Strathclyde, Scotland, 1–4 August.

Waine, L. and Kime, S. (2005) "Practical aspects of assessment", in G. Backhouse and K. Morris (eds), *Dyslexia? Assessing and Reporting*, London: Hodder Murray.

Yuen, M., Westwood, P. and Wong, G. (2005) "Meeting the needs of students with specific learning difficulties in the mainstream education system: Data from primary school teachers in Hong Kong", *The International Journal of Special Education*, 20(1): 67–76.

11 The inclusive secondary school teacher

Michelle Pearce

Chapter objectives

- To present the characteristics, knowledge and skills of an inclusive secondary school teacher.
- To examine how teachers learn to be inclusive.
- To provide examples of the systemic support necessary for teachers to be inclusive.

Focus questions

1. What are the attributes, attitudes, knowledge and skills of inclusive teachers in secondary schools?
2. How can teachers acquire the attributes, attitudes, knowledge and skills of inclusive teachers?
3. What support do schools and systems in the Asia-Pacific region need to provide for teachers to become inclusive?

Introduction

Since discrimination and segregation became issues in the 1960s during the civil rights movement in America, many cultures, countries and education systems have started to move towards a more inclusive approach as advocated by UNESCO (1994) in the Salamanca Statement. Governments and education systems, however, have interpreted and responded differently to inclusion. Countries such as Italy and some American states such as Vermont no longer have special education facilities, which were rejected as discriminatory relics of institutional segregation (Hallahan and Kauffman, 2005). In Australia, legislation gives parents of all children the right to choose regular class options, but most jurisdictions continue to offer a range of special education facilities (Foreman, 2001). Although the Australian experience demonstrates that legislation may be necessary to give inclusion impetus, the Asia-Pacific region is starting to develop more inclusive education policies (Forlin, 2007).

Education systems in the Asia-Pacific region can prepare for inclusion by developing an awareness of the challenges inclusion has posed in countries such as Australia, and learning from their successes, failures and research. What is learned from hindsight in one country becomes foresight for others considering the same pathway. Primary schools in Australia have generally been more receptive to inclusion than secondary schools (Pearce and Forlin, 2005). The primary school culture is more conducive to inclusion because it is child centered with teachers being experienced in catering for the needs of individual students and managing multiple learning activities at the same time. The class teacher has knowledge of each student and can communicate with parents, special education teachers, past and present teachers and other professionals. The curriculum focuses on all aspects of the child's development: social skills, physical, health, literacy and numeracy. Intervention services are available and teaching assistants are more likely to be employed. As children progress through primary school, the curriculum increasingly concentrates on academic development and differences between children with learning disabilities and their peers become more evident.

It is secondary school education, however, that poses the greatest challenges. The structure of secondary schools is problematic (Cole and McLeskey, 1997) as they are curriculum centered (McLeskey and Waldron, 2002). Like schools in the Asia-Pacific region, timetables and curricula are inflexible and dominated by exams. Schools are divided into subject-based departments, which can thwart collaboration and integration of the curriculum. Teaching is specialized and teachers are autonomous (Dieker and Murawski, 2003). Each teacher may be responsible for over 100 students per week. Thus it is difficult to acquire knowledge about each student and it takes a considerable amount of time to develop learning profiles and strategies. Lessons tend to be short and teachers must focus on covering the curriculum to maximize the potential of their students to pass exams. Teachers do not have time to stop lessons to resolve the social, learning, emotional or behavioral problems of individual children that may interfere with the learning of the other students.

Secondary schools have been likened to factories because they focus on the curriculum for large groups of students rather than individuals (DiMartino *et al.*, 2002). Teachers are trained to teach curriculum and content rather than pedagogy and children at all stages of development. An exam-driven system may not permit differentiation, and may be more conducive to didactic teaching. The close relationship students had with primary teachers is lost. Students are expected to learn independently, which presents a hurdle for students with disabilities. Teenagers may also be reluctant to support peers with disabilities and may reject them socially. The size of the school and the number of teachers discourages parents from involvement and impedes communication; and support services for students and teachers are often minimal.

Secondary teachers, who were trained to teach in a segregated system, may resist inclusion because they lack special education expertise and confidence when interacting with children with disabilities (Pearce and Forlin, 2005). If teachers with special education training are teaching special education classes, they are unlikely to have time to support the regular teacher. While some would argue that teachers need training in special education to include students with disabilities into secondary schools (Kauffman and Hallahan, 2005), others propose that inclusion is simply a matter of good teaching practice (Ainscow, 2005; Skrtic, 1995). If teachers are to be prepared for inclusion, it is important to identify the attributes, attitudes, knowledge and skills of inclusive teachers in secondary schools and how teachers learn.

An inclusive secondary teacher

The following perspective of an inclusive secondary teacher is based on an analysis of the views of 50 leading educators in the fields of special and inclusive education. Extensive interviews were undertaken with academics, consultants, psychologists, administrators, executive staff, Learning Support Coordinators (LSC) and teachers. Leaders from government, Catholic and independent schools and universities participated in the research. Interviewees were questioned about their experiences in secondary schools and were asked to identify the characteristics of an inclusive secondary teacher.

Attitude

During the last decade, research has shown that a positive attitude is the most crucial factor in becoming an inclusive teacher (Sharma *et al.*, 2006). Leading educators agreed, and claimed that attitude is even more important than knowledge and skills. Without an inclusive attitude, teachers will not be motivated to learn the knowledge and skills they need. Some teachers seem to be inclusive by nature, or possibly through nurture, and welcome the opportunity to teach every child. Inclusive teachers think it is important that children with and without disabilities interact and learn values from each other. Differences are accepted as a normal part of life. There are teachers who become inclusive after they have successful experiences in teaching children with disabilities. Improving pedagogy, therefore, increases the chances of teachers having successful experiences. Some teachers respond positively once they understand the philosophy of inclusion, which is emotionally appealing. Some teachers, however, reluctantly change their attitudes only when legal requirements give them no option. Teachers may not always agree with the choice of setting by the parents, but they do need to respect and accept the parents' legal right to make the choice.

Attributes

Inclusive teachers love teaching. They are described as compassionate, approachable, friendly, warm and kindhearted. The word soft is not mentioned because inclusive teachers demand high standards of behavior and work. They believe that all students can learn, so they have high expectations. Accordingly, opportunities are created for everyone to succeed. Successful learning builds the self-esteem and status of students with disabilities amongst their peers. Students can improve their status when they are given responsibilities in the classroom, leadership roles or age-appropriate praise. The inclusive teacher celebrates even small achievements. They do not blame the child for failing but change their teaching methods or strategies until they find one that works. Well-organized, inclusive teachers manage their classrooms efficiently and work comfortably with other adults in the room. Inclusive teachers accept responsibility to teach all the children in their classes rather than try to give their responsibilities to an assistant or recommend that the student with disabilities selects another course. They are hard working and prepared to devote the extra time and effort required to plan work for students who need differentiation. Their understanding of inclusion motivates them to devote the extra time and effort required to differentiate the curriculum or support the student. Calm personalities and a good sense of humour help teachers maintain a positive outlook.

Having a student with a disability in a secondary class does not mean that the child's needs are the most important or that they have to dominate the learning activities of the class. The needs of all the students and how the teacher can support everyone in the class must also be considered. There is awareness that adjustments made to include one student have the potential to help many others. The child with a disability blends into the class and is not singled out by being isolated with a teacher assistant at the back of the class. The students are helped to understand that everyone learns differently and that there are different ways of achieving goals.

In an inclusive secondary school, relationships in the classroom are respectful, positive and supportive. Disparaging comments are not tolerated. The teacher models appropriate attitudes for the students. The inclusive teacher does not pretend the student does not have a disability but helps the other students understand and support their peer. This could require the student with a disability, parents, a teacher or a disability support group providing peers with information and ways they can assist the student. Permission from the student with the disability and the parents is necessary and the awareness raising must be handled sensitively. Acceptance and understanding can be enhanced through the curriculum. For example, the class may study a novel featuring a person with a disability. Alternatively, students can study a disability in Science or famous people in History, some of whom just happen to have disabilities. A guest speaker may talk about their own experience of having a disability.

Effective communication skills are essential for a teacher to work collaboratively. A problem-solving approach is applied by an inclusive teacher when it comes to a student with a disability. The teacher remains confident that a simple solution can be found and thinks creatively. When a solution is elusive, the teacher openly expresses concern and seeks knowledge and assistance from others. Therefore, learning how to teach a student with a slightly different learning profile is inspiring rather than daunting.

Knowledge and skills

Student knowledge

A secondary school teacher's subject knowledge of curriculum and content is important, but so too is student knowledge. Student knowledge directs all other forms of teacher knowledge. Despite the increased difficulty of acquiring student knowledge with so many students to teach per week, inclusive teachers do their best to get to know their students personally in the same way as primary teachers. The whole child is considered by an inclusive teacher: academically, socially and emotionally. Teachers can gain personal knowledge by observing students in various contexts like the classroom, school excursions and the playground. Inclusive teachers listen to their students and their parents to learn about student interests. Teachers need time to get to know their students personally before they can understand how to apply effective strategies. This explains why even the best preparation for the transition of a student with a disability from primary to secondary school does not have immediate results.

In a similar way to inclusion in the primary school, some students will need quite different learning goals built into the curriculum. For example, the whole class may be conducting a science experiment. While the majority will learn about the properties of gas and liquid, the student with an intellectual disability may learn about science, but also to concentrate, help his peers and practise his communication skills. No matter how difficult the content or tasks may be, simple goals can be woven throughout. Inclusive teachers find out how their students learn best, assess their learning styles and use Gardner's (1999) multiple intelligences approach. They access or develop learning profiles of their students by gathering information from past teachers, parents and the school psychologist. Standardized tests, curriculum-based assessment and observation increase their knowledge. Inclusive teachers want to understand why the students are experiencing learning difficulties. Even more importantly, they want to identify the students' strengths because these can be used to improve learning. If a student is a visual learner, for example, the teacher knows to provide diagrams, pictures, photos, posters and visual material on the computer or in books.

Knowledge of the educational implications of the disability is essential to inclusive secondary teachers because it provides an understanding of how the curriculum, content and pedagogy will need to be changed if the student is to learn. The label or category of disability is of little benefit without specific information about the child. A child with cerebral palsy, for instance, may have minor problems with fine and gross motor skills or may be unable to walk. In this respect, parents have expert knowledge to share with teachers. Schools need to have an efficient means of accumulating and storing information so that teachers can quickly gain student knowledge. Student databases are very effective if they are kept up to date. The school psychologist may be the person who can explain medical reports or assessments related to the student's disability. On occasions, teachers will find a student's disability has such an impact on behavior or learning that they need further assistance.

Pedagogical knowledge

Inclusive teachers have a wide repertoire of teaching strategies, which gives them the flexibility to match student knowledge to pedagogy and to apply another strategy quickly if the first does not work. They do not rigidly use the same lessons and same methods each year but change them to suit the needs and interests of their students in different classes. They use good teaching practices such as giving clear instructions, breaking tasks into smaller components, demonstrating the task, providing opportunities for guided practice and independent practice, monitoring progress, giving feedback, reviewing learning at the end of one lesson and again at the beginning of the next. Adept with technology and computers, they use technology to boost learning and student motivation.

To be able to include a student with a learning disability academically, the inclusive teacher must differentiate the curriculum, teaching strategies, assessment methods and reporting. The teacher understands that children learn at different times, and there are many different pathways to learning the same outcomes. A student is not included by merely sitting in the classroom but actively participates in the program and learns. The student moves along the learning continuum. To guide differentiation, teachers may break the curriculum into "must know, should know and could know." All the students "must learn" core knowledge. Once this knowledge has been learned, students may move on to the knowledge that they "should know." It is possible that only the most gifted students learn the "could know" knowledge.

Social and emotional inclusion is just as important to the inclusive secondary teacher as academic inclusion. Social inclusion can be promoted by providing opportunities for students to interact with each other. Good social practices can include cooperative learning, working in pairs or groups, using peer tutors, team activities, structured games and changing seating arrangements. If a student appears to be isolated from peers, social groups can be established to support the student. Buddy or peer support systems offer opportunities for interaction. If a teaching assistant is allocated to the class to support the student, the assistant must be careful to work with all the students to avoid isolating or labeling the student with the disability.

Managing challenging behavior is another skill that inclusive teachers are always striving to improve. Well aware of the link between learning and behavior, they think of ways to engage their students. A disability may affect a child's behavior so the inclusive teacher makes sure they understand the connection.

Independence is a goal for all children. The inclusive teacher does not allow the student with a disability to become dependent on the teacher, teaching assistant or peers. The student who needs to improve organizational skills is taught to use checklists, colour-coded timetables or memory books. Prompts and assistance are gradually withdrawn. The teacher talks to the student about their strengths. Students are given strategies to help them learn so that they can take responsibility for their own learning. In doing so, students develop self-awareness, which can prepare them for life. Discussion between the teacher and the student occurs privately or with parents rather than in front of peers. Learning goals and strategies are negotiated between the teacher and the student. A student who has difficulty writing may negotiate to present his or her work alternatively through a PowerPoint presentation, an oral report or a video clip. All students are given choices. The student with a disability helps to develop the Individual Education Plan (IEP) or behavior plan. Feeling ownership of the plan is more likely to produce a positive outcome. Having a long-term vision guides the inclusive teacher in curriculum delivery. Students may need to learn functional skills such as eating or living skills such as money management and literacy through the curriculum. They could learn the skills by attending alternate courses within the school or community. If available, a job coach can support the student initially during work experience.

Teacher learning

Preservice

Attitudes, knowledge and skills can become more inclusive during preservice courses and throughout teachers' careers. It is important that a teacher emerges from preservice training with an inclusive attitude because negative attitudes are difficult to reverse. There is a marked difference in attitude when trainee teachers are aware that they will be teaching children with disabilities compared to those who never expected to do so. Listening to parents of children with disabilities talk about their children and their aspirations, or to adults with disabilities about their school experiences builds empathy amongst teachers and can become a valuable part of training.

Strategies for preparing teachers to work with students with disabilities are best infused through all education courses rather than designated as "special education" and taught separately. Courses that focus on disability categories need to concentrate on strategies, but even these will not be able to prepare teachers because the knowledge and skills they require are so student specific. Two students with autism, for example, may have completely different learning needs. As the roles of special and regular teachers merge in inclusive contexts, the knowledge and skills of teachers expand. Special education teachers need knowledge of curriculum, and subject teachers need pedagogical practices that were formerly regarded as the special educator's domain. Preservice courses have to give teachers an understanding of all stages of child development and the knowledge of how to teach literacy and numeracy from the early years to the final years of schooling.

Collaboration

The majority of teachers require new knowledge and skills to be able to include students with disabilities in their classes and to become inclusive secondary school teachers. Professional development in the form of one-day workshops or conferences has limited value. Knowledge is so student specific, that it is best learnt at the point of need through collaboration with others in a child's life. The relevant person will vary depending on the child, the disability and the situation, but could be medical professionals, therapists, disability support groups, teaching assistants, colleagues with experience in teaching the student, special education teachers or consultants. Inclusive teachers develop partnerships with parents who have so much knowledge of their own child to share. There is an honest exchange of opinions.

Access to special education expertise is essential for teachers to learn. For example, teachers with special education expertise or external consultants can be used to lead their colleagues through the Individual Education Plan process, the development of behavior management or social skills plans or differentiation of the curriculum. Many schools have learning support teams, comprising the deputy principal, psychologist, special education or learning difficulties teacher and one or two other experienced teachers. To function well the team should meet regularly to listen to the concerns of teachers of students with learning or behavioral difficulties. Members of the team suggest strategies the teacher can try. The teacher trials their recommendations and reports the results to the team. If the teacher needs further advice, the team may arrange for a person with specialist knowledge to visit the school. The ideal support is a full-time support teacher with specialist knowledge placed within the school.

Colleagues have a wealth of knowledge to share. To facilitate inclusion in secondary schools teachers need to move from being autonomous and teaching behind closed doors to being far more collaborative and collegial. Collaborative learning can be as simple as asking colleagues for advice in the staffroom or via email. The advantage of colleagues working within departments is that they can learn content knowledge and pedagogy from their peers. For example, they may focus on differentiating the Year 9 curriculum to cater for a group of students with learning difficulties and several who are gifted. Teachers can share units of work they have created or store them in a central file or on the intranet for colleagues to use. Teachers from different departments may work together to develop integrated units of work based on a student's strengths or interests. Teachers can observe their colleagues teaching to discover how to support a particular student or apply a new strategy. Colleagues can combine their experience and knowledge to brainstorm possible solutions to any problem. A teacher with more experience in a particular area can act as a mentor to a colleague, help plan lessons, give demonstration lessons, provide feedback on their colleagues' lessons or team teach. Professional networking with teachers from other schools and visits to other schools inspire teachers to try new ideas and explore other possibilities.

Inclusive teachers not only draw on the strengths of their colleagues, but on the strengths of their students. They highly value peer support and make maximum use of this resource. Students may be called upon to support their peers socially and academically. To help students learn, teachers carefully allocate students to groups based on their strengths. As part of their own learning programs, some students utilize and improve their skills by producing computer programs or art work for peers with disabilities. Students with learning disabilities may tutor younger students, or be tutored by older students or peers.

Teaching assistants and teachers work in partnership in an inclusive classroom. They have clear role statements and understand their responsibilities. The teacher is responsible for developing the curriculum and directing the assistant. There is effective communication between the two. The teacher is always consulted before changes are made to the program or problems occur and is given feedback on the student's progress. The assistant often works with groups of students and the student with disabilities, or with other students in the class so that the student is not stigmatized. Assistants are encouraged to attend planning meetings. Their contribution and experience is valued and respected.

Inclusive schools and systems

Participants in this study reported that some secondary schools are impressive in their inclusivity. Their principals are committed to inclusion and provide strong and courageous leadership. Inclusive schools have reviewed their policies and practices to make sure they are inclusive. The school culture is inclusive and the school community actively promotes inclusion as a value. Through the employment of additional staff, teachers are given time, that most precious of resources, to collaborate, plan and learn the skills they need. Effective teaching and inclusion are professional development priorities. The school builds close relationships with the community so that it can access vocational courses and workplaces to prepare students for life after school. Partnerships with universities are fostered. Timetables are flexible so that students can access any classes or external courses that suit their needs. There is a genuine desire to support students in achieving their post-school goals, whether these are to attend university or to enjoy their leisure time.

Leaders stressed that it is very difficult for teachers to be inclusive if their schools and the education system are not similarly inclusive. Inclusion must be a systemic priority or policies will be tokenistic and funding will not be forthcoming. Education systems must offer inclusive policies, funding, resources, expertise, professional development and curricula that promote and facilitate inclusion. Consultants and specialist services related to high incidence disabilities need to be available to provide support to special education and regular teachers.

Conclusion

It is important for education systems in the Asia-Pacific region to understand the attributes, attitudes, knowledge and skills of the inclusive secondary teacher and how they can be acquired so that they can plan for the necessary support to be in place. First and foremost, inclusive teachers have positive attitudes to inclusion. Teachers are more likely to become inclusive if they are supported with time, resources, and assistants and expertise as they develop their knowledge and skills.

Attributes such as good problem-solving skills, confidence, creativity, flexibility and really enjoying teaching are common to inclusive teachers. Although good teaching practice is essential, teachers will need access to special education expertise for the foreseeable future whilst they expand their skills. According to education leaders in inclusion, secondary teachers with a wealth of knowledge to share will learn the knowledge and skills to be inclusive if they work in collaborative schools that are learning communities, and if they are given the time and opportunities to do so.

This portrait of an inclusive secondary school teacher is an idealistic representation. The relative simplicity of the primary school structure compared to the secondary system has meant that success tends to be more evident in the primary setting. As schools in the Asia-Pacific region can observe, however, it is possible for secondary schools to become inclusive, even in systems dominated by external examinations, shortages of funding and teachers who are mostly untrained in special education and concerned with constant curriculum change. It does, however, require greater determination and commitment to inclusion on the part of the system and teachers. It is to be hoped that the needs of children with disabilities will lead reforms to providing a more relevant, responsive secondary school system for all children in the Asia-Pacific region.

References

Ainscow, M. (2005) "Looking to the future: Towards a common sense of purpose", *Australasian Journal of Special Education*, 29(2): 182–6.

Cole, C. M. and McLeskey, J. (1997) "Secondary inclusion programs for students with mild disabilities", *Focus on Exceptional Children*, 29(6): 1–15.

Dieker, L. and Murawski, W. W. (2003) "Co-teaching at the secondary level: Unique issues, current trends, and suggestions for success", *The High School Journal*, 86(4): 1–13.

DiMartino, J., Clarke, J. and Lachat, M. A. (2002) "Creating student-centered high schools", *Principal Leadership*, 2(5): 44–50.

Foreman, P. (2001) *Integration and Inclusion in Action*, Sydney: Harcourt Australia.

Forlin, C. (2007) "Classroom diversity: Towards a whole school approach", in S. N. Phillipson (ed.), *Learning Diversity in the Chinese Classroom: Contexts and Practice for Students with Special Needs*, Hong Kong: Hong Kong University Press, pp. 95–123.

Gardner, H. (1999) *Intelligence Reframed: Multiple Intelligences for the 21st Century*, New York: Basic Books.

Hallahan, D. P. and Kauffman, J. M. (2005) *Exceptional Learners: Introduction to Special Education*, 10th edn, Boston, MA: Allyn & Bacon.

Kauffman, J. M. and Hallahan, D. P. (2005) *Special Education: What Is it and Why We Need it*, Boston, MA: Pearson.

McLeskey, J. and Waldron, N. L. (2002) "Inclusion and school change: Teacher perceptions regarding curricular and instructional adaptations", *Teacher Education and Special Education*, 25(1): 41–54.

Pearce, M.V. and Forlin, C. (2005) "Challenges and potential solutions for enabling inclusion in secondary schools", *Australasian Journal of Special Education*, 29(2): 93–106.

Sharma, U., Forlin, C., Loreman, T. and Earle, C. (2006) "Pre-service teachers' attitudes, concerns and sentiments about inclusive education: An international comparison of the novice pre-service teacher", *International Journal of Special Education*, 21(2): 80–93.

Skrtic, T. M. (1995) "The special education knowledge tradition: Crisis and opportunity", in E. I. Meyen and T. M. Skrtic (eds), *Special Education and Student Disability: An Introduction*, 4th edn, Denver, CO: Love.

United Nations Educational, Scientific and Cultural Organization (1994) *The Salamanca Statement and Framework for Action on Special Needs Education*, Salamanca, Spain.

12 The changing roles and responsibilities of school principals relative to inclusive education

Umesh Sharma and Ishwar Desai

Chapter objectives

- To examine the impact of inclusion on the role and responsibilities of school principals.
- To provide an overview of the leadership styles that are most compatible for leading inclusive schools.
- To identify and describe the various functions that principals of effective inclusive schools are required to perform on a regular basis.
- To review and discuss the implications of research findings with respect to principals' academic backgrounds and formal training in special and inclusive education.

Focus questions

1 How are the roles and responsibilities of school principals changing as a result of a growing number of students with a disability seeking enrolment in regular schools?
2 What leadership styles help to promote inclusive practices in a school?
3 Are school principals adequately trained to fulfill their role as inclusive school leaders?

Introduction

Public schools around the world today are being called upon to serve a much more heterogeneous student population than ever before. In this regard, including students with disabilities in regular schools continues to attract much controversy. Bringing about change in education is difficult, especially when it involves a redefinition of roles and responsibilities on the part of school personnel towards a group of people whom society has only relatively recently accorded dignity and basic human rights.

Schools around the world have gone through major reforms during the last 50 years. Schools that were considered effective in the early 1970s and 1980s are no longer considered effective. Students from multi-ethnic backgrounds or with disabilities were rarely represented in such schools. The situation in the more developed parts of the world is slightly different today. Many schools in the West (e.g. in the United Kingdom, Europe, USA) have implemented inclusive education for more than ten years now but for many of the Asia-Pacific regions they are only just beginning to consider such changes (e.g. Vietnam, Cambodia, Indonesia). Schools are considered effective if they are inclusive (Ryan, 2006). According to Stainback and Stainback (1990) in an inclusive school "everyone belongs, is accepted and is supported by his or her peers and other members of the school community in the course of having his or her education needs met" (p. 3).

There is a belief in such schools that they are "enriched when they reflect the diversity of society and when all learners, including those with disabilities and diverse cultural/linguistic needs, become integral members of the learning community" (Salisbury and McGregor, 2005, p. 2). This chapter provides an overview of the leadership styles that are most compatible for leading inclusive schools; it presents a framework documenting functions performed by inclusive leaders on a regular basis and the key skills required to perform such functions; and finally, reviews research that examines principals' academic backgrounds and formal training relative to inclusive education, in order to highlight some of the challenges that lie ahead in training the future generation of school leaders.

Leadership style

Leading effective and inclusive schools requires school principals to adopt unique leadership styles and assume new roles and responsibilities. Inclusive school leaders are more democratic and transformative. They exercise their power by working with rather than over their staff (Blase and Anderson, 1995). This approach is democratic in its processes of decision making as well as in meeting the goals of equity and justice within education institutions (Blase and Anderson, 1995). Leadership in such schools does not reside within one individual but it is shared by all staff in fulfilling their roles and responsibilities. Gronn (2002) describes this kind of leadership as distributed leadership. Ryan (2006) argues that "concentrating leadership power in a single individual is exclusive; those who are not considered leaders are left out of leadership related activities" (p. 8). He adds that "the influence of single individuals on institutions is generally limited, and as a consequence, it does not make sense to rely heavily on single leaders" (p. 8).

Closely related to the democratic style of leadership is transformative leadership. Commenting on some of the attributes of transformative leaders, Jahan (2000) states that:

> transformative leaders make consultation and participation a part of the organization routine. The institutional decisions are not handed down in a bureaucratic top down manner. Instead, democratic participation by all members is emphasized. Decision making processes are open and transparent and not set behind closed doors. The leadership is responsive and accountable to the general members of the organization. The leaders are as much committed to means as ends, setting high standards of non corrupt behavior. They work towards building consensus through consultation and

> participation though these processes are time consuming and challenging. Instead of manipulating and controlling people, transformative leaders attempt to empower them.
>
> (Jahan, 2000, p. 4)

In an extensive review of the literature on school effectiveness and school leaders, Hallinger and Heck (1998) identified some of the key attributes of transformative school leaders. These principals are better at supporting staff, providing recognition, knowing the problems faced by school teachers, and are more approachable. They also follow through, seek new ideas, and spend considerable time in finding resources to support their school's mission. This leadership style allows staff to be more creative and risk taking and increases teacher enthusiasm in implementing a new education reform such as inclusive education. The staff also feels more willing to contribute in achieving the vision of the school.

Building on the ideas advanced by Sergiovanni (1992), Armstrong (2006) proposed that transformative principals lead schools through moral change. The moral change requires teaching staff to change their beliefs and expectations about students. In such leadership environments, teachers need to believe that they could teach all students. In order to bring about moral change in a school, Armstrong (2006) proposes that the principal needs to adopt a spiritually driven leadership style. She defines spirituality as a powerful force that helps one to see beyond one's limited self-interests into the possibilities of deeper connections not only for one's own good but also for others. Thus spirituality provides a way to embrace student diversity. This approach guides the principal in working through the most crucial questions: why and how to inspire the school to be inclusive. These principals lead from the heart, enabling them to inspire not only themselves, but also everyone working in their schools. Their strong beliefs guide all their actions, which creates an environment where everyone belongs and is valued. Principals in such schools are reflective and they encourage their staff to be reflective. They use a process-driven approach where each member of the school contributes. Most importantly, the journey to embrace inclusively is taken by the entire school and not just by the principal.

It would appear that such leadership styles have a positive and symbolic influence on everyone working in the school. Principals' actions, statements and expectations communicate what practices will be maintained and rewarded and what behaviors and actions by the staff will be condoned. Research indicates that in schools where the inclusion of students with disabilities into regular school programs has been implemented successfully, principals have clearly supported the policy guidelines and values underpinning inclusion (Burrello and Wright, 1992).

Symbolic leaders, that is, those who focus the attention of others on matters of importance to the school, lead to the creation of an environment of acceptance of student diversity (Sergiovanni, 1992). These leaders display positive behaviors and inclusionary practices by visiting integrated classrooms, seeking out and spending time with students with disabilities, and showing educational concerns for all students, with and without disabilities. Such leadership behaviors inspire other school staff to work diligently towards successfully integrating students with disabilities. There is growing evidence that indicates that where principals have facilitated initiatives to include students with disabilities, teachers have demonstrated a motivation to perform beyond expectation (Armstrong, 2006). Sharma (2001) also emphasized that principals play a significant role not only in shaping the overall school environment but also in shaping community attitudes.

One other key role that principals of inclusive schools perform is that of an instructional leader. Effective inclusive principals provide leadership in instruction, coordinate instructional programs, and most importantly emphasize high academic standards and expectations for all students but more specifically for students with disabilities. To fulfill this role efficiently, they must support teachers, maintain focus on the tasks, coordinate instructional programs, spend time in classrooms, and provide opportunity for staff to learn new skills to meet the education needs of all students. The availability of this support directly influences teachers' attitudes and practices about including children with disabilities into regular school programs.

A number of studies have also focused on what effective leaders do on a regular basis to make their schools more inclusive (e.g. Armstrong, 2006; Guzmán, 1997; Kugelmass and Ainscow, 2004). We used these observations as well as other relevant literature on leadership to conceptualize a framework that readers might find helpful in gaining an understanding of the key tasks that are performed by effective inclusive leaders. The proposed framework is devised to answers two crucial questions:

1 What are some of the key functions that effective inclusive leaders perform on a regular basis?
2 What are the key skills that are required of them to perform these functions?

Functions of effective school leaders

Figure 12.1 provides an overview of the various functions that principals of effective schools are required to perform on a regular basis.

Some of the most commonly performed functions of inclusive school leaders include:

- developing and selling a vision of inclusion;
- seeking and supporting active involvement of parents and family members;
- obtaining and providing resources;
- modifying school policies to support inclusion;
- developing a plan of professional development;
- monitoring the progress of inclusive efforts;
- supporting staff in their efforts to implement inclusive practices.

Developing and selling a vision of inclusion

This is one of the key tasks that leaders of inclusive schools have to perform. According to Regan and Brooks (1995) vision is the "ability to formulate and

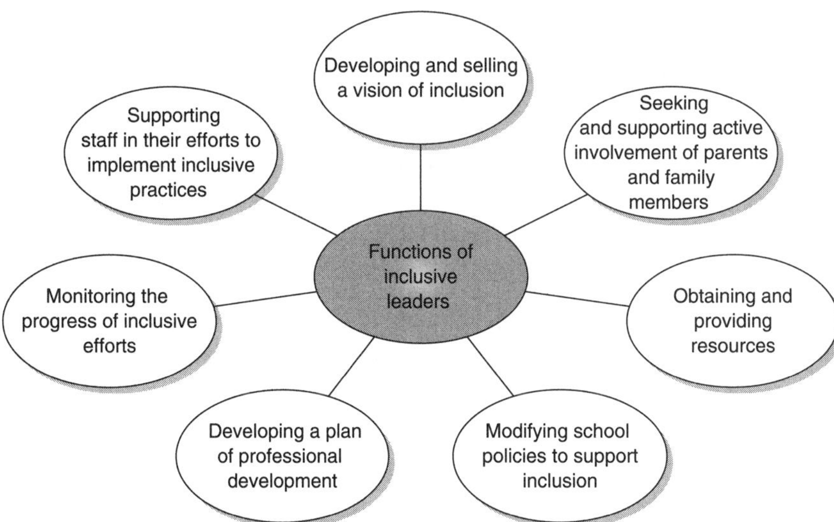

Figure 12.1 Functions performed by inclusive leaders.

express original ideas, enabling others to consider options in new and different ways" (p. 36). Beare *et al.* (1997) emphasize that school leaders must have an absolute commitment to a vision. School principals' every word and action must reflect that vision. They suggest that principals should be able to sell their vision not only to their staff but also to parents. They also suggest that the vision must be provided in both conceptual and operational forms. One challenge that principals of inclusive schools are likely to face are staff members who do not believe in the vision. For example, some teachers may believe that students with severe disabilities do not belong in their school and that such students should be referred to special schools. Similarly, some parents of typical children may resist the inclusion of students with disabilities in the school. Principals need to have mechanisms to deal with such challenges. If no attention is paid to such issues it is likely that the concerns expressed by teachers and parents will influence other staff in the school and result in resistance from even more staff to implement inclusive practices. Blair (2002) suggests that principals need to exercise tact, patience and resilience in order to address any opposition that may occur regarding the implementation of inclusive practices in their school.

Seeking and supporting the active involvement of parents and family members

Inclusion works best in those schools where parents and family members, particularly of those students who have disabilities, are actively involved. In order to seek active involvement from parents, it is important that they feel a part of the school community. School leaders can communicate this message through a number of overt and covert behaviors. Principals should actively participate in education planning meetings for students with disabilities. They should also spend time in classrooms with such students. This would convey a message to parents and to everyone associated with the system that such children are valued in their schools. They should also create an accepting environment for everyone, including parents of children with disabilities. They can achieve this by arranging meeting times that are appropriate for parents, by providing interpreters for those parents who cannot communicate in the same language as that spoken by the school community, and by establishing a system of communication that keeps parents informed of daily activities in schools (particularly those relevant to the parents). These principals can also occasionally call parents to inform them of the progress of their children.

Obtaining and providing resources

Implementation of inclusive practices requires principals to obtain and provide necessary resources. These can range from: technical, for example, access to experts such as special educators and speech pathologists; materials, such as computers and software, brailed books, and FM (frequency modulated) systems for students with a hearing impairment; human, such as integration aides; and organizational, such as additional time for planning. School leaders need to be creative in providing these resources as it is rare that all these resources will be available to support inclusive practices. This is particularly true for most schools in the Asia-Pacific region. It is, therefore, important that schools undertake a "restructuring of existing resources, change the way staff are assigned, and change the roles of existing staff" (Salisbury and McGregor, 2005, p. 8). It may also be necessary to collaborate with other schools in the community to share resources that are too expensive (e.g. printers to convert text into Braille or vice versa) or those resources that are in limited supply (e.g. paraprofessionals).

Often a lack of time to undertake a number of tasks associated with implementing inclusive practices can frustrate teachers. A significant contribution that school principals can make in this regard is to support teachers so that they can collaborate and engage with each other. Structuring the school schedule to allow for planning time for teachers could also be an important strategy. School leaders have to be creative as well as resourceful to ensure that teachers have sufficient time to work with each other, to modify materials, and to participate in various other activities such as consultations with parents and teacher aides.

Modifying school policies to support inclusion

Modifying standard practices and operating procedures is crucial to successfully include students with disabilities into regular school programs. One area that principals should pay attention to in this regard relates to assessment policies. Teachers around the world are being asked to raise the overall academic achievements of schools. If students with disabilities, more specifically those who have severe disabilities, are to be included in a school's academic evaluation, teachers are likely to express concerns about their school's academic performance declining (Sharma, 2001; Sharma and Desai, 2002; Sharma *et al.*, 2003). Ideally, therefore, assessment of academic performance of students with severe disabilities should be tied to individual goals identified by the family and the school. The data arising from such an assessment of students with disabilities can then be incorporated in evaluating a school's overall performance. Making such drastic changes in a school's assessment policy requires the support of school communities as well as departments of education.

One other area where schools may need to modify their practices relates to discipline and behavior policies. Some schools have a policy of "zero tolerance" against any kind of disruptive behavior. Such policies disadvantage all students but more so students with disabilities. Schools need to invest heavily in this area and need to have "whole school policies" based on principles of Positive Behavior Support (PBS) (Janney and Snell, 2000). Positive Behavior Support (PBS) approaches use collaborative problem-solving processes to develop individualized interventions that focus on prevention of problem behaviors through effective education programming. The goals of PBS include "helping students to 1) develop new communication, social and self control skills; 2) form more positive relationships with classmates, teachers, and other community members; and 3) take more active roles in their classrooms, schools, and communities" (Janney and Snell, 2000, p. 2). School principals need to ensure that such policies are in place as this is likely to result in a more conducive learning environment for all learners.

Developing a plan of professional development

In order to lead inclusive schools, principals will need to take on new roles and responsibilities. It is important that principals have a plan for their own professional development. They need to prioritize those skills that they will require to fulfill their added responsibilities efficiently. In a recent study of over 1300 school principals from the state of Virginia, USA, a large majority identified student learning as an area in which they felt that they needed more professional development (DiPaola and Tschannen-Moran, 2003). Some other areas where principals have been found to express a serious lack of knowledge is in legislation and policies related to students with disabilities (Desai, 1995; Sharma, 2001).

While school leaders develop a plan for their own professional development, it is equally important that they provide ample opportunities for their staff to engage in appropriate professional development (PD) activities. Commenting on the need for PD for staff, Ryan (2006) states, "If everyone is to meet the challenges associated with inclusion, then they will have to acquire new knowledge, understandings and attitudes. To do so, all members of the school community have to assume the role of both teacher and learner" (p. 10). In general, one-off professional development activities are not as useful as those delivered in a number of sessions, as these allow staff to resolve issues in subsequent sessions that they find difficult to implement in their classrooms.

Monitoring the progress of inclusive efforts

School leaders need to continuously monitor their efforts in successfully implementing inclusive education. Often it is believed that if the needs of students with disabilities are met, the school is inclusive. In this narrowly defined criterion to measure success of inclusive education, some of the key players are ignored. Inclusion should lead to the overall growth and satisfaction of the whole school community. The needs of typical children in the school should also be successfully met. There has to be a mechanism to monitor all these aspects through the use of hard data (e.g. staff and parent surveys) and soft data (e.g. informal feedback). It is important that any monitoring aimed at evaluating inclusive practices is guided by the school's overall vision of inclusion.

Supporting staff in their efforts to implement inclusive practices

According to Gameros (1995), providing administrative support to teachers who are involved in working with students with disabilities is an important trait of an effective inclusive school principal. The availability of this support can accordingly directly influence teachers' attitudes and opinions about integrating children with disabilities.

Skills required of school leaders to be inclusive

This section provides answers to the second question that we outlined in our framework: What key skills do school principals require to perform the multitude of functions identified above? It is important to highlight here that the list of skills that is outlined in Figure 12.2 should be considered compensatory to the existing literature on school leadership (e.g. Hallinger and Heck, 1998).

Conflict resolution skills

The implementation of reforms such as inclusive education is often accompanied by a number of conflicts. The conflicts may arise from issues within the school (e.g. teacher resistance to team teaching) or because of issues that arise from outside the school (e.g. parents of typical children resisting inclusion or demands imposed by education departments). It is critical that school leaders are equipped with conflict resolution skills. Kugelmass and Ainscow (2004) examined the leadership attributes of three exemplary school leaders in England, Portugal and the USA. They found that all three leaders of these schools reported that conflicts within their schools were inevitable. These school leaders believed that working with one another, children and parents may sometimes cause conflicts

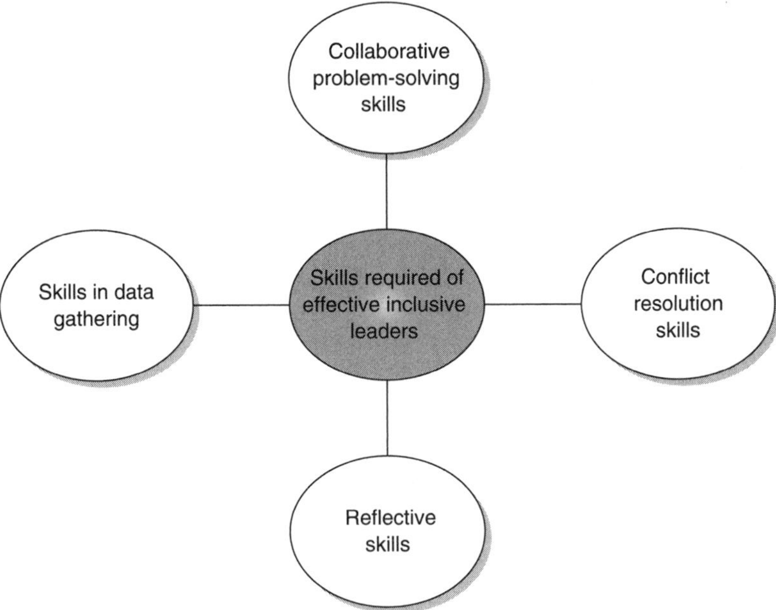

Figure 12.2 Skills required of inclusive leaders.

amongst staff members. It was their role to ensure that such conflicts were resolved as soon as possible.

Effective conflict resolution requires listening to the other person and looking at the problem from the other person's perspective. Conflict resolution may result in positive or negative responses depending on how effectively the skills of conflict resolution are used. If principals do not feel confident in resolving conflicts, then this should be an area that they need to prioritize for their professional development. It will also be useful for all staff to have training in these skills. Having a school policy to deal with difficult issues and resolving interpersonal differences can be a useful strategy.

Collaborative problem-solving skills

Collaborative problem-solving is an activity that is central to the success of inclusive schooling (Kugelmass and Ainscow, 2004). It is essential that principals organize their schools in such ways that encourage interaction and participation among staff and children. This allows staff to share expertize in areas that they are not fully prepared to deal with. Graden and Bauer (1992) emphasize that to be most effective in problem-solving, components of both collaboration and problem-solving, must be used simultaneously. Problem-solving involves six steps.

Step 1 Define the problem in observable, measurable and objective terms so that all team members have a mutual understanding of the problem.
Step 2 Analyze the problem to understand causes.
Step 3 Formulate alternative strategies based on the analysis of the problem.
Step 4 Select strategies based on the availability of resources and ease with which teachers can implement them.
Step 5 Implement strategies with support from specialist staff.
Step 6 Evaluate the success of alternative strategies to solve the problem and decide whether to continue, redesign or discontinue the program.

(Gutkin and Curtis, 1990)

Reflective skills

In recent years there has been an increased emphasis for school principals to become reflective leaders. Salisbury and McGregor (2002) identified reflectivity and an enquiring mind as the key attributes of leaders who are able to create a climate of acceptance in schools. They contend that reflective practices hold great promise as strategies for promoting the inclusion of students with disabilities in regular school programs.

Reflective leadership is based on the premise that "people make mistakes and these mistakes should be acknowledged and discussed in a constructive manner" (Ryan, 2006, p.11). These mistakes should be seen as learning opportunities to make progress and to move the school forward. Reflective leaders engage themselves with the school community (parents and teachers), which allows them to look critically at their practices and to be open to new ideas.

Skills in data gathering

In a data-driven culture of education, school leaders are expected to have a basic understanding of collecting and interpreting data. In her study of six effective inclusive school leaders in the State of Colorado, USA, Guzmán (1997) found that these leaders demonstrated skills in data gathering, listening, observation and interpreting data. She further added that these leaders frequently reviewed their school action plans and evaluation reports, suggesting that they were skilled in synthesizing and interpreting data from a wide variety of sources. One other skill that has significant relevance for inclusive leaders is the knowledge of conducting action research. Action research is a process in which researchers (e.g. school leaders) examine their own education practice systematically and carefully, using tools such as asking questions, gathering data, reflection and deciding on a course of action. It is based on the following assumptions:

1 Teachers and principals work best on problems they have identified for themselves.
2 Teachers and principals become more effective when encouraged to examine and assess their own work and then consider ways of working differently.

3 Teachers and principals help each other by working collaboratively.
4 Working with colleagues helps teachers and principals in their professional development.

(Watts, 1985, p. 118)

Principals' academic backgrounds and formal training relative to inclusive education

International perspective

Many countries seem committed to inclusive education in their rhetoric and have acknowledged, in their policy documents, the central role of the school principal in designing, leading, managing, and implementing programs for all students, including those with disabilities. However, there is currently very little research that indicates whether principals have the necessary knowledge, skills and attitudes to implement such programs in their schools. What little research exists, and much of what does appears to have been conducted largely in the USA, indicates that most principals have little or no academic background in special/inclusive education or in teaching children with disabilities.

In one of the earliest studies that examined this issue, Bullock (1970) found that 65 per cent of the 92 elementary school principals that he surveyed in a large Midwestern city school district in the USA had received no coursework in special education. Of those who had elected to take some courses in special education, only 23 per cent had taken one course, 8 per cent had taken two courses, and 4 per cent had taken three or more courses. In cumulative terms, this finding meant that the 92 elementary school principals had earned a total of 114 semester hours of special education credit. The mean number of college hours for the entire group was 1.24 hours.

One would expect that the situation would have improved in the years following the passage of *The Education of All Handicapped Children Act* in 1975 in the USA, which required all public schools to include students with disabilities into mainstream settings. However, studies published since the passage of this legislation appear to indicate that there has been little progress in this regard.

Recently published investigations bearing on this issue continue to paint an unprepossessing picture, as the study by Lasky and Karge (2006) clearly illustrates. The purpose of their study was to examine the formal training and experience of principals working in a variety of school districts in Southern California. More specifically, they were interested in finding out how much direct experience principals had with children with a disability during their formal administration credential course work, and how important these principals felt formal training in special education and mainstreaming was in courses for school administrators.

Two hundred and five principals from 28 different districts participated in the study. The majority of the respondents were elementary school principals. The remaining worked at a high school, junior high school or middle school level. Approximately 80 per cent of the principals held a master's degree, 2 per cent had a bachelor's degree and 17 per cent had a doctorate degree. Of the total number of these principals, less than 10 per cent were certified in special education.

The researchers found that the respondents had limited ability and knowledge related to children with special needs, regardless of how long they had worked in the position of school principal. This issue of inadequate preparation of school principals was also raised by a number of other researchers during the intervening years (e.g. Armstrong, 2006).

Almost 40 years ago, Bullock (1970) had suggested in his study of elementary school principals that, unless principals elected to take a course in exceptional child education, they would have little formal background to guide their decision making relating to children with special needs. At that time, none of the 50 states in the United States, nor the District of Columbia or Puerto Rico, that he had surveyed, required courses in special education for certification as a school principal. Findings from recent research indicate that not much has improved in this regard. According to Patterson *et al.* (2000), there are only five states within the United States that require any special education instruction for administrator certification.

Asia-Pacific perspective

During the past two decades or so, almost every system in the Asia-Pacific region has shown a growing commitment to inclusive education. Given the differences in the histories, cultures, resources, political and economic systems, and the demographics of these countries, it is not surprising to find, note Mitchell and Desai (2005):

> that the pattern of provisions for students with special education needs is extremely diverse, ranging from negligible to comprehensive, from highly segregative to various mixes of segregated and inclusive programs, from coordinated to uncoordinated services, from untrained to well trained personnel and from poorly resourced to well resourced provisions.
>
> (Mitchell and Desai, 2005, pp.166–7)

In line with the situation that exists in North America, England and Western Europe, there has also been a paucity of research in the Asia-Pacific region on the skill levels and knowledge base of principals relative to inclusion. For example, Center *et al.* (1985), who examined the attitudes of principals in New South Wales, Australia, towards mainstreaming, concluded that the number of special education courses taken and the extent of in-service program experience related to exceptional children were significant predictors of a positive attitude. Another Australian study that examined the attitudes of principals working in a variety of schools, covering pre-primary, primary and secondary, in the state of Queensland, was conducted by Bailey and du Plessis in 1998. They found that principals who had previous special education teaching experience had more positive attitudes towards inclusion.

Following a major *Ministerial Review of Educational Services for the Disabled in Victoria*, Australia, in 1984, which recommended far-reaching changes, including the "right of every child to be educated in a regular school", Desai (1995) surveyed a sample of 353 primary school principals to identify their attitudes towards the integration of students with a disability into their local school settings. The subjects for this study were drawn from two large metropolitan and one large country region in the state of Victoria. Each of the three regions covered both rural and urban environments with facilities ranging from one teacher primary schools to post-primary schools that were amongst the largest in the state. Pertinent to the issues discussed in this chapter were some of the following findings that emerged from this study. Of the 353 principals surveyed, 87.5 per cent held no qualifications in special education; 82 per cent had not participated in any in-service training programs related to special education or integration; and 82.1 per cent reported that they had either none or only some exposure to the education of students with disabilities in their formal study programs. Yet what was interesting was that those principals who either had formal training in special education or had completed some form of in-service training in special education or integration were significantly more positive in their attitudes towards the inclusion of students with a disability than principals who had no such training.

Of the few remaining studies recently conducted in this region that have included data on principals' education backgrounds and experiences in special/inclusive education was an investigation conducted in India by Sharma (2001). Among a range of measures proposed in the *Persons with Disabilities Act* (1996) for implementation in India was the increased emphasis to be given to integrated education as the preferred way to educate students with disabilities. This required all school principals to take on new roles and responsibilities. However, Sharma's study, which examined the attitudes, concerns and knowledge about inclusive education of 302 school principals, found that less than 10 per cent of such leaders had any training in special education. It was also found that a large majority of principals had less than positive attitudes towards inclusion and a very high level of concern about implementing inclusive practices in their schools. It is, therefore, not surprising that implementing inclusive education in government schools in the state of Delhi may not become a reality, as the principals are neither well prepared nor have the necessary attitudes to support the implementation of inclusive practices.

In a recent study, Sharma and Chow (in press) investigated the attitudes to integration of 130 Hong Kong primary school principals, finding that they were slightly negative. They concluded that the negative attitudes of school principals to some extent reflect the views of society in Hong Kong. Students with disabilities are not seen to belong to regular schools. This also reflects the invisible pressure on school principals in Hong Kong to ensure that their schools continue to perform better academically, even if it means that students with poor academic performance are refused entry into their schools. Perhaps there is a need in Hong Kong to review education policies where schools are encouraged to enrol students with disabilities. This will, however, require fundamental shift in attitudes not at just the school level but also at the district and society levels.

Conclusion

Given the current education backgrounds and experiences of school principals and their increasing roles and responsibilities in this era of school reform we can not resist asking some of the following fundamental questions that were raised by Davis (1980) almost three decades ago. First, should principals be expected to assume such a critical role in the mainstreaming process, as is widely suggested in the literature, when, in fact, they have had such minimal prior training in special education and/or exposure to children with disabilities? Second, is much of the negativism frequently attributed to principals regarding special education programs related to their feeling of inadequacy in this area as a result of lack of exposure to the field? Third, should all training programs for prospective school principals require work in the field of special education?

Clearly, if inclusion is to become a viable alternative to the present entrenched dual system of education we have in many countries in the Asia-Pacific region, as indeed, in several other parts of the world, serious attention will need to be given to the training of principals, so that they will be able to implement effective programs for all students in their schools and become catalysts for change.

There are several approaches that can be taken in the training of principals in order to redress the present situation. To begin with a concerted effort needs to be made to review current training programs and modify them, so that individuals preparing to be school principals can be ensured of receiving appropriate training and experience in special education and inclusion. Second, training in those aspects of special/inclusive education that would be helpful to principals in meeting the needs of students with disabilities in regular school settings should be infused into and made an integral part of a principal's regular training program and course offerings in school administration. To meet the more immediate and critical training needs of principals in the area of special/inclusive education, particularly in the Asia-Pacific regions, a viable short-term measure would be to provide a series of short intensive workshop experiences. Furthermore, it is important that principals are provided with opportunities to observe model programs in well-established inclusive schools as well as having opportunities to participate in meaningful interactions with students with disabilities and their parents. Apart from sensitizing principals to the needs of students with disabilities and their families, we also believe that such forms of training, especially if undertaken in inclusive settings, would make it possible to identify training needs as perceived by the principals themselves and thus make the training more contextually relevant.

References

Armstrong, J. (2006) "How principals lead to promote inclusive practices: A descriptive study", unpublished doctoral dissertation, School of Education, Duquesne University, Pennsylvania.

Bailey, J. and du Plessis, D. (1998) "An investigation of school principals' attitudes toward inclusion", *Australasian Journal of Special Education*, 22(1): 12–29.

Beare, H., Caldwell, B. and Millikan, R. (1997) "Dimensions of leadership", in M. Crawford, M. Kydd and C. Riches (eds), *Leadership and Teams in Educational Management*, Buckingham: Open University Press.

Blair, M. (2002) "Effective school leadership: The multi-ethnic context", *British Journal of Sociology of Education*, 23(2): 179–91.

Blase, J. and Anderson, G. (1995) *The Micropolitics of Educational Leadership*, London: Cassell.

Bullock, L. M. (1970) "An inquiry into the special education training of elementary school administrators", *Exceptional Children*, 36: 770–1.

Burrello, L. C. and Wright, P. T. (1992) *The Principal Letters: Practices for Inclusive Schools*, Bloomington, IN: The National Academy/CASE.

Center, Y., Ward, J., Parmenter, T. and Nash, R. (1985) "Principals' attitudes toward integration of disabled children into regular schools", *The Exceptional Child*, 32(3): 149–61.

Davis, W. E. (1980) "An analysis of principals' formal training in special education", *Education*, 101(1): 89–94.

Desai, I. (1995) "Primary school principals' attitudes toward mainstreaming in Victoria, Australia", *International Journal of Special Education*, 10(2): 22–36.

DiPaola, M. and Tschannen-Moran, M. (2003) "The principalship at a crossroads: A study of the conditions and concerns of principals", *National Association of Secondary School Principals*, 87(634): 43–65.

Gameros, P. (1995) "The visionary principal and inclusion of students with disabilities", *NASSP Bulletin*, 79: 15–7.

Graden, J. L. and Bauer, A. M. (1992) "Using a collaborative approach to support students and teachers in inclusive classrooms", in S. Stainback and W. Stainback (eds), *Curriculum Considerations in Inclusive Classroom*, Baltimore, MD: Paul H. Brookes.

Gronn, P. (2002) "Distributed leadership", in K. Leithwood and P. Hallinger (eds), *Second International Handbook of Educational Leadership and Administration*, Dordrecht, The Netherlands: Kluwer.

Gutkin, T. B. and Curtis, M. J. (1990) "School-based consultation: Theory and techniques", in T. B. Gutkin and C. R. Reynolds (eds), *The Handbook of School Psychology*, 2nd edn, New York: John Wiley and Sons.

Guzmán, N. (1997) "Leadership for successful inclusive schools: A study of principal behaviours", *Journal of Educational Administration*, 35(5): 439–50.

Hallinger, P. and Heck, R. H. (1998) "Exploring the principal's contribution to school effectiveness: 1980–1995", *School Effectiveness and School Improvement*, 9(2): 157–91.

Jahan, R. (2000) "Transformative leadership in the 21st century", paper presented at the Asia-Pacific Women Parliamentarians' Conference on Transformative Leadership for Good Governance in the 21st Century, Bangkok, March.

Janney, R. E. and Snell, M. E. (2000) *Teachers' Guides to Inclusive Practices: Behavioral Support*, Baltimore, MD: Paul H. Brookes.

Kugelmass, J. and Ainscow, M. (2004) "Leadership for inclusion: A comparison of international practices", *Journal of Research in Special Educational Needs*, 4(3): 133–41.

Lasky, B. and Karge, B. D. (2006) "Meeting the needs of students with disabilities: Experience and confidence of principals", *NASSP Bulletin*, 90(1): 19–35.

Mitchell, D. and Desai, I. P. (2005) "Diverse socio-cultural contexts for inclusive education in Asia", in D. Mitchell (ed.), *Contextualising Inclusive Education: Evaluating Old and New International Paradigms*, London: Routledge.

Patterson, J., Marshall, C. and Bowling, D. (2000) "Are principals prepared to manage special education dilemmas?", *NASSP Bulletin*, 84: 9–20.

Regan, H. B. and Brooks, G. H. (1995) *Out of Women's Experience: Creating Relational Leadership*, Thousand Oaks, CA: Corwin Press.

Ryan, J. (2006) "Inclusive leadership and social justice for schools", *Leadership and Policy in Schools*, 5(1): 3–17.

Salisbury, C. and McGregor, G. (2002) "The administrative climate and context of inclusive elementary schools", *Exceptional Children*, 68(2): 259–74.

Salisbury, C. and McGregor, G. (2005) *Principals of Inclusive Schools*, Denver, CO: National Institute of Urban School Improvement.

Sergiovanni, T. J. (1992) *Moral Leadership: Getting to the Heart of School Improvement*, San Francisco, CA: Jossey-Bass.

Sharma, U. (2001) "The attitudes and concerns of school principals and teachers regarding the integration of students with disabilities into regular schools in india", unpublished doctoral dissertation, University of Melbourne: Melbourne, Australia.

Sharma, U. and Chow, E. W. S. (in press) "Hong Kong primary school principals' attitudes toward integrated education", *Asia Pacific Education Review*.

Sharma, U. and Desai, I. (2002) "Measuring concerns about integrated education in India", *Asia and Pacific Journal on Disability*, 5(1): 2–14.

Sharma, U., Ee, J. and Desai, I. (2003) "A comparison of Australian and Singaporean preservice teachers' attitudes and concerns about inclusive education", *Teaching and Learning*, 24(2): 207–17.

Stainback, W. and Stainback, S. (1990) *Support Networks for Inclusive Schooling*, Baltimore, MD: Paul H. Brookes.

Watts, H. (1985) "When teachers are researchers, teaching improves", *Journal of Staff Development*, 6(2): 118–27.

13 General classroom strategies to enhance the inclusion of students with learning difficulties

Bruce Allen Knight, Anne Bellert and Lorraine Graham

Chapter objectives

- To outline research findings related to the main obstacles to successful learning that students with learning difficulties encounter.
- To discuss successful research-based strategies that meet the learning needs of students with learning difficulties.

Focus questions

1 What characteristics might students with learning difficulties display?
2 How can teachers work with students to enhance their learning skills?
3 What are the main principles of instruction that can be developed from research-based classroom strategies and applied to meeting the needs of students with learning difficulties?

Introduction

The philosophy of inclusion is difficult to translate into practice. Forlin (1998) and Knight (2000, 2007) have reported that inclusion makes considerable demands on teachers. For special needs education to work effectively, it is essential that teachers accept responsibility for managing students' special needs and their learning. This chapter builds on the work of Bellert and Graham (2006) in exploring how teachers can meet the needs of students with learning disabilities in their classrooms. In this chapter we emphasize the role of the teacher as the manager of students' learning based on "the recurrent educational research findings that in school differences outweigh any other factor in the performance of either individual students or indeed institutions and that teacher intervention in student learning is correlated with student success" (Smith *et al.*, 2007, p. 2). Specifically, this chapter will consider the characteristics of students with learning difficulties, approaches to overcoming obstacles to these students' successful learning and discuss research-based strategies that support students in inclusive classrooms.

Learning difficulties

Learning difficulties as a term lacks a clear definition (Chan and Dally, 2001; Scott, 2004). Definitions of learning disabilities and learning difficulties vary from country to country and controversies over identification procedures persist (e.g. Scott, 2004). In Australia, there is no national operational definition of learning difficulty and there is considerable overlap in the use of the terms learning difficulty and learning disability (Scott, 2004). The percentage of students identified with learning disabilities or difficulties continues to increase. Currently, about 7 per cent of the school-age population in North America is considered to have some form of learning disability (Gersten *et al.*, 2001). In Australia, where the definition of learning difficulties is broader and includes students with various learning difficulties, at least 20 per cent of school students are considered to have problems in academic areas (Westwood and Graham, 2000). Of these students 5 per cent are considered to have specific learning difficulties (Westwood and Graham, 2000).

For the purpose of this chapter, students with learning difficulties (LD) are considered to be those who do not have a diagnosed disability but who underachieve, both in comparison to their same-age peers and to their individual learning potential. Many students with LD are unique in their learning needs because they may have developed secondary learner characteristics due to persistent and often unaddressed primary LD. These skill deficits develop over time (Lenz and Deschler, 2004) and can affect students' social and emotional adjustment. Our chapter, then, has two aims. The first part provides more current and relevant information about the nature of LD and how deficiencies in academic and social skills, as well as cognitive processing, impact on students and affect their learning. The second part describes instructional strategies that are effective in meeting the needs of students with LD in the context of contemporary classroom teaching and learning.

Obstacles to classroom success for students with learning difficulties

Many classroom teachers would agree that students with LD are particularly hard to teach. The persistent nature of these students' LD makes it difficult for them to keep pace in terms of achievement with their peers. The gap in academic achievement between students with LD and their peers becomes wider during the crucial middle years of schooling when, for many students, meaningful engagement with curriculum content decreases. Further, inherent social, emotional and cognitive factors associated with LD increasingly take their toll on students. At times, classroom teachers can be bewildered by the wide range of learning needs in their classrooms and concerned about their levels of professional knowledge to assist them in catering for students with special learning needs (Westwood and Graham, 2003).

According to many recent research findings, the main obstacles to the successful learning of students with LD are due to (1) a lack of automaticity in basic academic skills, (2) reading difficulties, (3) mathematics difficulties, (4) affective difficulties, (5) general cognitive factors, (6) working memory, and (7) the non-awareness of intelligent learning behaviors.

Automaticity in basic academic skills

Though students with LD can develop understandings about basic academic concepts and procedures, many such students are unable to apply this information easily because of their poor literacy and numeracy skills. This lack of automaticity in basic skills such as reading and calculating can be readily observed in the effortful behavior of these students.

Automaticity in basic academic skills was initially thought to require almost no cognitive resources but more recently researchers have linked automaticity to extremely efficient cognitive processing. From this perspective the most important feature of automaticity is not that it enables fast recall, but rather that it reflects increasingly fluent, efficient and effective cognitive processing.

Expert learners utilize highly automatized component sub-skills of tasks, while their novice learner peers, such as students with LD, need to work effortfully on component skills, even those they have encountered many times before (Stanovich, 1990). Therefore, a lack of automaticity with basic academic skills frequently precludes students with learning problems from being able to focus on higher order skills or tackle the advanced procedural requirements of academic tasks. Automaticity is enhanced by providing an appropriate number of practice opportunities and by encouraging an orientation towards active learning. Effective learners adopt active learning approaches and tend to interact with task materials using self-monitoring and self-evaluation skills.

Reading difficulties

Difficulties in reading are the most common learning problem experienced by students with LD (Westwood and Graham, 2000). This lack of proficiency underlies their difficulties in all other domains of literacy, numeracy and academic learning. Poor readers commonly experience problems with the component reading skills of phonological awareness, orthography and reading fluency, all of which have an impact on their comprehension of text (Wolf *et al.*, 2000).

Many middle school students with learning problems can comprehend spoken language at, or close to, their age-appropriate levels, yet their poor reading skills deny them similar access to written texts and this has an impact on their performance across key learning areas. Thus, these students need to use their cognitive resources, specifically their time and attention, to decode words and process text. This often occurs at the cost of inherently attention-demanding higher order thinking and learning, such as comprehension and problem-solving (Walczyk, 2000). Reading comprehension is amenable to improvement through strategy instruction and training (Gersten *et al.*, 2001), but for students with LD the biggest barrier to reading for meaning is their poor automaticity of basic academic skills and the allocation of most of their cognitive resources to lower level thinking tasks.

Alongside these underlying difficulties, an increasing lack of experience or engagement with texts explains, in part, why poor readers lag further and further behind their peers as they progress through school. As Galletly and Knight (2004, p. 4) observe, poor reading accuracy becomes a major obstacle to successful learning in the middle school years, with potentially life-long consequences, "if reading accuracy is not mastered effectively by mid primary school, it becomes one of the most powerful blocks to academic and life progress that a person can experience."

Mathematics difficulties

Students with LD in reading, often also experience difficulties in numeric calculations. These students experience failure in mathematics for a variety of reasons, including poorly developed number sense, poor processing abilities, language and literacy difficulties, maths anxiety and inefficient memory processes. Students in the middle school years with difficulties in mathematics are considerably behind their normally achieving peers. In particular, they exhibit difficulties in several areas, such as basic computation skills, word problems, understanding the language of mathematics and mathematical reasoning (Milton, 2000).

Geary (2004) suggests that disruptions in the ability to retrieve basic facts from long-term memory might, in fact, be considered a salient feature of mathematical learning disabilities. Just as effortful decoding of words uses up cognitive resources and renders them unavailable for comprehension of text, effortful calculation of basic arithmetic facts precludes some students from focusing on procedures and problem-solving. As a result, content area learning in mathematics can be much less accessible for students with LD.

Affective factors

Meeting the challenges of long-term LD can be a trial for students and their parents. Research indicates what many teachers, parents and students already know; that such experiences can have a serious and negative impact on students' emotional health and can detrimentally affect their social interactions. In general, students with LD also have an increased likelihood of displaying inappropriate social skills (Elbaum and Vaughn, 2003) and tend to be less popular with their peers than non-LD students. In fact, for many students with LD poor social competence is a confounding factor in their lives that impacts on their school experience and constitutes yet another obstacle to their school success.

Perhaps one of the strongest ways of understanding students' self-systems is through research exploring their notions of self-concept, locus of control, self-esteem and self-efficacy. For example, research indicates that children and adolescents with LD can have lower academic self-concepts and a more external locus of control orientation than their normally achieving peers, but equally good self-concepts in non-academic areas (Knight *et al.*, 1998). Academic self-concept appears to act as an important variable that mediates academic achievement

(Elbaum and Vaughn, 2003). Likewise, the development of a realistic internal locus of control orientation reinforces active learning and indicates to students that they are responsible for the outcomes of their behavior. Such an orientation reinforces the importance of self-directed learning.

The feeling of powerlessness that leads students with learning problems to believe that they are unable to succeed has been termed "learned helplessness" (Diener and Dweck, 1978). Learned helplessness behavior has a debilitating effect on academic performance. Specifically, if students perceive that they cannot achieve success because of factors beyond their control, then their levels of participation, engagement and performance on any task decreases (Bellert and Graham, 2006; Knight, 2007).

Learned helplessness and low self-efficacy can result in learner characteristics, which can be displayed by many students with LD, such as: reduced motivation including a lack of persistence in the face of failure; negative expectations about the future; a tendency not to develop a strategic approach to learning; avoidance strategies; and a generally negative affect (Westwood, 2004).

General cognitive factors

In addition to deficits in basic academic skills and the impact of the affective factors already described, many students with LD also have particular cognitive characteristics that influence their learning experiences. Generally, for example, these students are very inefficient in their approaches to learning (Westwood, 1993). Thus, students with LD in the classroom often use lower order strategies, such as counting on fingers to work out number facts or using sounds to decode previously encountered words because of their inefficient cognitive habits or ways of thinking that may be amenable to change.

Working memory

In terms of cognitive processing, students with LD seem to lack the flexibility required to coordinate several memory stores and are likely to have reduced or inefficient working-memory function (Swanson and Siegel, 2001). The processes and functions of working memory have been identified as key underlying factors in all LD (Keeler and Swanson, 2001). Students with LD not only experience inefficiencies within and between the components of working memory, but also their working-memory capacity (i.e. the amount of information they can hold in mind) is thought to be less than that of their non-LD peers (Swanson and Siegel, 2001). Limitations in working-memory functions or processes pose significant obstacles to successful learning for students with LD.

Working memory can be enhanced by introducing strategies to students and teaching them to use them efficiently. This is achieved by first teaching learning strategies (declarative knowledge or "knowing that"), the procedural knowledge ("knowing how") involved in using the strategy and also the conditional knowledge ("knowing when") required about when and how to best use the strategy.

Table 13.1 The SPEW strategy

	Strategy	*Questions to be asked*
S	Setting	Who's involved? What are you doing? Where does it take place? When does it take place?
P	Problem	What's the situation to be solved?
E	Effects of the problem	How did it make you feel?
W	What?	What would you like to have happen now or next time? What are some possible solutions?

Source: Knight, B. A. *et al.*, 1998, p. 40.

Strategy use

Let's take the following example (see Table 13.1) of the strategy "SPEW" (Knight *et al.*, 1998, p. 40), a social problem-solving strategy that, as its name suggests, is very popular with primary and secondary students. The purpose of this strategy is to provide a framework to give direction for students to systematically analyze a social problem (e.g. threatening behavior on the school oval or in the classroom) and identify possible solutions.

For students to effectively use this strategy so as to enhance social relationships with their peers, they must first understand what each letter of the mnemonic means. From our experience, students have no problem remembering the catchy term but they must also know that S = setting, etc., and what is involved in the setting. Next, the procedural knowledge must be used and followed in the correct order. Students who follow this strategy become actively involved by thinking about the situation by brainstorming solutions to the problem. They are not being told that their behavior is unacceptable and against the school rules (they already know this) but rather they become actively involved in ensuring a number of solutions to the problem at hand. SPEW is a general strategy and could be applied to other situations; for example inappropriate borrowing of a pen, ruler or textbook without a peer's approval in the classroom.

Intelligent behaviors

Although debate rages as to whether intelligence can be modified, Campbell (2006, p. 2) maintains that intelligent behaviors can be taught and "have the potential to build students' capacity to learn, which is essential if learners are to stay abreast of the rapidly changing aspects of work, technology and society."

Such behaviors, forming part of Costa's (1985) "Habits of Mind" include:

A Persevering when there is no immediate solution to a problem. Too often students who experience LD give up when a solution is not readily apparent. These students need explicit teaching and practice in the use of strategies so that they persevere when problem-solving. An example of a strategy

Table 13.2 The ROSES strategy

	Strategy	*Activity*
R	Read	Read the problem to yourself.
O	Organize	Organize the information contained in the paragraph. What is important? What do I deal with first?
S	Select	Select the appropriate operation. Add? Subtract? Divide? Multiply?
E	Estimate	Estimate the answer you might get.
S	Solve	Solve the problem.

Source: Knight, B. A. *et al.*, 1998, p. 36.

specifically designed for such problem-solving situations is the ROSES (Knight *et al.*, 1998, p. 36) strategy (see Table 13.2).

B Decreasing impulsivity. The use of open-ended problems encourages students to consider different alternatives. Impulsivity is encouraged by teachers when they ask closed questions that require an immediate answer.

C Listening to others with understanding and empathy. Exercising empathy means that students attempt to understand another's point of view. This is a much underestimated skill for all learners, which is underpinned by the need to learn and practice strategies for active listening. For example, the CARING strategy (Knight *et al.*, 1998, p. 24) as outlined in Table 13.3 can be useful in inclusive classrooms.

D Developing flexibility in thinking. Rather than presenting problems requiring one answer, teachers are encouraged to set open-ended problems that allow students to discuss, develop arguments to support their answers, listen to others' viewpoints and evaluate different methods of solving problems. Once again, students need to be taught strategic ways to evaluate information and arguments. For example, a Strengths and Weaknesses (SW) strategy encourages students to consider the strengths and weaknesses of problems using an evaluative framework.

E Metacognition involves students in developing an awareness of their own thinking and thus leads to them becoming more in control of their learning processes. When metacognitively aware, students plan, monitor and evaluate their completion of tasks. For example, teachers often give homework in the form of a project to be completed over a period of extended time. To be successful in this task, students with LD need to be explicitly taught planning skills (e.g. drawing up timelines, considering the accessibility of resources), implementation (e.g. skills of how to find the information and execute the required task) and evaluation criteria to enable them to judge the work they put into the project (e.g. what they did, how they did it and the result they got).

F Checking for accuracy and precision is a skill that encourages students to reflect upon their work. By using appropriate strategies students can be encouraged to learn to self-monitor and set appropriate standards for their work.

Table 13.3 The CARING strategy

	Strategy	*Activity*
C	Cares about the message	Tune in to the message and think about the feelings of the speaker.
A	Always looks at the speaker	Keep eyes on the person or people speaking.
R	Remains comfortably seated	Don't fidget or move around.
I	Is quiet	Don't make any noise while someone is speaking to you.
N	Notices detail	Pay attention to detail so that questions or replies can be formulated.
G	Greets speaker with an open mind	Try to think only about what is being said.

Source: Knight, B. A. *et al.*, 1998, p. 24.

G Questioning and problem-posing. A good understanding of a task is necessary to ensure that appropriate questions about it can be formulated. Students need to be encouraged to not only ask literal questions where the answer is readily apparent, but also to ask critical and creative questions where they need to read between the lines and to think creatively by seeking multiple responses to different questions.

H Drawing on past knowledge and applying it to new situations. These skills are critically important to ensure students move their thinking towards actively solving a problem by connecting it with prior knowledge. For example, the ROSES strategy outlined above could be used or modified by students to solve problems in content areas such as Science or Liberal Studies.

I Inquisitiveness, curiosity and the enjoyment of problem-solving. Students not only need to have a realistic locus of control orientation evidenced by an "I can do this attitude", but they also need to be motivated to enjoy the challenge of complex tasks because they have the declarative knowledge of a toolkit of strategies.

The focus of these intelligent behaviors is to enable students to be actively involved in their own learning. However, it is important that students with LD are not always being told to go away and *try harder* or *do it again* or *concentrate more*. Instead these students should be given the tools (the explicit teaching and practice of using strategies) so that they have a framework for approaching classroom tasks.

In summary, students with LD display particular learner characteristics and face many obstacles to achieving age-appropriate learning outcomes. These difficulties are often artifacts of social and emotional difficulties, basic skills deficits and constraints, and inefficiencies in cognitive processing. Having an understanding of these characteristics of students with LD can guide classroom teachers in developing instructional approaches that are effective for students with LD.

Research-based strategies for meeting the learning needs of students with LD

Classroom teachers can do a great deal towards ensuring that students with LD participate meaningfully in quality teaching and learning experiences. The effective teaching of students with LD generally does not require new or specific instructional strategies but rather relies on what many practitioners would call just good teaching or what Westwood (1993, p. 92) calls "the tried and true basics of skilled teaching". Considered in this way, instructional strategies that enhance learning outcomes for students with LD result in improved outcomes for all students (Vaughn *et al.*, 2000b).

Effective teaching necessitates a focus on teacher actions and decision making, in order to maximize student learning. Thus, effective teaching is concerned with the things teachers do to increase student participation and learning. Frequently, effective teaching for students with LD requires direct or explicit instruction of basic academic skills (Westwood, 2001). Explicit instruction is especially necessary when teaching new or difficult information and when the content is critical to subsequent learning.

Strategies to support the development of literacy, numeracy and content knowledge

Effective, explicit teaching involves showing, telling, using think-aloud protocols and self-talk, as well as modeling and demonstrating by both teacher and peers, so that a systematic and structured approach to instruction leads students towards mastery and success. Effective teaching also requires that the purposes of lessons and their intended outcomes are made clear to students, and that regular opportunities to practice and revise previous work are presented.

Strategies to support the development of literacy and numeric skills and content knowledge for students with LD include:

- Providing pre-teaching and practice in saying, reading and writing key vocabulary relevant to topics.
- Adjusting the level of task difficulty so students can succeed at the tasks.
- Providing abundant amounts of practice with formative feedback.
- Using graphic organizers to provide an overview of the content to be covered and the links between known and new information.

QuickSmart is an example of an intense, focused program designed to improve the basic reading and numeric skills of low achieving middle school students. The studies conducted to date (e.g. Graham *et al.*, 2007) have investigated the effects of improved automaticity of basic skills on higher order processes such as comprehension and problem-solving. The *QuickSmart* intervention delivers small group instruction three times per week for up to three school terms to students with difficulties in reading or numeracy.

The *QuickSmart* programs in both reading and numeracy follow a structured lesson sequence based around a "focus set" of number facts or words. Most lessons conclude with an assessment on the *Cognitive Aptitude Assessment System* (Royer *et al.*, 1993) to provide the student and the instructor with information about each student's accuracy and speed of recall of basic academic facts. Students aim to increase their accuracy and decrease response times as a means of demonstrating increasing automaticity. The *QuickSmart* program extends for up to three consecutive school terms, or 30 weeks. All students participating in the intervention attend three half-hour *QuickSmart* lessons each week, in pairs, with the same instructor. Where possible, the pairings of students match individuals with similar levels of achievement in either reading or numeracy.

The main ideas of the approach are also presented to the students embedded in a mnemonic associated to the pathway metaphor. The key word, PATH stands for Practice, Attention to understanding, Time, and How to. By using the PATH, participants in the *QuickSmart* intervention learn to develop effective strategy use (How to) that flows from clearer understandings (Attention to understanding) as they participate in focused practice activities (Practice) that externalize time as a dimension of instruction (Time). The program also provides students with opportunities to monitor their own learning and to receive and record immediate, formative feedback.

An example of the *QuickSmart* numeracy lesson format is provided below:

1 Understanding check: Focus Number Facts (2–5 minutes)
To begin the lesson, review and discuss the current Focus Number Facts. Examine patterns in the number facts and how they make sense.

2 Automatic recall of Focus Number Facts (5 minutes)
Using a pack of flashcards of current Focus Number Facts challenge each student to see how many facts each student can get correct in 1 minute. Graph results and discuss improvements and errors.

3 Independent Speed Sheet challenge (5 minutes)
In this part of the lesson the students will work as fast and correctly as they can to complete Speed Sheets of the current set of Focus Number Facts in a prescribed time period (usually 2 minutes). Feedback will be given on any errors from the previous *QuickSmart* session.

4 Strategy development: Independent work sheets (5 minutes)
These sheets provide students with the opportunity to apply automatic recall of number facts to relevant work sheets. During this section the instructor will work with students to develop helpful strategies that will assist in recalling basic number facts more quickly.
Note. To devote more time to the strategy development needed to solve word-based mathematical problems, a whole session may need to be devoted each week to the modeling of the strategy use that is required for explicit

understanding of each step that is needed to visualize and conceptualize the process and steps required in problem-solving.

5 Assessment (5 minutes) (one student per *QuickSmart* session)
   (a) Individual students complete a computer-based assessment and graph results.
   (b) Each student discusses results with the instructor and sets goals for next time.

6 Games (5–10 minutes)
   Play some maths games to help students become quick and smart at automatically recalling number facts. Games include Three in a Row, Same Sums, Double O, QuickSmart Bingo or QuickSmart Dominoes. These games provide opportunities for using extension facts, approximations and applications of number facts to life-skill mathematical learning activities.

Instructional methods used in the *QuickSmart* intervention focus on a variety of practice and recall strategies to develop understanding and fluency with basic academic skills.

Each *QuickSmart* lesson involves:

- revision of the previous session;
- a number of guided practice activities featuring overt self-talk;
- discussion and practice of memory and retrieval strategies;
- games and worksheet activities;
- timed independent practice activities.

Some useful procedures for overcoming learning obstacles are features in the *QuickSmart* program. Many of these procedures are also identified in the research literature relating to effective instruction for students with LD (e.g. Gersten *et al.*, 2001; Swanson and Hoskyn, 2001; Vaughn *et al.*, 2000b).

Useful *QuickSmart* procedures include:

- a structured and predictable lesson sequence;
- content based on topics of high interest to the students;
- repeated opportunities for students to succeed and to know they are improving, e.g. recording and graphing of results;
- graduated and faded prompting that is responsive to students' needs;
- externalizing time in a low key but focused and consistent way, e.g. through the use of stopwatch, timers, repeated tasks, etc.;
- individually focused timed recall activities;
- explicit strategy instruction;
- instruction focused on developing metacognitive awareness through asking students to become aware of, and explain, their thinking processes;
- long-term, intensive instruction;
- the use of an explanatory metaphor to focus students' attention on their learning processes and the purpose of the intervention.

Explicit teaching behaviors

It must be emphasized that direct, explicit teaching of declarative knowledge is necessary for all learners. Successful teachers engage students actively with their work so that they operate at the instructional level within their zone of proximal development (Vygotsky, 1978). The instructional level of engagement involves teachers building learning scaffolds by teaching strategies to students that actively involve them in the learning process. Operating in this way will be different for each student and will also be dependent on each individual's profile of abilities, approach to learning, learning context and the necessary declarative knowledge of the concepts being taught.

Research on teacher-directed explicit methods of teaching reports strong evidence regarding its effectiveness for students' learning, especially for those experiencing LD (Westwood, 2006). Explicit teaching has had such an impact that one public education provider in one state of Australia now mandates that "all students are provided with the explicit and scaffolded teaching they need for success in schooling and beyond" (Education Queensland Inclusive Education Statement, 2005, p. 3).

Westwood (2004) discusses the concept of dyspedagogia or bad teaching as an indicator of why students with LD are struggling to achieve in their classrooms. If teachers take an active approach to teaching by working with students within their zone of proximal development, then the following teacher behaviors are related to the likelihood of student success.

Teacher behaviors related to the likelihood of student success:

1 explicit teaching of basic skills;
2 in-depth coverage of topics to ensure mastery of content;
3 close monitoring of students' responses to learning tasks;
4 appropriate expectations of students' work and behavior;
5 feedback that is appropriate to the task;
6 good demonstrations of the required students' behaviors;
7 appropriate resources.

The following literacy teaching examples demonstrate how the above listed teaching behaviors can be effectively implemented in the classroom. Active and explicit teaching examples include:

- Actively modelling literate behavior by such methods as reading aloud to students every day and using students' own writing examples to model the writing process.
- Teaching students skills such as phonics and sight word vocabulary that are essential in the development of automatcity in reading.
- Presenting many forms of literature that is read to and by students.
- Creating opportunities for students to use language in authentic ways, such as completing application forms online and reading and writing recipes.

- Using a wide variety of reading materials in different forms, such as online text as well as traditional written forms that relate to students' interests and which motivate them to want to read.
- Challenging students by adopting a program framework that allows students choice and opportunities to negotiate decision making through such activities as choosing a class novel to write, selecting dust covers for books, writing and reading different reviews of the same piece of work, creating illustrations to demonstrate different understandings, writing letters, etc., to display on a "graffiti" board.
- Completing running records on students' reading so that students' reading behaviors are accurately monitored.
- Working with students to determine their prior knowledge of a topic, such as what is known of the features of non-fiction genre, so informed teaching decisions are made.
- Teaching through multiple demonstrations the features, for example, of non-fiction text and allowing students to practice writing text that fits within this genre. An emphasis is given to the text features and not specific content until the student is familiar with the features of the particular genre.
- Allowing students opportunities to practice their literary skills and give relevant ongoing feedback. For example, if students have written a text poorly, rather than correct every mistake that relates to surface features of the text, teachers can indicate that feedback will first be given specifically on the correct use of punctuation, and possibly even more specifically, on the use of commas in enhancing the flow and meaning of the text.
- Encouraging students to develop literacy skills by building up their repertoire of pleasurable experiences with books, and allowing time for free choice reading and writing.
- Building students' self-esteem by attributing successful results to effortful and strategic engagement with learning tasks. For example, by learning an editing strategy the student can have actively "edited" a piece of writing.
- Being in control of the classroom learning environment by developing and selecting resources related to students' literacy needs rather than using a pre-set structured and inflexible program to organize the teaching and sequencing of tasks.

Social strategies to support students with learning difficulties

Improving students' academic skills can lead to significant gains in academic self-concept, self-esteem and self-efficacy (Westwood, 2004).

Strategies that can support students with LD overcome affective obstacles include:

- Using groupings and cooperative learning strategies to facilitate good social modeling and foster skill development among peers.
- Valuing effort over achievement.

- Having a structure and routine that underpins lesson presentation and allows students to develop a sense of security regarding expectations about how they can be expected to contribute and participate in their own learning.
- Ensuring the level of task difficulty is appropriate so students can succeed at classroom tasks.

Strategies that support efficient cognitive processing

Swanson and Hoskyn's (2001) meta-analysis of instructional components that best predict positive outcomes for students with LD identified (1) advanced organizers (i.e. statements or strategies that direct students to preview instructional material and provide information about the learning task at the beginning of a lesson) and (2) explicit review and practice, as the two most important instructional components related to high effect sizes for instructional interventions. These effect sizes highlight the practical significance of using advanced organizers and practice as components of good instruction that will produce outcomes for students with learning disabilities.

Both of these instructional components enable students to compensate for any obstacles to efficient cognitive processing that they may have. Specifically, review and practice encourages the development of a reliable knowledge base that can be efficiently accessed, and the use of advanced organizers provides students with a mental scaffold of the targeted learning content.

Strategies to help students with LD ameliorate their cognitive inefficiencies include:

- Making connections between the content to be taught and students' prior knowledge and experiences.
- Chunking content and tasks into achievable, carefully sequenced steps.
- Teaching task-specific cognitive strategies, i.e. "how to" step by step procedures.
- Developing and using mnemonics (e.g. presenting the 3H strategy "Here, Hidden and in my Head" as a prompt for answering questions after reading a passage, see below) and other memory aids.

The 3H strategy is an example of a cognitive strategy with mnemonic and met cognitive features. While many strategies direct students to re-read or look back in the text if they cannot respond confidently to questions after a passage, simply re-reading or returning to the text in a random way does not help students with LD improve their comprehension. Instead, these students have to learn to re-read strategically. Graham and Wong's (1993) teaching of the 3H strategy compared self-instructional training with more traditional teaching of a question–answer relationship strategy. Their results indicated that instructing students with LD to ask themselves three focus questions as a strategy to guide re-reading was more effective and resulted in better maintenance of learning.

The three self-monitoring questions used in Graham and Wong's study were: (1) How will I answer this question? (select a strategic approach); (2) What kind of question is this? [literal (Here), inferential (Hidden) or creative (In my Head)]; (3) Is my answer correct? (justify or prove the answer). The 3H strategy has been used successfully by students in Canada and Australia (Graham and Wong, 1993; Graham, 2002) as a self-instructional comprehension strategy to guide re-reading and answering questions and would be just as applicable in other Asia-Pacific regions.

Differentiating instruction

Differentiated instruction is variously referred to as curriculum adjustment, curriculum differentiation, adaptation or modification. Curriculum adjustment occurs mainly in terms of content, process and product (Tomlinson and Allen, 2000) but also includes factors related to classroom management, the learning environment, assessment procedures and grading practices (Westwood, 2001).

As mentioned previously, modifying content by adjusting the level of task difficulty, so that students with LD have an opportunity to successfully develop and practice desired skills or strategies, rather than failing at difficult tasks, has great potential in positively influencing student learning outcomes.

Examples of curriculum adjustments for students with LD include:

- re-phrasing directions and instructions;
- providing more time to complete tasks;
- accepting alternative formats for responses;
- increasing the use of visual aids, hands on materials and concrete examples;
- adapting or modifying resource materials.

Sharon Vaughn's Pyramid Planning Model (Vaughn *et al.*, 2000a) has great potential as a cohesive framework to help teachers plan for differentiating instruction. This model illustrates the notion that all students are capable of learning but not all students will learn everything presented in classroom instruction. The pyramid model consists of a base (essential information for all students to learn by being taught explicit strategies), a middle section (important information that not all students will be able to access) and a top section (containing complex information that will only be accessed by a few students). This model is useful in tracking adjustments that are made to students' instructional needs and learning experiences.

Conclusion

In this chapter we have outlined the characteristics of students with LD, discussed potential obstacles to learning and presented effective research-based strategies that can be used with students who experience LD in the regular classroom. The benefits to students, teachers and education systems of catering to the needs of all students are easy to see. However, the challenge of embedding these classroom practices into school culture is going to vary as schools need to consider their local context and teacher experiences, skills and commitment to their teaching role. In the Asia-Pacific region, where enormous diversity ensues, it is important to carefully consider these ideas in order to tease out those that are likely to be accepted and workable in local school communities.

We would suggest that the information we have outlined in this chapter is good teaching practice for all teachers across the entire Asia-Pacific region in order to support the academic development of students with LD. Effective implementation of the strategies and the teaching role discussed here takes time. There will undoubtedly be some practices and strategies that are not as successful as others, as they are dependent on the students' abilities, behaviors and learning contexts, but by developing a repertoire of successful strategies and practices for supporting the academic achievement of students with LD different learning needs may be addressed.

Although students with LD face significant obstacles to learning, including basic skills deficits, social and emotional difficulties and cognitive inefficiencies, with effective, explicit classroom teaching and appropriate adjustments these students can, and do, make progress towards achieving meaningful learning outcomes. Effective teaching does not leave learning to chance for vulnerable students. The understanding of student characteristics and provisions for their learning outlined in this chapter are necessary as a universal means of responding to the education needs of the diverse student populations found in general classrooms across the whole Asia-Pacific region.

References

Bellert, A. and Graham, L. (2006) "Caught in the middle: Reaching and teaching middle years students with learning difficulties", *Australian Journal of Middle Schooling*, 6(1): 3–10.

Campbell, J. (2006) "Theorizing habits of mind as a framework for learning", *Proceedings of the Australian Association for Research in Education Conference*, Adelaide, South Australia.

Chan, L. and Dally, K. (2001) "Learning disabilities: Literacy and numeracy development", *Australian Journal of Learning Disabilities*, 6(1): 12–9.

Costa, A. (1985) "The behaviors of intelligence", in A. Costa (ed.), *Developing Minds: A Resource Book for Teaching Thinking*, Alexandria, VA: Association for Supervision and Curriculum Development.

Diener, C. and Dweck, C. (1978) "An analysis of learned helplessness: Continuous changes in performance, strategy, and achievement cognitions following failure", *Journal of Personality and Social Psychology*, 36: 451–62.

Education Queensland Inclusive Education Statement (2005) Online. Available at: education.qld.gov.au/studentservices/learning/docs/inclusedstatement2005.pdf

Elbaum, B. and Vaughn, S. (2003) "Self-concept and students with learning disabilities", in H. L. Swanson, K. R. Harris and S. Graham (eds), *Handbook of Learning Disabilities*, New York: Guildford Press.

Forlin, C. (1998) "Teachers' personal concerns about including children with a disability in regular classrooms", *Journal of Developmental and Physical Disabilities,* 10(1): 87–106.

Galletly, S. and Knight, B. (2004) "The high cost of orthographic disadvantage", *Australian Journal of Learning Disabilities,* 9(4): 4–11.

Geary, D.C. (2004) "Mathematics and learning disabilities", *Journal of Learning Disabilities,* 37(1): 4–15.

Gersten, R., Fuchs, L. S., Williams, J. P. and Baker, S. (2001) "Teaching reading comprehension strategies to students with learning disabilities: A review of research", *Review of Educational Research,* 71(2): 279–320.

Graham, L. (2002) *The 3H Strategy, in Follow-Up to Basic Skills Tests,* Sydney, NSW: Department of Education.

Graham, L. and Wong, B. Y. L. (1993) "Comparing two modes in teaching a question-answering strategy for enhancing reading comprehension: Didactic and self-instructional training", *Journal of Learning Disabilities,* 26(4): 270–9.

Graham, L., Bellert, A., Thomas, J. and Pegg, J. (2007) "QuickSmart: A basic academic skills intervention for middle-years students with learning difficulties", *Journal of Learning Disabilities,* 40(5): 410–19.

Keeler, M. and Swanson, H. L. (2001) "Does strategy knowledge influence working memory in children with learning disabilities?", *Journal of Learning Disabilities,* 34(5): 418–34.

Knight, B. A. (2000) "Educating learners with special needs in the regular classroom", in T. Maxwell and P. Ninnes (eds), *The Context of Teaching,* 2nd edn, Armidale, NSW: Kardoorair Press.

Knight, B. A. (2007) "Teaching students with special needs", in R. Smith, D. Lynch and B. Knight (eds), *Transitioning Teachers to National and International Change,* Frenchs' Forest, NSW: Pearson Education Australia.

Knight, B. A., Paterson, D. and Mulcahy, R. (1998) *Strategies Program for Enhancing Learning and Thinking (SPELT),* Melbourne: Hawker Brownlow Education.

Lenz, B. K. and Deschler, D. D. (2004) "Adolescents with learning disabilities: Revisiting the educator's enigma", in B. Wong (ed.), *Learning about Learning Disabilities,* 3rd edn, New York: Elsevier Academic Press.

Milton, M. (2000) "How do schools provide for children with difficulties in numeracy?", *Australian Journal of Learning Disabilities,* 5(2): 23–7.

Royer, J. M., Cisero, C. A. and Carlo, M. S. (1993), "Techniques and procedures for assessing cognitive skills", *Review of Educational Research,* 63(2): 201–43.

Scott, W. (2004) "Learning difficulties and learning disabilities: Identifying an issue – The issue of identification", in B. Knight and W. Scott (eds), *Learning Difficulties: Multiple Perspectives,* French's Forest, NSW: Pearson Sprint, pp. 1–15.

Smith, R., Lynch, D. and Knight, B. A. (2007) *Learning Management: Transitioning Teachers for National and International Change,* Frenchs' Forest, NSW: Pearson Education Australia.

Stanovich, K. E. (1990) "Concepts in developmental theories of reading skill: Cognitive resources, automaticity and modularity", *Developmental Review,* 10: 72–100.

Swanson, H. L. and Hoskyn, M. (2001) "Instructing adolescents with learning disabilities: A component and composite analysis", *Learning Disabilities Research & Practice,* 16(2): 109–19.

Swanson, H. L. and Siegel, L. (2001) "Learning disabilities as a working memory deficit", *Issues in Education*, 7(1): 1–48.

Tomlinson, C. A. and Allen, S. D. (2000) *Leadership for Differentiating Schools and Classrooms*, Alexandria, VA: Association for Supervision and Curriculum Development.

Vaughn, S., Bos, C. S. and Schumm, J. S. (2000a) *Teaching Exceptional, Diverse and At-Risk Learners in the General Education Classroom*, 2nd edn, Boston, MA: Allyn & Bacon.

Vaughn, S., Gersten R. and Chard, D. (2000b) "The underlying message in LD intervention research: Findings from research syntheses", *Exceptional Children*, 67(1): 99–114.

Vygotsky, L. S. (1978) *Mind in Society: The Development of Higher Psychological Processes*, Cambridge, MA: Harvard University Press.

Walczyk, J. J. (2000) "The interplay between automatic and control processes in reading", *Reading Research Quarterly*, 35(4): 554–66.

Westwood, P. (1993) "Striving for positive outcomes for students with learning difficulties", *Special Education Perspectives*, 2(2): 87–94.

Westwood, P. (2001) "Differentiation as a strategy for inclusive classroom practice", *Australian Journal of Learning Disabilities*, 6(1): 5–11.

Westwood, P. (2004) "The affective components of difficulty in learning: Why prevention is better than attempted cure", in B. A. Knight and W. Scott (eds), *Learning Difficulties: Multiple Perspectives*, French's Forest, NSW: Pearson Sprint.

Westwood, P. (2006) *Teaching and Learning Difficulties: Cross Curricular Perspective*, Camberwell, Victoria: Australian Council for Educational Research.

Westwood, P. and Graham, L. (2000) "How many children with special needs in regular classes: Official predictions vs teachers' perceptions in South Australia and New South Wales", *Australian Journal of Learning Disabilities*, 5(3): 24–35.

Westwood, P. and Graham, L. (2003) "Inclusion of students with special needs: Benefits and obstacles perceived by teachers in New South Wales and South Australia", *Australian Journal of Learning Disabilities*, 8: 3–15.

Wolf, M., Miller, L. and Donnelly, K. (2000) "Retrieval, automaticity, vocabulary elaboration, orthography (RAVE-O): A comprehensive, fluency based reading intervention program", *Journal of Learning Disabilities*, 33(4): 375–86.

14 Including children with autism in the culture of play with typical peers

Pamela Wolfberg

Chapter objectives

- To consider education reform and teacher training for inclusive education that is responsive to the unique needs of children with autism spectrum disorders.
- To provide an overview of teacher preparation focused on a research-based model that supports the social inclusion of children with autism in educational settings.
- To articulate the clear connection between theories, research and practice in preparing educators to design and implement high quality inclusive programs for children with autism.

Focus questions

1 What are the factors that impact on the need for education reform and teacher preparation in inclusive education for children with autism spectrum disorder?
2 What are the key components of the Integrated Play Groups model that draw on theory, research and practice in the areas of autism, peer relations and play?
3 What types of knowledge, skill and dispositions describe teachers who achieve mastery in guiding children with autism and typical peers in inclusive play experiences?
4 How might teachers apply and adapt the practices of the Integrated Play Groups model to diverse populations and inclusive communities?

Introduction

This chapter focuses on preparing teachers in Integrated Play Groups (IPG), a research-based model for including children with autism in play with typically developing peers within inclusive education settings. The chapter begins by highlighting the importance of preparing teachers to support the inclusion of children with autism in peer relations and play. Drawing on current theory, research and practice, the major features of the IPG model are described while delineating the phases of the training program. An overview of the knowledge and skill that teachers gain while progressing through the various phases of the training program is provided. A case illustration of an inclusion teacher facilitating an IPG with elementary-aged students is then presented. The chapter concludes with an overview of efficacy research focusing on the perceptions and experiences of teachers trained in applying the IPG model.

Autism spectrum disorders (ASD) is one of the fastest growing special education populations, which presents unprecedented challenges in teacher education. As such, there is a pressing need to prepare qualified educators to effectively meet the unique needs of students with autism in inclusive education settings (Yell *et al.*, 2005). This chapter considers education reforms and teacher training for inclusive education by focusing on the IPG model that is designed to support the social inclusion of children on the autism spectrum with typical peers.

The complex nature and wide spectrum of variability in ASD poses distinct challenges for preparing educators to work effectively with this population, particularly in inclusive settings [National Research Council (NRC), 2001]. ASD refers here to a broad definition of autism and related conditions, including classic autism, Asperger Syndrome and other pervasive developmental disorders, all of which share many core characteristics. The result of a neurological condition, autism affects a person's capacity to interact socially with others, communicate basic needs, feelings and ideas, understand and use language effectively, develop play and imagination, and form peer relationships [American Psychiatric Association (APA), 2000]. While changing over the lifespan, the presence of behaviors may manifest in a wide variety of combinations and degrees of intensity, ranging from mild to severe.

To maximize learning, development, independent functioning and full participation in social, cultural and quality of life experiences, each student requires a mosaic of specialized education services and supports, carefully configured by highly knowledgeable and skilled professionals in collaboration with families. In a comprehensive review of empirical research and evidence-based practices, the NRC (2001) ranked the teaching of social skills and play with peers among the six types of interventions that should have priority in the design and delivery of effective education programs for children with autism. Thus, a critical piece of the mosaic involves preparing educators with the corresponding knowledge and skill.

Preparing teachers in the Integrated Play Groups (IPG) model

The IPG model is designed to support the social inclusion of children with autism in play experiences with typical classmates or peers (Wolfberg, 2003; Wolfberg and Schuler, 2006). This multi-dimensional model specifically draws on current theory, research and evidence-based practices, incorporating parameters pertinent to promoting social interaction, communication, play and imagination. Table 14.1 gives an overview of the key features of the IPG model, which involves a number of implementation phases.

Table 14.1 Key features of the Integrated Play Groups model

	Description
Mission	To provide a haven for children with diverse abilities to create genuine play worlds together, where they may reach their social and imaginative potential, as well as have fun and make friends.
IPG program design	
Objectives	• Foster spontaneous, mutually enjoyed, reciprocal play with peers • Expand/diversify social and symbolic play repertoire • Enhance peer mediated play activities with minimal adult guidance
Service delivery	• Preschool–elementary aged children (3–11 years) • Customized as part of education/therapy program • Led by trained adult facilitator (play guide)
Play group composition	• 3–5 children per group – higher ratio of expert to novice players • Novice players – children of all abilities on the autism spectrum and with related special needs • Expert players – typically developing peers/siblings
IPG environmental design	
Schedule	Play group sessions meet two times per week for 30–60 minutes over a 6–12 month period
Play setting	• Natural integrated settings – school, home, therapy or community • Specially designed play spaces – wide range motivating materials, activities, themes encourage interactive and imaginative play
Play session structure	Consistent routines, rituals, visual supports foster familiarity, predictability and a cohesive group identity
IPG assessment	
Observation	Naturalistic observation of children at play
Framework	• Social play styles • Symbolic dimension of play • Social dimensions of play • Communicative functions and means • Play preferences – diversity of play
Assessment tools	• Play questionnaire • Play preference inventory • Integrated play groups observation • Profile of individual play development • Record of monthly progress in IPG (with sample goals) • IPG summative report

(Continued)

Table 14.1 (Continued)

	Description
IPG intervention	
Guided participation	System of support to facilitate social interaction, communication, play and imagination by skillfully applying the following practices: • Monitoring play initiations • Scaffolding play • Social-communication guidance • Play guidance

Phase I: Embracing the spirit of play –conceptual foundation

In the first phase of training, teachers participate in a seminar series that provides the theoretical framework. Teachers gain a deep understanding of the nature of autism and the complex problems children encounter learning how to play and socialize with peers (for recent reviews, see Boucher and Wolfberg, 2003; Wolfberg and Schuler, 2006). Hallmarks of autism include a lack of varied and imaginative or imitative play, as well as a failure to develop peer relationships appropriate to developmental level. Problems in these areas are intricately tied to characteristic impairments in reciprocal social interaction, communication and imagination (APA, 2000).

In sharp contrast to the rich social and imaginary play of typically developing children, the play of children with autism is strikingly detached and stark. Children with autism tend to pursue repetitive activities in isolation. Many children get stuck on one or a few activities, which may last hours and continue over months and even years. Some children are attracted to conventional activities while others develop fascinations or preoccupations focused on unusual objects or pedantic subjects. They are less inclined to spontaneously engage in functional play and rarely produce pretend play (Jarrold, 2003).

Socializing with peers in the context of play and other shared activities is particularly problematic for children with autism. Overall, they direct fewer obvious social initiations to peers as well as inconsistently respond to peers when they initiate with them. When children with autism do make attempts to interact with peers, their initiations have a tendency to be subtle, obscure or poorly timed. Some children present social play styles in which they are considered *aloof*, as they distance themselves from peers or act as though they are unaware of their presence. Others are considered *passive* as they follow along or watch what their peers are doing, but rarely initiate interaction in obvious ways. Still others are considered *active and odd* in the sense that they attempt to engage peers, but do so in an idiosyncratic or one-sided manner – such as by talking excessively about one topic.

Knowledge of the role of play in learning, development and culture

Teachers also become familiar with a prominent body of literature documenting the importance of play for children's learning, development and cultural participation. A major focus is on the work of Vygotsky (1978) who ascribes a pivotal role to play in the social lives of children. According to his view, play's significance extends beyond that of merely reflecting development to that of leading development. Vygotsky further emphasized that social factors mediate all learning and development. He recognized play, and particularly pretend play, as a primary social activity through which children acquire symbolic capacities, interpersonal skills and social knowledge.

When children join together for play, they construct a peer culture that is uniquely their own. An essential feature of this peer culture is that children develop a sense of collective identity in which they recognize themselves as members of a group created exclusively by and for children. Although the adult world is often represented within the content of children's peer culture, children pursue social activity that is most meaningful to them on their own terms regardless of adult expectations. Since play is the leading social activity in the lives of children, it is the very essence of their peer culture.

Play culture more accurately describes that realm in which children create and live out their social and imaginary lives (Mouritsen, 1996). It is based on active participation in those social activities that are most valued by the peer group. In a sense, play culture is living folklore that manifests itself in the rituals, narratives and creations children produce and pass on to one another. The skills, values and knowledge acquired through peer play experiences are a part of the cultural tradition transmitted to each new generation of children.

It is within the culture of play that children learn and develop in a multitude of ways (for reviews, see Wolfberg, 2003). When it comes to play, peers in particular perform a distinct role in children's socialization and development by offering learning opportunities and experiences that cannot be duplicated by adults. While playing together, children acquire many interrelated skills that are necessary for attaining social competence and ultimately, establishing mutual friendships. Through jointly constructed activity, children refine their social communication strategies, learn to negotiate and compromise, resolve conflicts, build trust, and develop other foundation social skills. Play further provides opportunities to express intimacy and affection with peers, the core ingredients of friendship (Rubin *et al.*, 1983).

Knowledge of peer influences on inclusion of children with autism

Teachers gain important insights into the role of peers and their influence on the inclusion of children with autism. Despite inherent problems, there is strong evidence to suggest that children with autism share many of the same desires and capacities for play, companionship and peer-group acceptance as typical children (Boucher and Wolfberg, 2003). What differs is that their intentions are expressed in ways that are uniquely their own. How the peer group responds to these children has an especially profound influence on the extent to which they may gain access to the play culture and reap the benefits of play. Unfortunately, their subtle or awkward attempts to socialize and play are frequently misinterpreted by peers as signs of deviance or limited social interest.

The reality for many children with autism is that they are frequently excluded from their peer group simply because their behavior does not conform to the conventions of the play culture. As a consequence, many children with autism become targets of bullying, teasing and taunting by intolerant peers (Heinrichs, 2003), while others are simply ignored or overlooked by peers who might otherwise be open-minded to the differences of others. These rejected and neglected children may become caught in a cycle of exclusion. The transactional nature of these influences poses a dilemma for these children; with limited capacities to socialize and play with peers, children with autism are likely to be excluded from participating in their play culture, yet without such participation, they are unlikely to develop the capacities to socialize and play that would be needed to escape their isolation. Without a system of support, they are thus deprived of opportunities to actualize their potential to socialize and play and be included by their peer group.

Phase II: Setting the stage for play –IPG program and environmental design

In the second phase of training, teachers are guided through a series of field exercises while learning tools and techniques for designing the IPG program and environment. Teachers learn to develop and execute a well-formulated individualized IPG program plan while working in close collaboration with other key professionals as well as parents. Each IPG is customized as a part of a child's individualized education plan. The groups are designed for three to five children with a higher ratio of expert (typical peers) to novice players (children with autism). The groups are scheduled to meet on a regular basis in an inclusive education setting at least twice a week for 30–60 minute sessions over the course of a school year. Times may vary depending upon the age and developmental stage of the participating children.

Teachers gain experience in selecting, organizing and training play group participants. Expert players include general education classmates and other typical peers who demonstrate competence in the areas of social interaction, communication and play with other children. Playmates ideally have some familiarity and attraction to one another and the potential for developing long-lasting friendships.

Special attention is given to training teachers to prepare the players through autism awareness or demystification activities that draw on the work of McCracken (2005a, 2005b). Prior to the first IPG session, both novice and expert players participate in specially designed puppet presentations, simulation games and follow-up discussions that foster awareness, understanding and empathy for children who relate, communicate and play in unique or different ways.

Teachers learn how to design play spaces and select play materials based on multiple factors. Play spaces are carefully configured with consideration of size, density, organization and thematic arrangements. Play materials include a wide range of highly motivating sensory motor, exploratory, constructive and sociodramatic props with high potential for interactive and imaginative play. Play materials vary in degree of structure and complexity to accommodate children's diverse interests, learning styles and developmental levels. Intrinsic motivation for peer participation derives from identifying play activities that will be mutually enjoyed by novice and expert players.

Teachers learn how to structure play sessions by establishing consistent schedules, routines and rituals and incorporating visual supports (consisting of words and/or pictures) that foster familiarity, predictability and a cohesive group identity. Basic rules for fair and courteous behavior and appropriate care of materials are presented at the outset of play groups. Personalized visual calendars and schedules help children anticipate the days and times of meetings and the sequence of the play session. Play sessions begin and end with an opening and closing ritual (e.g. greeting, song and brief discussion of plans and strategies).

Teachers learn how to design visual choice boards, which consist of a variety of preferred activities from which children may select to get started in play. Visual role tags may be worn by children, which depict their different characters or roles, such as cashier, customer and cook while playing restaurant. Story books are also created to help children review play activities and themes as well as to teach new play schemes. Group membership is established by creating play group names and associated rituals, which also serve to provide the intrinsic motivation for true peer participation.

Phase III: Observing children at play –IPG assessment

In the third phase of training, teachers become well versed in the range of assessment tools and techniques specifically developed. Teachers must refine their observation skills to effectively understand, interpret and guide children's participation in IPGs. Systematic and ongoing observations provide a basis for setting realistic and meaningful goals, guiding intervention strategies, and documenting and analyzing children's progress.

Another fundamental aspect of the IPG assessment approach involves insightful interpretation that taps into the unique developmental potential of each child. The assessments are especially sensitive to the unique qualities rather than deficiencies observed in the play of children with autism. They do not focus on what is missing or wrong with the way children socialize or play, but rather on present and emerging abilities. Teachers must therefore acquire a broad and deep understanding of patterns of play development in typical childhood compared with noted variations among children on the autism spectrum.

Teachers gain extensive and repeated practice in conducting assessments that follow an explicit observation framework focused on children's play preferences and diversity of play, symbolic and social dimensions of play, and social communication (Wolfberg, 2003). These are designed to interface with the overall goals and objectives of each child's individualized education plan.

Documenting the play preferences of both novice and expert players in play groups offers a means by which to identify and match children's play interests as well as assess diversity of play. Symbolic dimensions of play refer to play acts that the child directs towards objects, self, or others and that signify events. These include exploratory play (manipulation), conventional object use and simple pretense (functional), and advanced pretense (symbolic/pretend).

Social dimensions of play focus on the child's distance to and involvement with one or more children. These include playing alone (isolate), watching peers (onlooker/orientation), playing beside peers (parallel/proximity), playing with peers in joint activity (common focus), and collaborating with peers in an organized fashion (common goal).

Social communication focuses on the functions of communication, i.e. what the child intends to convey (e.g. requests for objects, peer interaction, affection, protests, declarations and comments), which may be accomplished through a variety of verbal and non-verbal communicative means (e.g. facial expressions, eye gaze, physical proximity, touching, gestures, intonation, vocalization, echolalia and simple or complex speech/sign/symbol/written word). Each child's communicative attempt (as expressed through any one or a combination of communicative functions and means) is recognized as a potential initiation to play with someone or something, even when expressed in a subtle or obscure form.

Phase IV: Guided participation in play –IPG intervention

The fourth and final phase of training prepares teachers for applying the intervention practices. The intervention, *guided participation*, involves a carefully tailored system of support that is responsive to each child's unique profile of development and socio-cultural experience, while also being sufficiently intensive to maximize the child's potential. The overall premise is to allow novice and expert players to initiate and incorporate desired activity into socially coordinated play, while challenging novice players to practice new and increasingly complex forms of play. To achieve this, the teacher guides novice and expert players toward engaging in mutually enjoyed play activities that encourage social interaction, communication, play and imagination, such as pretending, constructing, art, music, movement and interactive games. Gradually, teacher support is decreased as the children learn to mediate their own play activities. To guide peer play, teachers learn how to apply the following key set of practices.

Monitoring play initiations involves the teacher in recognizing, interpreting and responding to the novice player's spontaneous attempts to socialize and play. Play initiations may include virtually any conventional or unconventional act or display (directed to objects, self and others) that indicates a child's interest or desire to play in the company of peers. Even acts that reflect unusual fascinations, obsessions, rituals or idiosyncratic language are recognized as play initiations. Play initiations are the foundation on which to build upon the child's social and symbolic play repertoire and the springboards for novice and expert players to find common ground in mutually engaging activities. The adult's capacity to monitor play initiations is essential for delivering support that is matched to the level of comprehension and ability within the child's zone of proximal development (Vygotsky, 1978).

Scaffolding play involves the teacher in systematically adjusting assistance to match or slightly exceed the level at which the child is independently able to engage in play with peers. Scaffolding is a fluid process that relies on finding that ever-so-delicate balance of knowing when to step in, when to step out and especially when to be quiet, while sustaining child engagement. At a more intensive level, the teacher directs the play event and models behavior by identifying and/or narrating common themes, arranging props and assigning roles and play partners. At a less intensive level, the teacher guides the children by posing leading questions, commenting on activities, offering suggestions and giving subtle reminders using verbal and visual cues. As the children grow increasingly comfortable and competent in their play, the teacher withdraws support and remains on the periphery of the group.

Social communication guidance involves the teacher in supporting novice and expert players in adopting conventional verbal and non-verbal strategies to elicit one another's attention and sustain mutual engagement in play. Directed to novice and expert players alike, these strategies are presented in the form of social communication cues focused on what the players may do and/or say to invite and join peers for play. Specifically, the strategies focus on (a) initiating play with peers (including persisting in enlisting reluctant peers), (b) responding to peer social bids, (c) joining or entering established play events with peers, and (d) maintaining and expanding reciprocal exchanges in play with peers. Relevant cues are selected based on observation and analysis. The cues are then introduced and reinforced with the aid of visual supports. The intent is for children to naturally incorporate these strategies into their repertoire, and to no longer rely on adult guidance or the presence of visual cues.

Play guidance involves supporting novice players in peer play experiences that are slightly beyond the child's capacity (i.e. within the child's zone of proximal development), while fully immersed in the whole play experience at his or her present level, even if participation is minimal. Strategies range from orienting (watching peers and activities), imitation and mirroring (mimicking the actions of a peer), parallel play (playing side by side in the same play space with similar materials), and joint focus (active sharing and informal turn taking in the same activity) to socially coordinated activity involving joint action (formal turn taking), role enactment (portraying real-life activities through conventional actions), and role playing (taking on pretend roles and creatively using objects while enacting complex scripts). By building upon play initiations, and encouraging participation in activities that are just slightly beyond the child's present abilities, novices may begin to explore and diversify existing play routines.

Case illustration of an inclusion teacher facilitating an integrated play group

The following case illustration is of a play group facilitated by an inclusion support teacher in an elementary school. The IPG is designed for Paulo, a nine-year-old boy with autism (Asperger's). He is fully included in a fourth grade class.

Based on goals identified in his IEP, Paulo participates twice a week for 30 minutes in an IPG with three of his typically developing classmates.

Assessments conducted by Paulo's teacher indicate that he has an active odd social play style. He expresses a genuine desire for peer companionship, but has had little success in developing a mutual friendship. His peers frequently ignore his attempts to engage them for social interaction and play. Paulo has a tendency to initiate in a one-sided and idiosyncratic fashion without consideration of his peers' perspectives. He typically approaches peers by asking them if they have read a particular book, and then proceeds to recite lines from the book no matter what the response.

Paulo's play interests are consistent with themes generated from his most beloved books. His current favorite is the Harry Potter series by J. K. Rowling. He enjoys collecting figures and other paraphernalia represented in these stories. He spends much of his time organizing these toys and generating lists that depict the characters and key events. Paulo has also recently begun wearing Harry Potter eye glasses that he picked up in a novelty shop.

The goals and objectives identified for Paulo focus on:

1 To maximize development in social play with peers. Paulo will demonstrate a common focus and goals in play by
   a engaging in reciprocal social exchanges
   b jointly planning and carrying out a common agenda, and
   c negotiating and compromising around divergent interests.
2 To maximize representational abilities (i.e. flexible imagination and creative expression). Paulo will demonstrate symbolic pretend play at an advanced level by role-playing scripts (real or invented) with age-appropriate props, self, peers and/or imaginary characters.
3 To maximize social communicative competence. Paulo will expand his language expression in play with peers by
   a carrying on conversations, and
   b narrating socio-dramatic pretend play scripts.
4 To expand and diversify his repertoire of spontaneous play preferences/ interests. Paulo will demonstrate
   a an increased number of self-selected play interests, and
   b an increased variety of self-selected play interests.

Adapted from Wolfberg (2003), Table 14.2 depicts an IPG session that took place at the start of the school year.

Efficacy of the IPG model

A series of experimental and exploratory studies have been carried out to examine the efficacy of the IPG model (for a recent review, see Wolfberg and Schuler, 2006), including cross-cultural research in the Asia-Pacific region (Opitz *et al.*,

Table 14.2 An IPG session at the beginning of a new school year

Play scenario	*Monitoring play initiations*	*Scaffolding play*	*Social-communication guidance*	*Play guidance*
The session opens with a ritual greeting and a recap of the last session. The teacher asks the children to come up with ideas and a plan of what they would like to play together. She prepares to write the different ideas on the board.	Recognize play initiation	Intermediate support: Verbal and visual cueing		
Paulo immediately tells Lisa, Lori and Ray (expert players) that the plan for the day is to make Harry Potter books.				
The teacher reminds Paulo, "One of the goals of play groups is to 'cooperate' – that means each member may make a suggestion (which may be different from your suggestion). The next step is to make a plan together that everyone agrees upon. So Paulo, your suggestion is to make Harry Potter books. Why don't you ask the others what they'd like to play?"	Interpret and respond to play initiations	Intermediate support: Verbal and visual cueing	Reinforce cues: What to do: "Face your friends when you talk to them" What to say: "What do you want to play?"	Joint focus

(Continued)

Table 14.2 (Continued)

Play scenario	*Monitoring play initiations*	*Scaffolding play*	*Social-communication guidance*	*Play guidance*
While facing the teacher, Paulo begins …The teacher quietly redirects him to the social-communication poster, "Don't forget that we need to face our friends when we talk to them." Paulo faces Lisa and asks, "What do you want to play?"				
Lisa suggests putting on a puppet show. Lori says she'd like to do the same…Ray begins, but Paulo interrupts.		Minimum support: Standing by		
The teacher points again to the social-communication poster and reminds the children to "take turns" when speaking. Ray continues and suggests making a space station model. The teacher writes the different ideas on the board and asks the children if	Interpret and respond to play initiations	Intermediate support: Verbal and visual cueing	Reinforce cue: What to do: "Take turns when speaking"	Joint action/role playing

(Continued)

Table 14.2 (Continued)

Play scenario	*Monitoring play initiations*	*Scaffolding play*	*Social-communication guidance*	*Play guidance*
they can think of a way to combine their different ideas.				
Ray suggests building a model of Hogwarts School instead of a space station. Lisa and Lori suggest making stick puppets of all the Harry Potter characters. Paulo adds that he will be Harry Potter and assigns the other children roles from the book. "Ray, you be Ron Weasly, Lisa, you be Hermione, and Lori, you be Professor McGonnegal."		Minimum support: Standing by		
The teacher coaches Paulo to ask each of the others if they agree with their roles, which they do. The teacher next provides the children with markers and a pad of paper to write out the different steps of their plan. "What is the first thing you are going to do?" Ray and Paulo agree to make		Intermediate support: Verbal and visual cueing	Reinforce cues: What to do: "Face your friends when you talk to them"	Joint action/role playing

(Continued)

Table 14.2 (Continued)

Play scenario	*Monitoring play initiations*	*Scaffolding play*	*Social-communication guidance*	*Play guidance*
the model while Lori and Lisa make the puppets. A discussion continues as to what materials they will need and how they will make their creations. After several minutes they come up with a simple plan.				
The teacher brings an assortment of art materials to the table and helps Ray and Paulo secure a cardboard base for the model.		Maximum support: Directing and modeling		Joint action
The children spend half the session creating the model and puppets. The teacher occasionally interjects to guide the conversation by suggesting the children ask questions, make comments, exchange materials and ideas – e.g. What are you making? That looks cool! May I borrow that? Please, help me…		Intermediate support: Verbal and visual cueing	Reinforce cues: What to do: "Take turns when speaking" What to say: (see examples in text)	Joint action

(Continued)

Table 14.2 (Continued)

Play scenario	*Monitoring play initiations*	*Scaffolding play*	*Social-communication guidance*	*Play guidance*
They next begin acting out a simple script directed by Paulo. Lisa and Lori deviate from the script with protests from Paulo.	Recognize play initiation	Minimum support: Standing by		Role playing
The teacher interjects by reminding the children (for Paulo's sake) that another goal of the play group is to be creative and use your imagination – that means it is okay to change the story so that it is different from the original. She suggests that next time they meet the children may write their own story script – Harry Potter can have new adventures.	Interpret and respond to play initiation	Intermediate support: Verbal and visual cueing		Role playing
Ray suggests that Harry Potter can do magic to go into outer space. Paulo appears a bit uneasy, but then adds, "Okay, Harry Potter can go to outer space, but only if he wears his invisibility cloak."		Minimum support: Standing by		

2004; Yang *et al.*, 2003). While much of this research has focused on evaluating outcomes for novice and expert players (including social validation with families) (e.g. Lantz *et al.*, 2004; Yang *et al.*, 2003), there is also research focused on teachers who were trained in the IPG model (O'Connor, 1999; Wolfberg and Schuler, 1992). The following provides a summary of findings based on this body of research with a more detailed overview of teacher-related research.

The accumulated findings provide consistent evidence that the children with autism spontaneously generated more diverse and complex forms of representational and social play than previously exhibited in unsupported peer play activity. Moreover, the children maintained these skills when adult support was withdrawn. Improvements in language were also documented in a few cases. Further, observational and social validation data indicated that the children's advances in play generalized beyond the specific play group to other peers and siblings, settings (school, home, community) and social activity contexts.

Positive outcomes were also noted for typical peers with respect to developing greater sensitivity, tolerance and acceptance of the novice players' individual differences. In addition, they articulated a sense of responsibility as well as an understanding of how to include the less skilled players by adapting to their unique interests and styles of communication. They further reported having fun and developing mutual friendships with novice players that extended beyond the play group setting to after school activities in the home and community.

The teacher-related research focused on perceived outcomes for the children as well as self-perceptions of the experience of facilitating IPGs. Expanding upon a pilot study with 19 elementary school teachers in the context of an initial research and demonstration project (Wolfberg and Schuler, 1992), O'Connor (1999) conducted an extensive investigation focused on ten preschool and elementary teachers at the beginning stages of facilitating IPGs with children ranging in age from three to eleven years. Through a questionnaire and interviews, this study sought to understand what teachers perceive in terms of (1) potential benefits for the novice and expert players; (2) influences on their own practice with children; and (3) the competencies needed to be a successful facilitator.

Consistent with the outcomes of the pilot study, the results of O'Connor's study indicated that all of the teachers perceived the novice players as benefiting from guided participation in IPGs. Many noted outward signs of sheer enjoyment on the part of the children with autism. More specific observations included increases in the novice players' eye contact, observation and imitation of peers, initiating behaviors, social responsiveness, social and symbolic play levels, communication and diversity of spontaneous play interests.

Benefits for expert players were also reported by the teachers in this study. They indicated that the expert players thoroughly enjoyed the experience of participating in IPGs as well as exhibiting the following: increased self-esteem and confidence; a sense of pride in accomplishments; greater empathy, patience and assertiveness; increased awareness and acceptance of differences in others; more compassion, empathy and patience; and greater initiation and responsiveness towards the novice players.

The teachers also reported that they themselves had benefited from the training and as facilitators of IPGs. They also noted that the experience had an impact on their own practice with children. They related that they had acquired new skills and realizations, including: better observation and assessment skills; more focused understanding of social and play goals; how not to underestimate the potential of children; how better to select and set up play activities; how to be more creative, facilitative and less directive/intrusive; and how better to explain to parents what they might do to support their children in play.

The teachers also made a variety of recommendations that may help to support future teachers, including: the need for ongoing supervision and consultation following initial training; creating collaborative IPG teams to meet and support one another on a regular basis; to have an opportunity to observe other IPGs in action; to reflect on one's practice by reviewing videotapes of oneself in action; and to involve parents more to enhance generalization, as well as to empower the families.

Conclusion

Dispositions are goals that describe students' desired behaviors and attitudes as an outcome of their education. These goals address student development as a whole and relate to real-world functioning. In light of the growing numbers of children with autism being educated alongside typical peers, there is a pressing need to prepare teachers in effective and meaningful inclusive practices. The core challenges of autism are accentuated by the developmental and socio-cultural significance of peer relations and play in the lives of children. This clearly has implications for children worldwide, including those representing diverse cultural and linguistic groups within the Asia-Pacific region. The Integrated Play Groups model was designed in an effort to bring together children with autism and typical peers within the context of socially and culturally relevant activity in inclusive settings.

The practices of the IPG model are currently being carried out across the Asia-Pacific region, including Australia, Indonesia, Singapore, Taiwan and Thailand. There is strong evidence to suggest that teachers who are effective in supporting children in IPGs draw from a number of different sources of knowledge and insight to accommodate varying developmental levels, learning styles, interests, experiences and cultures. It is hoped that the information presented in this chapter will inspire teachers to refine and reflect on their practice in an effort to support the inclusion of the many children who might otherwise remain on the fringes of peer groups.

References

American Psychiatric Association (2000) *Diagnostic and Statistical Manual of Mental Disorders –IV (TR)* , Washington, DC.

Boucher, J. and Wolfberg, P. J. (eds) (2003) "Special issue on play", *Autism: The International Journal of Research and Practice*, 7(4): 339–46.

Heinrichs, R. (2003) *Perfect Targets: Asperger Syndrome and Bullying – Practical Solutions for Surviving the Social World*, Shawnee Mission, KS: Autism Asperger.

Jarrold, C. (2003) "A review of research into pretend play in autism", *Autism: The International Journal of Research and Practice*, 7(4): 379–90.

Lantz, J. F., Nelson, J. M. and Loftin, R. L. (2004) "Guiding children with autism in play: Applying the Integrated Play Group model in school settings", *Exceptional Children*, 37(2): 8–14.

McCracken, H. (2005a) "Friend 2 Friend: Fostering mutual friendships for children with ASD", *Autism-Asperger Digest*, (Jan–Feb): 6–15.

McCracken, H. (2005b) "Friend 2 Friend programs help children with autism feel safe to say, 'I'm autistic too.' ", *Autism Spectrum Quarterly*, 2: 13.

Mouritsen, F. (1996) *Play Culture: Essays on Child Culture, Play and Narratives*, Odense, Denmark: Odense University.

National Research Council (2001) *Educating Children with Autism. Committee on Educational Interventions for Children with Autism. Division of Behavioral and Social Sciences and Education*, Washington, DC: National Academy Press.

O'Connor, T. (1999) "Teacher perspectives of facilitated play in integrated play groups", unpublished Master's thesis, San Francisco State University, California.

Opitz, V. B., Ing, S. and Kong, T.Y. (2004) "Comparison of behavioral and natural play interventions for young children with autism", *Autism: The International Journal of Research and Practice*, 8(3): 319–33

Rubin, K. H., Fein, G. and Vanderberg, B. (1983) "Play", in P. Mussen and E. M. Hetherington (eds), *Handbook of Child Psychology*, 4th edn, *Socialization, Personality, and Social Development*, New York: Wiley, pp. 693–774.

Vygotsky, L. S. (1978) *Mind in Society: The Development of Higher Psychological Processes* (translation from 1932), Cambridge, MA: Harvard University Press.

Wolfberg, P. J. (2003) *Peer Play and the Autism Spectrum: The Art of Guiding Children's Socialization and Imagination*, Shawnee, KS: Autism Asperger.

Wolfberg, P. J. and Schuler, A. L. (1992) *Integrated Play Groups Project: Final Evaluation Report* (Contract # HO86D90016), Washington, DC: Department of Education, OSERS.

Wolfberg, P. J. and Schuler, A. L. (2006) "Promoting social reciprocity and symbolic representation in children with ASD: Designing quality peer play interventions", in T. Charman and W. Stone (eds), *Early Social Communication in Autism Spectrum Disorders*, New York: Guilford Publications.

Yang, T., Wolfberg, P. J., Wu, S. and Hwu, P. (2003) "Supporting children on the autism spectrum in peer play at home and school: Piloting the Integrated Play Groups model in Taiwan", *Autism: The International Journal of Research and Practice*, 7(4): 437–53.

Yell, M., Drasgow, E. and Lowrey, K. (2005) "No child left behind and students with autism spectrum disorders", *Focus on Autism and Other Developmental Disabilities*, 20(3): 130–9.

15 Including students with attention-deficit hyperactivity disorder and autistic spectrum disorders

Neil Humphrey

Chapter objectives

- To provide an up-to-date overview of evidence-based strategies that can be used by teachers to facilitate the inclusion of students with *attention-deficit hyperactivity disorder* (ADHD) and *autistic spectrum disorders* (ASD).
- To discuss the notion of inclusive education in relation to ADHD and ASD.

Focus questions

1 What do we mean by inclusive education in relation to students with ADHD and ASD?
2 What can I do to promote the inclusion of students with ADHD and ASD in my classroom?

Introduction

Reforms in relation to special education needs in the Asia-Pacific region appear to have followed a similar trend to those in the West. In many ways this is not surprising, given that delegates from several countries in this region were amongst those who met in the formation of the Salamanca Statement (Forlin, 2006). In parallel to this, the publication of *Provision for Children with SEN in the Asia Region* by the World Bank (Lynch, 1994), and the gradual emergence of legislation for people with disabilities in Asia-Pacific regions throughout the 1990s (Asia-Pacific Development Centre on Disabilities, 2007), has meant that the notion of inclusion has gathered support in the region. However, as has been the case in the West, the degree to which legislation has been fully implemented as planned varies considerably (Forlin, 2007). There are also clear differences to be acknowledged though, such as the influence of philosophy (e.g. the Confucian philosophy that has so greatly influenced many Eastern countries is considerably more tolerant and accepting than the individualist paradigm that has dominated Western thinking) and economics (e.g. the influence of poverty).

Attention-deficit hyperactivity disorder (ADHD)

Attention-deficit hyperactivity disorder (ADHD) is considered to be a medical condition characterized by *inattention* (e.g. difficulty sustaining attention in tasks, easily distracted, does not seem to listen when spoken to), *hyperactivity* (e.g. often fidgets with hands or feet, talks excessively, has difficulty playing or engaging in leisure activities quietly) and *impulsivity* (e.g. often has difficulty awaiting turn, often interrupts) [American Psychiatric Association (APA), 2000]. Although such symptoms are expected to be consistent across settings, recent research in Australia has found low levels of agreement in parent and teacher ratings of children with ADHD (Gomez, 2007). How does ADHD present at home and in the classroom? It may be useful to consider the following (hypothetical) case study:

> Jamie is a nine-year-old boy attending a primary mainstream school. He has recently been referred to an educational psychologist as a result of his behavior in school. Jamie is an extremely boisterous child and is considered to be the class clown. His teacher reports that he is constantly up and out of his seat, tearing round the classroom and disturbing the other children. Once he climbed on to a table in an attempt to reach an overhead lighting panel. Even when he is in his seat he squirms and fidgets, struggling to maintain his attention in class activities. Jamie's teacher reports that she usually has to repeat instructions several times as he does not seem to listen to her. Jamie is described as constantly on the go, but he has not been able to direct his seemingly boundless energy into his academic pursuits. His grades have been steadily declining, and he often makes careless mistakes in his written work. Jamie's behavior was initially considered amusing by his classmates, some of whom would give him dares, knowing that he would struggle to resist. However, more recently he has become isolated from his peers, and has been unable to sustain any enduring friendships.
>
> Jamie says that he cannot control his behavior, and that he always tries his best to pay attention in class. He says that with the exception of Physical Education and Science (two subjects in which his grades have not been declining) he finds schoolwork boring. Jamie's mother and father report that he has always been extremely active since he was a toddler. They say that he is very difficult to control, and he is often in trouble at home, most recently for trying to climb out of an upstairs window. However, in certain activities Jamie's behavior appears to be transformed. For instance, when watching his favorite cartoon, Spider-Man, he sits transfixed for a full half an hour. Also, when helping his father repair an antique motorcycle, a hobby activity they engage in every weekend, Jamie dutifully obeys instructions and is largely well behaved. His father, a mechanic, says that Jamie shows a real aptitude for engineering and is generally fascinated by how things work. This fascination often lands him in trouble though, as last month he disassembled his sister's CD player.

Do you think Jamie has ADHD? What alternative explanations are there for his behavior at home and in school? Estimates suggest that between 2 and 6 per cent of students are affected by ADHD (Cooper, 2005). These rates also appear to hold true for the Asia-Pacific region, in such countries as China (Leung *et al.*, 1996). Discrepancies in prevalence can be due to a range of factors, including differences in diagnostic systems, the overlap between ADHD and other externalizing disorders (Purdie *et al.*, 2002), technological, organizational and cultural factors, and different notions of what constitutes normal and acceptable behavior. Around three times more boys than girls receive a diagnosis of ADHD (although the ratio may be as high as 9:1) (Phares, 2003). Up to 75 per cent of students with ADHD are prescribed stimulant medications, with methylphenidate (Ritalin™) being the most common drug used (Virginia Department of Health, 2003). These rates, however, can vary tremendously across time and according to geographical location. For instance, a study conducted in Australia reported a dramatic rise in new prescriptions from 1990–5 but a steady decline thereafter; this pattern was strongly mediated by geographic variation (Reid *et al.*, 2002).

Research by Reid *et al.* (1994) suggested that up to 80 per cent of children diagnosed with ADHD are educated in mainstream settings, although again this is dependent upon a number of factors, including whether they are on medication and whether they also have learning difficulties. Children with ADHD certainly appear to be over-represented in certain sectors of the special education system. For instance, Place *et al.* (2000) found a prevalence rate of 70 per cent in special schools for children with emotional and behavioral difficulties.

Cooper (2005) suggests that teachers in mainstream schools may be prone to "typing" of such students; that is, placing students into ready-made categories relating to perceived ability, behavior, motivation, etc., based upon limited interactions and observations (this practice, of course, may lead to a self-fulfilling prophecy). This typing may be related to the high media profile that ADHD has received in recent years (Norris and Lloyd, 2000). As with ASD (see below), it is generally accepted that students with ADHD are considered amongst the most difficult to effectively include, a trend also seen in some Asia-Pacific regions, such as Brunei (Bradshaw and Mundia, 2006) and Australia (Subban and Sharma, 2006). Mainstream teachers report a lack of appropriate training as a key barrier to success in this area (West *et al.*, 2005). Interestingly, there appear to be differences in teacher attitudes towards (and perceptions of) ADHD between Western and Asia-Pacific regions. For instance, Norvitilis and Fang (2005) found that Chinese teachers were more likely to cite psychosocial factors (e.g. parenting, boredom) as influences in the presentation of ADHD than their American colleagues (although interestingly, a higher proportion of Chinese teachers suggested that medication should be used as a first line of treatment).

Students with ADHD are more likely than others to experience social isolation, with fewer reported friendships and greater levels of peer rejection (Bagwell *et al.*, 2001). Unlike ASD, statistics for exclusion rates of ADHD are not available, although they are considered to be at "a higher than average risk" (Watling,

2004, p. 17), a proposition that has been verified by recent research (Wilkin *et al.*, 2005) that suggests that students with ASD are also over-represented in exclusion figures. Research from the perspective of students themselves suggests that many experience "confusion, anxiety, blame, [and] guilt" (Hughes, 2007, p. 79) in relation to their education.

Autistic spectrum disorders (ASD)

Autism is seen as a spectrum of difficulties rather than a singular condition (hence the use of autistic spectrum disorder (ASD) throughout this chapter) (Humphrey and Parkinson, 2006). At the lower functioning end of the spectrum are those who would previously have been described as having classic (or "Kanner's") autism, many of whom fail to develop functional speech and often have additional learning difficulties. At the other end of the spectrum are those described as having Asperger Syndrome and high-functioning autism, who usually develop adequate linguistic and intellectual faculties. All individuals on the autistic spectrum share a common difficulty in making sense of the world. More specifically, they experience problems in communication (e.g. delay in, or lack of language development, stereotyped use of language) and social development (e.g. failure to develop peer relationships, impairments in non-verbal behaviors such as eye to eye gaze), and often display ritualistic and stereotyped behavior (e.g. preoccupation with parts of objects, hand flapping or twisting) and resistance to change (e.g. rigid reliance upon routine) (APA, 2000). How does ASD present at home and in the classroom? It may be useful to consider the following (hypothetical) case study:

> Umar is an eight-year-old boy who has recently been referred to an educational psychologist as a result of difficulties experienced at his mainstream primary school. Umar's teacher reports that, whilst she feels he is very academically able, he has extremely poor social skills and appears to lack any real understanding of people's emotions. Although he is occasionally active in seeking social contact with his peers, his methods are often inappropriate. For instance, he will initiate conversations, but only about dinosaurs (his favourite topic). When others try to steer the topic away to something of mutual interest, he ignores them. Umar will play alongside other children, but rarely engages in the kind of spontaneous, imaginative make-believe play observed in his peers; instead, he prefers to line up his dinosaur toys in a row.
>
> Umar has a very large vocabulary for his age, but his understanding and use of language are relatively weak. In particular, he takes the meaning of utterances in a very literal sense. For instance, after putting his hand up to answer a question in class last week, his teacher told him to hold that thought and Umar was then observed holding his head tightly with both hands. Instances like this, along with an unusual gait and very serious, monotonous voice, have meant that some classmates have begun to tease him, and he is viewed as a geek. His parents report that Umar is a generally well-behaved child who has always been extremely reliant upon particular routines. For instance, he insists upon a very restricted diet consisting of fish fingers and potato croquettes,

and will only eat from a special dinner plate. When such routines are broken, he becomes very distressed. For example, two months ago his dinner plate was broken by accident and he threw a tearful tantrum that lasted for two hours.

Around 1 per cent of students are thought to be affected by ASD (Green *et al.*, 2005), although, as with ADHD, prevalence rates differ across studies and according to a range of factors. This figure also appears to be true of the Asia-Pacific region in such countries as Japan (Honda *et al.*, 1996). However, some very able students with ASD may never come to the attention of services because they have developed strategies to overcome their difficulties (National Autistic Society, 2006a). The ratio of males and females affected by ASD is also similar to ADHD, i.e. approximately 3:1.

Research suggests that just over half of children with ASD are educated in a mainstream setting, although this figure varies greatly depending upon a number of factors (e.g. availability of specialist provision in the local area, and presence or absence of additional learning difficulties) (Humphrey and Parkinson, 2006). Mainstream education of children with ASD may be less likely in certain Asia-Pacific regions. In China for instance, where the diagnosis of ASD is a relatively recent phenomenon (and where special education services are still developing); many parents report that their children are refused entry into public schools (McCabe, 2007).

Around 21 per cent of students with ASD are excluded from school at least once (National Autistic Society, 2003). This is a significantly higher rate than students with other special education needs (SEN), and 20 times that experienced by students without SEN (Department for Education and Skills, 2006). Furthermore, teachers in mainstream schools report that they do not have the necessary training and support to provide adequately for such students (Robertson *et al.*, 2003). This problem is also reflected in parts of the Asia-Pacific region. For instance, Aluri (2002) reported on the lack of availability of specialist training and support for children with ASD in Bangalore City. Current practices within mainstream schools may, therefore, contribute to disaffection and social exclusion in these students. Furthermore, such children also tend to experience a high degree of bullying and social isolation (National Autistic Society, 2006b) and it is perhaps not surprising that they are at an increased risk of developing mental health problems as a consequence. In light of this, parents' confidence in the effectiveness of inclusion diminishes as students with ASD progress through the different phases of education. Recent research conducted in the United Kingdom (Humphrey and Lewis, 2008) suggests that the students themselves generally find school to be a stressful and anxiety-provoking place, particularly at secondary school level.

Strategies and approaches to facilitate the inclusion of students with ASD

The ideas and strategies that follow are based upon research and professional knowledge in this area. They are all based upon the principle that by creating a better fit between the school environment and the student with ASD, we are creating opportunities for him or her to succeed. Consider the insightful words of a young man with ASD:

> People with AS (Asperger's Syndrome) are like salt water fish that are forced to live in fresh water. We're fine if you just put us into the right environment. When the person with AS and the environment *match*, the problems go away and we even thrive. When they don't match, we seem disabled.
>
> (Baron-Cohen, 2003, p. 180).

Challenge stereotypes and raise expectations

A good place to start is to take some time to consider your pre-conceived notions and expectations of students on the autistic spectrum. Most of us have an idea of how we expect a person with ASD to behave, but all too often we have only basic templates to work from, often imposing stigmas and stereotypes to the diagnostic labels that are applied. As Singer (1999) argues, the autistic spectrum is often, "associated in the public mind with images of rocking, emotionally cut off, intellectually impaired children and 'Rainman'-like savants" (p. 63). Every person with ASD is different, and it is important to look beyond the label, such that students do not become "defined by their diagnosis" (Molloy and Vasil, 2002, p. 661). If we fail to see past the label our expectations of what a child is capable of are bound to be lowered. There is evidence to suggest that this can have a knock-on effect on a child's view of him or herself – leading to a self-fulfilling prophecy. In a recent study about life in mainstream school a student with ASD told us:

> I'd prefer they didn't know because everyone treats me differently and I don't like being treated differently. But I don't like being treated differently as though as if I'm retarded but.... That's how some look at it is that I'm retarded and I really don't like that, it really bugs me.
>
> (Humphrey and Lewis, 2008)

Create order from chaos

Most students with ASD show a strong preference for routine and predictability. Indeed, this preference is etched into the diagnostic criteria for ASD (e.g. adherence to specific...routines or rituals, APA, 2000). This puts them at odds with the noisy, bustling and often chaotic environment of the average school, particularly the average high school (Humphrey and Lewis, 2008; Moore, 2007). As a result, the school environment itself can be a considerable source of anxiety. In the aforementioned study of life in school, one student told us, *"I'm upset every second, every second I've got tears in my eyes"*. When faced with such anxiety, students struggle to access the curriculum. Another student wrote in his diary,

"In English there was so much noise. I just wanted the class to be quiet and I can get on with my work". There is, however, evidence of simple adaptations that can be made to help students cope with this aspect of school life. For instance, one school in our recent study routinely selected quiet, well-behaved classes for students with ASD who had particular difficulties coping with noise and disruption. In other schools there were often certain areas (such as resource rooms or libraries) that were used as a refuge for students wanting to escape the chaos of the corridor. Another way to help students feel more at ease with the school environment is to create a schedule that allows them to know the daily routine and be aware, in advance, of what events will be happening on a given day.

Promote peer understanding

The relationships students with ASD have with their peers can be both a barrier and an enabler to their successful inclusion in school. In our recent study, nearly all students reported being bullied at different levels of severity and frequency. One student told us: *"People in my class know about my autism at school that's why they likely pick on me".* Although it is already recognized that those with special education needs are more likely to be bullied than other students (e.g. Norwich and Kelly, 2004), it may be argued the difficulties in communication and interaction experienced by those with ASD place them at an even higher risk. Their behavior is often seen as odd by other children, making them an immediate target. They may also lack the necessary resilience to help them overcome the problems associated with being bullied, and the thought of school itself can become distressing. In the short term, this can mean that such students experience increasing levels of social isolation, and, indeed, we found evidence of this with our sample.

The social isolation and bullying experienced by students with ASD can be counteracted by support from (and often enduring friendships with) peers. One student stated, *"I do have friends who very often stick up for me"*. The importance of such support in facilitating a positive sense of self (and therefore increasing resilience to feelings of depression) cannot be overstated: *"Yeah if people are nice to you, you feel better. When I was in school when people didn't like me it was rubbish and now many more people like me it's easier".* How might one go about promoting more positive peer relationships? Gus (2000) suggests that Circles of Friends (CoF) activities can be a successful strategy. Circles of Friends works by building relationships around vulnerable children to establish support networks that then develop into natural friendships. In this case, there may be a particular need to focus upon developing peer understanding of ASD. Educating peers about ASD in a CoF framework is also useful because it challenges the attitudes and stereotypes they often hold about the condition.

Develop social skills

Students with ASD often struggle to understand the unwritten rules that permeate everyday social interactions. Myles and Simpson (2001) refer to this as the hidden curriculum, i.e. a set of skills that are not taught directly but are taken for granted in schools and everyday life. An example of such a skill can be seen in body language. The majority of people understand that when speaking to a peer, we tend to keep our hands to ourselves, maintain a small distance (thereby respecting their personal space), and do not usually need to speak too loudly (Betts *et al.*, 2007). This type of implicit knowledge about the way we govern social interactions may be lacking in students with ASD and as a consequence it may need to be explicitly taught.

One increasingly popular way in which such understanding and skills can be taught is through social stories. A social story

> ... describes a situation, skill, or concept in terms of relevant social cues, perspectives, and common responses in a specifically defined style and format. The goal of a social story is to share accurate social information in a patient and reassuring manner that is easily understood by its audience.
>
> (Gray, 2007)

Thus, they are a means of enabling students with ASD to understand the difficult and complex social world in which they find themselves, presented in a format that is appealing to their preferred ways of learning (hence the emphasis on structure). Social stories can be tailored to any skill, situation or concept desired. All social stories include three key types of sentences: descriptive, directive and perspective. Descriptive sentences define a situation/event and introduce characters and their roles (e.g. "The bell rings for students to come in from lunch. The students go to their classroom where the teacher reads a story."). Perspective sentences provide information regarding the internal states of characters (e.g. "When the bell rings for lunch to end, the teacher is happy to see all the students line up quietly and walk to their classroom. Many students are excited that they get to hear a story. The teacher likes to see the students listen. The teacher likes it when students are quiet during the story."). Directive sentences define what is expected in response to a particular cue or behavior (e.g. "I am playing during lunch. The bell rings for me to come in. I stop playing and line up to come in. I follow the other students and quietly go to the classroom. When we get to the classroom, I go to my desk and sit down. I listen as my teacher reads a story.") (Howley and Arnold, 2005). Additional cues, such as photographs, can be used to provide contextual information for the student.

Writing social stories to use with a student with ASD is by no means the only way of developing their social skills, but it is an empirically validated and widely used approach. Whatever the approach taken, Krasny *et al.* (2003) recommend that educators need to incorporate several key principles, including:

1 make the abstract concrete, e.g. by providing visual cues and prompts;
2 provide structure and predictability, e.g. by using consistent opening and closing formats;

3. provide scaffolded language support, e.g. providing language models and scripts;
4. provide multiple and varied learning opportunities, e.g. using multisensory techniques;
5. include other focused activities, e.g. by highlighting peers' preferences and interests;
6. program in a sequential and progressive manner, e.g. simplifying complex behaviors into specific skills; and
7. provide opportunities for generalization, e.g. by providing activities that can be carried out in the home as well as in school.

Adapt academic subjects

Like all other children, students with ASD are entitled to a broad and balanced curriculum. The typical pattern of strengths and weaknesses experienced by such students do present teachers with a particular set of challenges in making that curriculum accessible, but these can be viewed as an opportunity to help ensure the success of all students.

Modify conversational language

Students with ASD tend to understand and use language in a very literal manner (Welton, 2004). As such, any non-literal use of language (e.g. metaphors, figures of speech) can be problematic for them. This is compounded by the fact that we use so many metaphors and figures of speech in our everyday interactions with students. For example, students who are not doing enough work might be told by a teacher, "Pull your socks up!" A student who has been in trouble a lot but is being given another chance by his school might be asked to, "Turn over a new leaf". These and the countless other examples of non-literal use of language are embedded in our daily interactions with others. For a student with ASD, a literal interpretation of such metaphors can often be interpreted as a sign of insolence or worse (consider, for example, how you might react to a student who bends down and physically pulls his/her socks up instead of actually doing what you expected and working harder).

It is important, therefore, for teachers to consider carefully their use of language in their interactions with students with ASD. Other pragmatic aspects of language also need to be considered, e.g. the use of sarcasm or irony, where the meaning intended by the speaker is modified by the tone and pitch of their voice. In addition to modifying our conversational language, there are strategies that can be used to help students gain a better understanding of these difficult aspects of language use. For example, resources are available that provide explanations of the meaning of metaphors in a structured, concrete and visual way. Welton (2004) suggests that to understand a metaphor, students with ASD need to know what was *said* (e.g. "Keep it under your hat."), what was *meant* (e.g. if you are told something and then asked to keep it under your hat, you are being asked not to tell anyone else), and given examples of appropriate use (e.g. "I'm looking for a new job, but I don't want my boss to find out yet. So, please keep it under your hat."). In addition, it may also be useful to explain *why* a certain metaphor is used (e.g. if you physically keep something under your hat it means that other people cannot see it).

Strategies and approaches to facilitate the inclusion of students with ADHD

As in the previous section, the ideas and strategies that follow are based upon research and professional knowledge in this area. Again, they are all based upon the principle that by creating a better fit between the school environment and the student, we are creating opportunities for him or her to succeed. Like students with ASD, those with ADHD often experience difficulties in mainstream classrooms and schools because the emphasis on meeting common needs means that their specific group needs are not addressed (Cooper, 2005).

Reframe ADHD

Cooper (2005) suggests that a useful strategy to aid the development of inclusive practice for students with ADHD is to reframe the way we view the concept itself. In particular, he suggests that if we view it as a particular cognitive style rather than a deficit, the logical corollary is that we begin to develop pedagogical strategies that exploit, rather than inhibit the common characteristics of such students. For instance, students are reported to be somewhat verbose, talking at inappropriate times. This aspect can be exploited by designing lessons that allow increased opportunities for verbal participation. The need to keep such verbal participation on task can be facilitated by adapting seating arrangements within the classroom, such as by seating students in a semi circle around a teacher or in small groups. Furthermore, the fact that students with ADHD struggle to sustain their attention over time more so than other students can be used as an opportunity to restructure lessons such that seatwork is punctuated by frequent periods of other, different activities. Research has shown that this kind of approach can lead to decreases in disruptive behavior and increases in on-task behavior (Pellegrini and Horvat, 1995). If sustained periods of seatwork are unavoidable, physical activities that can be carried out at the student's desk (e.g. squeezing a ball) are reported to be beneficial in helping to maintain focus.

Another corollary of a reframing of ADHD is that the practice of typing described by Cooper (2005), although still evident, is much more likely to relate to *positive* expectations regarding ability, behavior, motivation, etc. This in turn will make for better staff–student relationships and a positive classroom ethos. Such a change in focus may be difficult to achieve, and indeed may represent a major paradigm shift for many teachers. Recent research by Ghanizadeh *et al.* (2006), has demonstrated that more tolerant and positive attitudes towards students with ADHD are associated with levels of knowledge of ADHD amongst teachers, suggesting that training to increase knowledge may need to be a priority if subsequent shifts in attitudes and practice are to occur.

Understand the role of medication

Since up to 75 per cent of students with ADHD are prescribed stimulant medication (Virginia Department of Health, 2003), it is important for their teachers to develop an understanding of the role it plays in their students' lives, and the subsequent implications for education. Indeed, teachers play at least two pivotal roles in relation to medication. First, they can provide detailed information that will help in the assessment that leads up to the prescription of medication; second, they should take an active role in monitoring the effects of medication observed in the classroom. Over and above these roles, a better understanding of the effects of stimulant medication, what it can and cannot do, how it is likely to impact upon a given student's behavior, etc., will enable the teacher to plan his/her pedagogical strategies in a way that takes these factors into account.

A key starting point is that medication should never be used as the sole means of intervention for a student with ADHD; thus, a student being prescribed Ritalin does not exonerate us of the responsibility for adapting our pedagogical approaches to better meet their needs. Stimulant medication takes effect very quickly, but its influence may not last throughout the school day. A range of factors including the individual student, type of stimulant, and dosage will influence the effects of the medication, but it is important to note that it will typically have differential effects on domains of functioning. For instance, its effects on behavior (in terms of activity level) are typically longer lasting than its effects on cognition (in terms of attention). As such, even though a medicated student may not be up and out of his/her seat or blurting out answers as much as usual, they may still not be accessing the curriculum because they are still struggling to maintain their focus on the material presented. Furthermore, medication may cause side effects (such as increased anxiety) that provide further barriers to learning and participation (Cooper and Ideus, 1996). Finally, although medication may be effective in managing the core difficulties experienced by those with ADHD (inattention, hyperactivity, impulsivity), it is less useful in alleviating secondary problems, such as social isolation and academic underachievement (Doggett, 2004).

Minimize distractions

Students with ADHD have a lower threshold for distraction than other students. As such, it is important to create a classroom environment that accommodates this difference whenever possible. For example, the student may need to be given preferential seating in a place that is as free from distraction as possible, e.g. away from doors and windows (Cooper and Ideus, 1996), and in an area of the classroom with a direct line of sight to the teacher (although not necessarily *directly* in front of the teacher's desk since this may be considered a punitive measure by other students and could therefore draw further unnecessary attention to the student's differences) (Levine, 2002a). This will mean that the teacher can easily monitor and reinforce a student's on-task behavior.

Although students with ADHD may have a greater need for quietness than other students to help them maintain their attention, it is important to note that having a classroom that is devoid of any sensory stimulation can also create difficulties. In such circumstances, students can become distracted by their own thoughts. What needs to be achieved, therefore, is what we might refer to as an optimal level of stimulation, wherein unnecessary distractions are removed but tasks and activities provided are still varied and rousing, enough to maintain students' interests (Levine, 2002b).

Provide predictability, structure and routine

Students with ADHD will benefit from being provided with a clear structure to each *day*, *lesson* and *task*. This is particularly crucial given recent research evidence that suggests a core underlying difficulty may be related to temporal perception (Smith *et al.*, 2002). At the level of the school day, dividing into broad units of time will make it seem more manageable to the student. At the level of each lesson, the Department of Education (2006) suggests that teachers need to provide a consistent structure that involves a routine of introducing the lesson, conducting the lesson and concluding the lesson. Whilst this basic structure may seem like common sense (it is!), the detail is critical regarding what kinds of instructional practice within each component will aid students. When introducing lessons, it is useful to:

(i) review the previous lesson (e.g. remind them of what the key topics and concepts were, and explain how they link to the current lesson);
(ii) provide an advance organizer (e.g. talk students through the order of the various activities planned for the current lesson);
(iii) set learning expectations (e.g. make clear what and how they will learn);
(iv) set behavioral expectations (e.g. what is and is not acceptable, and how and when this could change during the lesson, such as that talking with other students is acceptable during a group activity, but not during an end of lesson test);
(v) state needed materials and resources (e.g. what will students need to complete the various activities? Where can they find these materials?); and
(vi) simplify instructions and choices (e.g. ensure that you communicate in a clear, uncomplicated manner).

(Department of Education, 2006, p. 4).

In relation to the conduct of a lesson, the concordance of research regarding the typical learning styles of students with ADHD suggests that they learn more effectively when they are able to actively experiment and are presented with concrete examples that are visual in nature (Brand *et al.*, 2002). Learning technologies that facilitate this style of learning, such as the use of overhead projectors, computers etc., should, therefore, be an integral part of lessons. Any directions given to the class should be followed up (either orally, or in writing on a white-board) and clarified to ensure that the student has understood what he/she is required to do. Lessons with frequent but short breaks between activities are also to be encouraged.

In relation to concluding a lesson, the Department of Education (2006) suggests that teachers of students with ADHD need to provide advance warnings (5 or 10 minutes prior to the end) of how much time remains in a lesson, check assignments and work, and preview the next lesson (e.g. give students a brief overview of the topic and any resources they will need). Such practices will help to circumvent the difficulties with transitioning that many students experience.

Although the nature of tasks and activities within lessons inevitably varies according to a wide range of factors (e.g. subject, resources available), there are some key design principles that can be applied to facilitate the learning of students with ADHD:

1 All tasks need to be broken down into small, manageable chunks as this helps to accommodate the shorter attention span of such students.
2 It may also be useful to provide models of completed work to provide a visual prompt of the goal for a task.
3 Key information should be highlighted (e.g. keywords or instructions on a worksheet presented in bold or in a different color) wherever possible, thus helping students who experience difficulties in selective attention (e.g. knowing what information to select for processing).
4 Over time, students can be taught to practice drawing focus to key information themselves.

Apply cognitive and behavioral strategies

Behavioral strategies use principles of reinforcement and punishment to reduce maladaptive behaviors and increase adaptive behaviors. Once a dominant force in education, the behavioral paradigm has fallen out of favor recently, but key techniques based on these principles do have a convincing evidence base. Indeed, a review of some 150 intervention studies (a large proportion of which were behavioral in nature) reported that such approaches can be successful in establishing behaviors conducive to classroom learning for students with ADHD (Fiore *et al.*, 1993). Within the range of specific approaches that are underpinned by behavioral principles, the authors concluded that there were three (*positive reinforcement*, where appropriate behavior is immediately rewarded, *behavior reduction strategies*, such as reprimands and redirection, and *response cost*, a form of punishment in which something important is taken away after an undesired behavior takes place) that appeared to be the most effective. This conclusion has been ratified by more recent research (e.g. Root and Resnick, 2003). However, Purdie *et al.* (2002) caution that: "Consequences or contingencies for ADHD children generally need to be more immediate, powerful, tangible, and frequent than those that teachers often use in their everyday work with other children in the classroom" (p. 67). It has also been observed that generalization can be problematic when behavioral approaches are used.

Cognitive-behavioral approaches emphasize reinforcement principles to alter thoughts or cognitions related to ADHD behaviors. In particular, they focus on the way internalized speech serves to regulate behavior. Students are taught to use self-talk, self-instruction, self-monitoring and self-reinforcement to develop self-control of their attention and impulsive behavior problems. Simple examples of the application of such techniques in the classroom include teaching children to subvocalize (e.g. repeating a piece of key information under their breath to help them maintain their focus on it), use self-testing strategies (e.g. when reading, students are encouraged to stop at key points and ask themselves questions about what they have just read), and use self-reinforcement (e.g. giving themselves praise for achieving targets, such as staying on-task for a specified period of time). A review of cognitive-behavioral approaches (Ervin *et al.*, 1996) concluded that they can be successful in achieving behavior change, but that they are more effective when combined with behavioral contingencies in the natural environment.

Conclusion

The overall aim of this chapter was to provide a current overview of evidence-based strategies that can be used by teachers to facilitate the inclusion of students with ADHD and ASD. In concluding this chapter, it is important for me to state that I have only covered the tip of the iceberg in this area. There are many books and websites produced each year on inclusive education, special education needs, ADHD and ASD that provide far more detail than I ever could in a single chapter, and I would encourage interested readers to seek these out (see Section 3 recommendations for further reading). Second, you may also have noted that the recommendations made in the latter half of this chapter are focused very much in and around the classroom. I have adopted this approach in the interests of brevity, but it is crucial to note that inclusion does not begin and end in the immediate school environment. Booth and Ainscow (2000) suggest that inclusive practices need to be underpinned by the production of inclusive *policies* and the creation of inclusive *communities and cultures.* As such, partnership with parents and the wider community within which a school resides are important elements of any attempts to promote the learning and participation of students.

The final, and perhaps most important point, is that inclusion is not reducible to a recipe of teaching tips. None of the strategies outlined here or elsewhere are likely to be successful unless they are underpinned by core values and attitudes that include respect for (and celebration of) diversity, a commitment to reaching out to all learners, a philosophy of excellence for all, and the notion that inclusion is a *process* rather than a *state* (Humphrey *et al.*, 2006). This is true for the Asia-Pacific context just as much as it is in Western educational settings, for although there may be differences in culture, language, etc., ultimately our goal as educators must be the same.

References

Aluri, U. (2002) "Rehabilitation facilities available for children with autism/PDD in Bangalore city: A survey", *Asia-Pacific Disability Rehabilitation Journal*, 13: 1–7.

American Psychiatric Association (2000) *Diagnostic and Statistical Manual of Mental Disorders*, (4th edn, revised), Washington, DC.

Asia-Pacific Development Centre on Disabilities (2007) *Country Profile*. Online. Available at: http://www.apcdproject.org (accessed 21 June 2007).

Bagwell, C. L., Molina, B. S. G., Pelham, W. E. and Hoza, B. (2001) "ADHD and problems in peer relations: Predictions from childhood to adolescence", *Journal of the American Academy of Child and Adolescent Psychiatry*, 40: 1285–92.

Baron-Cohen, S. (2003) *The Essential Difference: Men, Women and the Extreme Male Brain*, London: Penguin.

Betts, S. W., Betts, D. E. and Gerber-Eckard, L. N. (2007) *Asperger Syndrome in the Inclusive Classroom*, London: Jessica Kingsley.

Booth, T. and Ainscow, M. (2000) *Index for Inclusion*, Bristol: Centre for Studies in Inclusive Education.

Bradshaw, L. and Mundia, L. (2006) "Attitudes to and concerns about inclusive education: Bruneian inservice and preservice teachers", *International Journal of Special Education*, 21: 35–41.

Brand, S., Dunn, R. and Greb, F. (2002) "Learning styles of students with attention deficit hyperactivity disorder: Who are they and how can we teach them?", *Clearing House*, 75: 268–73.

Cooper, P. (2005) "ADHD", in A. Lewis and B. Norwich (eds), *Special Teaching for Special Children?*, Buckingham: Open University Press, pp. 123–37.

Cooper, P. and Ideus, K. (1996) *ADHD: A Practical Guide for Teachers*, London: David Fulton.

Department for Education and Skills (2006) *Permanent and Fixed period Exclusions from Schools and Exclusion Appeals in England 2004/05*, Nottingham: DfES Publications.

Department of Education (2006) *Teaching Children with ADHD: Instructional Strategies and Practices*, Washington, DC.

Doggett, A. M. (2004) "ADHD and drug therapy: Is it still a valid treatment?" *Journal of Child Health Care*, 8: 69–81.

Ervin, R. A., Bankert, C. L. and DuPaul, G. J. (1996) "Treatment of attention-deficit/hyperactivity disorder", in M. A. Reinecke and F. M. Dattilio (eds), *Cognitive Therapy with Children and Adolescents: A Casebook for Clinical Practice*, New York: Guildford Press, pp. 38–61.

Fiore, T. A., Becker, E. A. and Nero, R. C. (1993) *Research Synthesis on Education Interventions for Students with ADD*, Research Triangle Park, NC: Research Triangle Institute.

Forlin, C. (2006) "Inclusive education in Australia ten years after Salamanca", *European Journal of Psychology of Education*, 21: 265–77.

Forlin, C. (2007) "Classroom diversity: Towards a whole school approach", in S. N. Phillipson (ed.), *Learning Diversity in the Chinese Classroom: Contexts and Practice for Students with Special Needs*, Hong Kong: Hong Kong University Press, pp. 95–123.

Ghanizadeh, A., Bahredar, M. J. and Moeini, S. R. (2006) "Knowledge and attitudes towards ADHD among elementary school teachers", *Patient Education and Counselling*, 63: 84–8.

Gomez, R. (2007) "Australian parent and teacher ratings of the DSM-IV ADHD symptoms", *Journal of Attention Disorders*, 11: 17–27.

Gray, C. (2007) *What is a social story?*. Online. Available at: http://www.thegraycenter.org (accessed May 2007).

Green, H., McGinnity, A., Meltzer, H., Ford, T. and Goodman, R. (2005) *Mental Health of Children and Young People in Great Britain, 2004*, London: Office for National Statistics.

Gus, L. (2000) "Autism: Promoting peer understanding", *Educational Psychology in Practice*, 16: 461–68.

Honda, H., Shimizu, Y., Misumi, K., Niimi, M. and Ohashi, Y. (1996) "Cumulative incidence and prevalence of childhood autism in children in Japan", *British Journal of Psychiatry*, 169: 228–35.

Howley, M. and Arnold, E. (2005) *Revealing the Hidden Social Code*, London: Jessica Kingsley.

Hughes, L. (2007) "The reality of living with ADHD: Children's concern about educational and medical support", *Emotional and Behavioural Difficulties*, 12: 69–80.

Humphrey, N. and Lewis, S. (2008) "'Make me normal': The views and experiences of pupils on the autistic spectrum in mainstream secondary schools", *Autism: An International Journal of Research and Practice*, 12: 23–46.

Humphrey, N. and Parkinson, G. (2006) "Research on interventions for children and young people on the autistic spectrum: A critical perspective", *Journal of Research in Special Educational Needs*, 6: 76–86.

Humphrey, N., Bartolo, P., Ale, P., Calleja, C., Hofaess, T., Janikova, V., Lous, A. M., Vilkiene, V. and Wetso, G. M. (2006) "Understanding and responding to diversity in the primary classroom: An international study", *European Journal of Teacher Education*, 29: 305–18.

Krasny, L., Williams, B. J., Provencal, S. and Ozonoff, S. (2003) "Social skills interventions for the autism spectrum: Essential ingredients and a model curriculum", *Child and Adolescent Psychiatric Clinics of North America*, 12: 107–22.

Leung, P. W. L., Luk, S. L., Ho, T. P., Taylor, E., Mak, F. L. and Bacon-Shone, J. (1996) "The diagnosis and prevalence of ADHD in Chinese schoolboys", *Journal of the American Academy of Child and Adolescent Psychiatry*, 28: 497–500.

Levine, M. (2002a) *Developing Minds: Attention*, Boston, MA: WGBH/All Kinds of Minds.

Levine, M. (2002b) *A Mind at a Time*, New York: Simon and Schuster.

Lynch, J. (1994) *Provision for Children with Special Educational Needs in the Asia Region*, World Bank Technical Paper 261, Washington, DC: The World Bank.

McCabe, H. (2007) "Parent advocacy in the face of adversity: Autism and families in the People's Republic of China", *Focus on Autism and Developmental Disabilities*, 22: 39–50.

Molloy, H. and Vasil, L. (2002) "The social construction of Asperger Syndrome: The pathologising of difference?", *Disability and Society*, 17: 659–69.

Moore, C. (2007) "Speaking as a parent: Thoughts about educational inclusion for autistic children", in Cigman, R. (ed.), *Included or Excluded? The Challenge of Mainstream for Some SEN Children*, London: Routledge, pp. 34–41.

Myles, B. S. and Simpson, R. L. (2001) "Understanding the hidden curriculum: An essential social skill for children and youth with Asperger Syndrome", *Intervention in School and Clinic*, 5: 279–86.

National Autistic Society (2003) *Autism and Education: The Ongoing Battle*, London.

National Autistic Society (2006a) *How Many People Have Autistic Spectrum Disorders?*, London.

National Autistic Society (2006b) *B is for Bullied*, London.

Norris, C. and Lloyd, G. (2000) "Parents, professionals and ADHD: What the papers say", *European Journal of Special Needs Education*, 15: 123–37.

Norvitilis, J. M. and Fang, P. (2005) "Perceptions of ADHD in China and the United States: A preliminary study", *Journal of Attention Disorders*, 9: 413–24.

Norwich, B. and Kelly, N. (2004) "Pupils' views on inclusion: Moderate learning difficulties and bullying in mainstream and special schools", *British Educational Research Journal*, 30: 43–65.

Pellegrini, A. and Horvat, M. (1995) "A developmental contextualist critique of ADHD", *Educational Researcher*, 24: 13–20.

Phares, V. (2003) *Understanding Abnormal Child Psychology*, Hoboken, NJ: John Wiley & Sons.

Place, M., Wilson, J., Martin, E. and Hulsmeier, J. (2000) "The frequency of emotional and behavioral disturbance in an EBD school", *Child Psychology and Psychiatry Review*, 5: 76–80.

Purdie, N., Hattie, J. and Carroll, A. (2002) "A review of research on interventions for ADHD: What works best?", *Review of Educational Research*, 72: 61–99.

Reid, R., Hakendorf, P. and Prosser, B. (2002) "Use of psychostimulant medication for ADHD in South Australia", *Journal of the American Academy of Child and Adolescent Psychiatry*, 41: 906–13.

Reid, R., Maag, J. W., Vasa, S. F. and Wright, G. (1994) "Who are the children with ADHD? A school-based survey", *Journal of Special Education*, 28: 117–37.

Robertson, K., Chamberlain, B. and Kasari, C. (2003) "General education teachers' relationships with included students with autism", *Journal of Autism and Developmental Disorders*, 33: 123–30.

Root, R. W. and Resnick, R. J. (2003) "An update on the diagnosis and treatment of attention deficit/hyperactivity disorder in children", *Professional Psychology: Research and Practice*, 34: 34–41.

Singer, J. (1999) "Why can't you be normal for once in your life? From a 'problem with no name' to a new category of difference", in M. Corker and S. French (eds), *Disability Discourse*, Buckingham: Open University Press, pp. 59–67.

Smith, A., Taylor, E., Rogers, J. W., Newman, S. and Rubia, K. (2002) "Evidence for a pure time perception deficit in children with ADHD", *Journal of Child Psychology and Psychiatry*, 43: 529–42.

Subban, P. and Sharma, U. (2006) "Primary school teachers' perceptions of inclusive education in Victoria, Australia", *International Journal of Special Education*, 21: 42–52.

Virginia Department of Health (2003) *The Prevalence of Methylphenidate and Amphetamine Prescriptions in the Commonwealth*, Richmond, VA.

Watling, R. (2004) "Helping them out: The role of teachers and healthcare professionals in the exclusion of pupils with special educational needs", *Emotional and Behavioural Difficulties*, 9: 8–27.

Welton, J. (2004) *What Did You Say? What Do You Mean? An Illustrated Guide to Understanding Metaphors*, London: Jessica Kingsley.

West, J., Taylor, M., Houghton, S. and Hudyma, S. (2005) “A comparison of teachers’ and parents’ knowledge and beliefs about ADHD”, *School Psychology International*, 26: 192–208.

Wilkin, A., Archer, T., Ridley, K., Fletcher-Campbell, A. and Kinder, K. (2005) *Admissions and Exclusions of Pupils with Special Educational Needs*, Research Report RR608, Nottingham: DfES Publications.

16 Transition for students with disabilities

Christie Gilson and Ming-Gon John Lian

Chapter objectives

- To discuss the services provided to students with disabilities as they transition from secondary school to adult life.
- To recognize the positive aspects and potential challenges of transition services.
- To propose promising practices for developing transition programs and services for youth with disabilities in the Asia-Pacific region.

Focus questions

1. How can teachers assist students with disabilities as they transition from secondary school to adult life?
2. What skills should students with disabilities possess when transitioning to adulthood?
3. Which components of transition listed in this chapter are most relevant to students with disabilities from your country?

Introduction

What opportunities are available for students with disabilities after they complete their senior secondary school in the Asia-Pacific region? Practitioners as well as parents of these students frequently worry about post-secondary life, and some even indicate the concern that these young people may end up going nowhere after school. Many regions have begun to seriously consider transition issues for students with disabilities as they start to provide extended years of study for them in secondary schools. For example, starting in 2003, the Hong Kong Government supported the Extended Year of Education (EYE) program, mainly for the purpose of providing 24 months of additional education programs for 14–16-year-old students that focus on transition [Education and Manpower Bureau (EMB), 2007].

Recently, Hong Kong's education reform has also moved towards changing the academic structure to include a new senior secondary (NSS) curriculum that emphasizes career-oriented study (COS) and experience-based learning. This is being developed for all students and includes a special NSS–Intellectual Disability curriculum for those with special education needs (EMB, 2006). The purpose of this chapter is to consider effective services employed internationally for students with disabilities as they transition from secondary school to adult life, including: the challenges and positive aspects; ways teachers can assist; skills that need to be developed in students; and related issues. In particular, both the EYE and NSS curricula and current programs employed in Hong Kong can benefit from a review of successful transition examples from the USA. This comparison will be used to consider transition programs that are especially appropriate for the Asia-Pacific region.

Development of transition services for students with disabilities

The development of transition services for students with disabilities to enable them to progress from school to the community has been rather slow to build up in many countries. While the construct of transition gained widespread popularity when suggested by the US Department of Education in the early 1980s, at that time the idea of transition applied mainly to employment outcomes. Similarly, early transition planning in most Western countries has continued to focus mainly on preparation for work. It is only in the most recent years that transition planning is being written into policy and legislation in Western countries where more current definitions of transition also now cover a wider scope of goals beyond employment.

In the Asian-Pacific region there has been little emphasis to date on the issue of transition, as opportunities for work are almost non-existent in the mainstream workforce for school leavers with disabilities. In addition, most children with disabilities have either not had the chance to attend school or have left well before senior secondary. Most preparation, when available, has focused on life-skills training to prepare students for working in sheltered workshops or similar industries.

Although it has been suggested that "the transition from 'child' to 'adult' status is viewed as an important achievement within society" (Mitchell, 1999, p. 753), this is not always the case for those with disabilities. Mitchell does acknowledge that "it is a complex, involved process, which evolves over a period of time" (p. 753). Clearly, it is possible to see how the stages of evolvement differ between the West and the Asian-Pacific region and it is also possible to use this as a way of considering how best to further the importance of transition issues in those regions that have not yet considered how to do this. If transition is characterized as a bridge between adolescence and young adulthood as proposed by Hudson (2006), and the purpose of transition for students with disabilities is that of integrating them into the community (Kinnison *et al.*, 2005), then there is much to be learned by the Asian-Pacific region from countries that have already attempted to do this.

Best practices in transition for students with disabilities

Taking the case of the USA as an example where transition planning has now been legislated in law, the following aspects of transition planning for students with disabilities are discussed in relation to how they might influence the development of future planning in the Asian-Pacific regions where such plans have not yet been instigated.

It has been found that student participation in transition planning is essential and is strongly encouraged by many researchers and government officials (Johnson *et al.*, 2002). Students' preferences and interests should be reflected in their transition plans (Heward, 2006). Although recognized as a crucial component of transition planning in the West, the applicability of self-determination to Asian cultures requires further study (Zhang *et al.*, 2005). Self-determination is defined by Field *et al.* (1998) as: "A combination of skills, knowledge, and beliefs that enable a person to engage in goal-directed, self-regulated, autonomous behavior" (p. 2). Field and Hoffman's (1994) model includes the following aspects: "Know Yourself, Value Yourself, Plan, Act and Experience" (p. 165).

Timelines are used throughout special education services to ensure that services for students with disabilities are delivered in an efficient manner. Transition services are no exception. The education program that is in effect when the student with a disability turns 16 in the United States for example, must contain a plan for transition under the current special education law (Heward, 2006).

The accountable, efficient service provision brought about by these timelines has changed the power dynamics present in the American model of transition. Students with disabilities and their parents may take legal action to ensure that schools comply with mandated transition timelines. Therefore, the authority that was traditionally vested in school administrators has shifted to include students with disabilities and their parents. Since objective third parties hear disputes between schools and parents of students with disabilities, fair judgments are often made. Rather than the use of the courts being characterized as shameful or undesirable, some of the most important antidiscrimination legislation in the United States has resulted from judicial rulings.

The specificity of American transition plans extends beyond timelines for service provision. Measurable goals related to employment, tertiary education, training and, where appropriate, independent living skills, should be written into the transition plan. Each time the transition plan is revisited, often annually, the goals written in the previous plan are examined to determine whether they have been met. Those that have been met are deleted from the next plan, but the components of any goals that have not yet been realized are addressed in the current plan. New goals deemed appropriate by members of the transition planning team are also generated and incorporated.

A list of services delivered by the school and other agencies collaborating to help the student achieve transition goals is written into the transition plan. Some outside service providers such as rehabilitation counselors, employers and adult service center staff are present during transition planning meetings to provide feedback related to adult services. These opportunities for networking serve many purposes, not the least of which is familiarizing students with disabilities and their parents with the differences between school-related services and those provided to adults with disabilities.

Components of transition services

Four components of transition are widely recognized as important within the academic literature (Thoma *et al.*, 2001). Clarification of these components and their importance in transition planning will provide a framework with which to compare the Asia-Pacific region of Hong Kong's transition services with those in the United States. Of course, cultural norms have influenced the development of these components in the United States and would similarly shape their provision in Hong Kong.

1 Procuring employment

First, procuring employment is the earliest component of transition recognized by policy-makers. In American society, which has been strongly influenced by the Judeo-Christian work ethic, employment is one of the central goals of any adult's life. Successful employment leads to economic self-sufficiency and residential independence. Despite the importance of employment for persons with disabilities, they continue to experience staggeringly high unemployment rates in the United States (Louis Harris & Associates, 2000). Many people with disabilities are still employed in sheltered workshops, in which they are paid much less than the minimum wage, and are rarely encouraged to transition to competitive employment settings. Thus, the importance of employment in transition planning cannot be overstated.

Similar situations exist in Hong Kong, with adult daycare and day training programs. Nevertheless, it is encouraging to find that, after the implementation of the "extended year education" in the past three years (EMB, 2007), the NSS curriculum (EMB, 2006) will have a focus on career-oriented study to go along with the reform in academic reform (i.e. to be changed to three years junior high school, three years senior high school, and four years tertiary education) for students with and without disabilities, and this will be implemented by 2009 [Curriculum Development Council and Hong Kong Examination and Assessment Authority (CDC and HKEAA), 2004; Lian, 2005].

2 Tertiary education and training

Second, tertiary education and training are seen as essential in today's service-oriented economy (National Council on Disability, 2003). Completion of a higher degree for persons with disabilities has been linked more highly with employment rates and income than for persons without disabilities (Jones, 2002). Individuals with disabilities have been attending tertiary educational institutions in the United States since their earliest existence. Since 1978, the percentage of college students self-identifying as having disabilities has quadrupled (Michaels *et al.*, 2002). The range of disabilities students have in tertiary education reflects the general population. Thus, in addition to students with more traditional sensory and mobility impairments, students with learning disabilities, attention-deficit hyperactivity disorder (ADHD), mental illnesses, intellectual disabilities, autism and multiple disabilities (Heward, 2006) have the opportunity to enroll in tertiary education in the United States.

The Equal Opportunity Ordinance (EOO) in Hong Kong helps to secure higher education opportunities for students with certain disabling conditions, such as visual, hearing and physical disabilities, as well as reading and writing difficulties. The advancements in assistive technology have increased the enrollment in post-secondary or tertiary institutions (Lian, 2005). However, further efforts are needed to make higher education a reality for students with special education needs, especially those who have severe and multiple disabilities, when they get to be involved in the new "three plus three plus four" academic structure.

3 Leisure and recreation activities

Third, as is the case with most adults without disabilities, those with disabilities engage in leisure and recreation activities. *The American Heritage Dictionary of the English Language* (2000) defines leisure as "Freedom from time-consuming duties, responsibilities, or activities." In contrast, recreation is defined by the same dictionary as "Refreshment of one's mind or body after work through activity that amuses or stimulates; play." Both the *Individuals with Disabilities Education Act* (IDEA) and the *Americans with Disabilities Act of 1990* (i.e. PL 101–336) stipulate that students and adults with disabilities should have access to recreation and leisure activities, especially if such activities are offered to the public in general. Engaging in recreational and leisure activities affords young adults with disabilities the opportunity to express their own choices and preferences – a key component of self-determination (Carter *et al.*, 2006). Typical leisure and recreation activities include individual and team sports, personal hobbies, social gatherings, community-based classes, fieldtrips, activities at local parks, arts and crafts, music and dance, and community theatre. These leisure and recreation activities can be categorized as active versus passive, structured versus non-structured, indoor or outdoor, and with versus without involvement of non-disabled peers.

Related transition and post-secondary programs for enhancing involvement of students with disabilities in inclusive leisure and recreational activities in Hong Kong are limited to those who have mild disabling conditions, while others may be included in isolated, center- or institution-based services.

4 Domestic and home-living

The fourth component widely recognized by transition experts are domestic and home-living skills and these are taught to young adults with disabilities in order to prepare them for functioning in their places of residence in as independent a manner as is desired. Wehman *et al.* (1985) define these skills as, "the activities that are engaged within the home (i.e. the place where an individual lives)" (p. 48). In fact, young adults who require more pervasive levels of support, such as those with more significant intellectual disabilities, may be able to access fewer living arrangement choices, should their domestic skills be lacking (Wehman *et al.*, 1985). Some group homes and other more autonomous living arrangements require that their residents are toilet trained, for example. Domestic and home-living skills include cooking, personal grooming, dressing (Wehman *et al.*, 1985), washing of laundry and house cleaning. A fairly recent curricular area addressed by educators is human sexuality education. Unfortunately, non-disabled caregivers are often reluctant to acknowledge the sexual needs of young adults with disabilities, especially when those disabilities are intellectual in nature (Whitehouse and McCabe, 1997).

Participation in one's community is an essential part of adult life. If the adult with a disability does not drive, learning how to safely access public transportation (Wehman *et al.*, 1985) in order to arrive at and return home from one's job is an essential skill. Purchasing groceries, mailing correspondence at the post office, accessing one's local recreational centers, and dining out are common activities engaged in by adults. For some transitioning young adults, many skills may need to be acquired before such activities can be fully engaged in.

The liberal study and elective components in the NSS curriculum for students with disabilities in Hong Kong may generally focus on self-help and daily-living skills, especially for those with severe disabling conditions. The post-secondary life is mainly in the model of adult daycare and day training services. Further follow-up investigation is needed to have a better picture about the potential of independent- and home-living, as well as participation in one's own community.

Questions to be addressed in transition planning

In order to provide an even more concrete idea of what transition plans may look like, Heward (2006) has suggested a set of questions that well-written transition plans should address in order to prepare students with disabilities for adult life:

- What are the student's dreams and vision of his life as a young adult?
- What are his strengths? How will he build on them to facilitate a successful transition?
- What skills does the student need to develop or improve to make progress toward her post-school goals?
- Will the student seek a regular high school diploma? If so, what course of study and proficiency tests will be required?
- Will she work toward a vocational certificate of completion instead of a regular diploma?
- Does he have an expressed career interest now? If not, what can the team do to help him explore career possibilities and discover his preferences?

- Is the student likely to remain in high school through the maximum age of eligibility for special education services? If so, what curriculum and work experiences will be needed after age 18?
- In what school and community activities will the student participate?

(Heward, 2006, p. 601)

Potential barriers to smooth transition

Numerous critiques of the current transition process as practiced in the United States have been identified in the academic literature. Hudson (2006) pinpointed several barriers to smooth transitions for students with learning disabilities in the United Kingdom, which also apply to students with many other disabilities and to those in the United States. Hudson suggests that competing priorities amongst service providers such as rehabilitation counselors, secondary school professionals, residential living staff and tertiary education institutions often result in fragmented service delivery (Dymond *et al.*, 2007). Parents and the students with disabilities themselves often fail to consider their future goals in time to adequately plan for transition. When students graduate from secondary school, therefore, the services designed to assist them in procuring employment, locating housing, and engaging in social activities are often not yet in place (Heward, 2006; Hudson, 2006).

Organizational turbulence and environmental complexity occur when agencies designed to provide transition services are keen to provide new, high-profile programs and services dictated by funders instead of those services most useful to transitioning youth (Hudson, 2006). Finally, some argue that skill deficits on the part of students with disabilities contribute to difficulties experienced when transitioning from adolescence to adulthood (Heward, 2006). This problem is perpetuated when such students choose to leave school before they obtain their secondary diplomas.

Future directions for the Asia-Pacific region

The promising practices and related implications mentioned above need to be considered when developing transition programs and services for youth with disabilities. This is especially urgent in regions such as Hong Kong where the academic structure will soon undergo reform i.e. the upward age extension in providing compulsory education for all students, with and without disabilities. The NSS curriculum has to go beyond the original EYE goals and program contents sponsored by the Education Department in the past three years (Lian, 2005). The goals of providing appropriate schemes of work and learning outcome frameworks for NSS students with disabilities will continue to be widely explored and discussed (CDC and HKEAA, 2004; EMB, 2006; Lian *et al.*, 2007). The core of career-oriented studies, liberal studies, electives, and experience-based learning content and strategies needs to be further studied and validated via research procedures with field trials, as well as to be compared with international models such as: the American transition model mentioned in this paper; the P-scale, PACE (i.e. the P-scales Assessment of the National Curriculum from EQUALS), and the EQUAL (i.e. Entitlement and Quality Education for Pupils with Severe Learning Difficulties) systems of the United Kingdom (Lian *et al.*, 2007); the Behavior Characteristics Progression (BCP) and Choosing Options and Accommodations for Children (COACH) packages of the United States; and the local Systematic Approach to Mainstream Education curriculum package. Future investigations need to be planned and carried out to validate the corresponding curriculum guides, schemes of work, learning outcome frameworks, and appropriate exit evaluation content and procedures, in order to achieve successful transition and, thus, improve the quality of life of students and adults with disabilities.

Conclusion

The transition experienced by young adults with disabilities from senior secondary school to adult life will continue to be fraught with challenges. Teachers and other service providers have an obligation to assist students with disabilities in negotiating this critical rite of passage. While promising practices from the United States have been identified in this paper, research-based practices for doing so in much of the Asia-Pacific region have yet to be disseminated in the academic literature. Until such time when best practices for transition in these regions are empirically validated, those from Western countries could be adapted for use in the Asia-Pacific Region.

References

Americans with Disabilities Act of 1990 (1991) PL 101–336, S 2, 104 Statute 32.

Carter, E. W., Lane, K. L., Pierson, M. R. and Glaeser, B. (2006) "Self determination skills and opportunities of transition-age youth with emotional disturbance and learning disabilities", *Exceptional Children*, 72: 333–46.

Curriculum Development Council and Hong Kong Examination and Assessment Authority (2004, October) *Proposed Core and Elective Subject Frameworks for the New Senior Secondary Curriculum*, Hong Kong: Education and Manpower Bureau.

Dymond, S. K., Gilson, C. L. and Myran, S. P. (2007) "Improving services for children with Autism Spectrum Disorders", *Journal of Disability Policy Studies*, 18: 133–47.

Education and Manpower Bureau (2006, August) *Action for the Future: Further Consultation on Career-Oriented Studies and the New Senior Secondary Academic Structure for Special Schools*, Hong Kong: The Government Logistics Department.

Education and Manpower Bureau (2007) *Curriculum Development on the Extension of Years of Education (EYE) Program for Students with Mental Handicaps*. Online. Available at: http://www.edb.gov.hk/ (accessed 5 October 2007).

Field, S. and Hoffman, A. (1994) "Development of a model for self-determination", *Career Development for Exceptional Individuals*, 17: 159–69.

Field, S., Martin, J., Miller, R., Ward, M. and Wehmeyer, M. L. (1998) *A Practical Guide for Teaching Self-Determination*, Reston, VA: Council for Exceptional Children.

Heward, W. L. (2006) *Exceptional Children: An Introduction to Special Education*, 8th edn, Upper Saddle River, NJ: Pearson Prentice Hall.

Hudson, B. (2006) "Making and missing connections: Learning disability services and the transition from adolescence to adulthood", *Disability and Society*, 21: 47–60.

Johnson, D. R., Stodden, R. A., Emanuel, E. L., Luecking, R. and Mack, M. (2002) "Current challenges facing secondary education and transition services: What research tells us", *Exceptional Children*, 68: 519–31.

Jones, M. (2002) *Providing a Quality Accommodated Experience in Preparation for and During Post-Secondary School. Minneapolis*, MN: National Center on Secondary Education and Transition (ERIC Document Reproduction Service No. ED466064).

Kinnison, R. L., Fuson, S. and Cates, D. (2005) "Rural transition: What are the limitations?" *Rural Special Education Quarterly*, 24: 1–10.

Lian, M-G. J. (2005, May) "Three plus three plus four: Advancing special education programs", *Centre for Advancement of Special Education (CASE) Newsletter*, 1(1): 3–6.

Lian, M-G. J., Tse, A. C. Y. and Li, M. C. A. (2007) "Special education in Hong Kong: Background, contemporary trends and issues in programs for learners with disabilities", *Journal of the International Association of Special Education*, 8(1): 5–19.

Louis Harris & Associates (2000) *The N.O.D. Harris Survey Program on Participation and Attitudes: Survey of Americans with Disabilities*, New York: Author.

Michaels, C. A., Pollock, F., Morabito, S. M. and Jackson, K. (2002) "Assistive and instructional technology for college students with disabilities: A national snapshot of postsecondary service providers", *Journal of Special Education Technology*, 17(1): 5–14.

Mitchell, W. (1999) "Leaving special school: The next step and future aspirations", *Disability & Society*, 14: 753–69.

National Council on Disability (2003) *People with Disabilities and Post-Secondary Education: Position Paper*. Online. Available at: http://ww.ncd.gov/newsroom/publications/ (accessed15 October 2003).

The American Heritage Dictionary of the English Language, 4th edn. (2000) Boston: Houghton Mifflin. Online. Available at: http://dictionary.reference.com/ (accessed 15 April 2006).

Thoma, C. A., Rogan, P. and Baker, S. R. (2001) "Student involvement in transition planning: Unheard voices", *Education and Training in Mental Retardation and Developmental Disabilities*, 36: 16–29.

Wehman, P., Renzaglia, A. and Bates, P. (1985) *Functional Living Skills for Moderately and Severely Handicapped Individuals* (pp. 45–72), Austin: Pro-Ed.

Whitehouse, M. A. and McCabe, M. P. (1997) "Sex education programs for people with intellectual disability: How effective are they?", *Education and Training in Mental Retardation and Developmental Disabilities*, 32: 229–40.

Zhang, D., Wehmeyer, M. L. and Chen, L.-J. (2005) "Parent and teacher engagement in fostering the self-determination of students with disabilities: A comparison between the United States and the Republic of China", *Remedial and Special Education*, 26: 55–64.

17 Inclusive education as a catalyst for special education reform in the Asia-Pacific region

Tim Loreman

Chapter objectives

- To consider the main themes identified in the preceding sections of this text.
- To comment on the Asia-Pacific region's relationship with itself and with the international community.
- To discuss the challenges for the Asia-Pacific region raised in preceding sections of this text.
- To raise for discussion some solutions to problems and possibilities for education reform in the Asia-Pacific region.

Focus questions

1 Which recurring themes are woven throughout various sections of this text?
2 How is teacher education linked to broader education reform?
3 What are the main challenges facing the Asia-Pacific region on the road to inclusive and special education reform?
4 How might these challenges be overcome?

Introduction

Using preceding chapters in the book as a foundation, this chapter comments on some of the major themes discussed and offers further reflections regarding inter-regional relationships, the Asia-Pacific region's relationship with the world, the need for progressive teacher education, and some of the unique challenges facing this region. Comments are made as to possible ways forward to more inclusive models of teaching and learning as education systems in the Asia-Pacific region undergo significant change in reform.

Inclusive education as a catalyst for education reform in the Asia-Pacific region

Each chapter of this book examines critical areas that must be addressed if meaningful education reform in the area of special education is to be achieved in the

Asia-Pacific region. To move forward, the Asia-Pacific countries must maintain a dialogue with the rest of the world, while at the same time retaining important and progressive aspects of their existing education systems. Policy and legislative support are required, along with practical support for schools and teachers in terms of resources and professional development, which help to ensure good practice. Positive attitudes towards the inclusion of children with disabilities in this part of the world must also be fostered and promoted both inside and outside the educational community, and especially in preservice teacher education. The task of education reform is large and complex, sometimes confounded and sometimes assisted by contextual variables, local views and practices. The chapters in this book clearly demonstrate that those looking for a quick fix for any given regional system will be disappointed. Rather, as in any part of the world, the journey towards education reform is likely to be lengthy and challenging. This process, however, might gather more momentum if education reform for inclusive and special education is seen as a catalyst for wider education reform in the Asia-Pacific region, rather than as a discrete field changing in isolation.

The chapters in Section 1 of this book address the need for law and policy in the area of special and inclusive education in the Asia-Pacific region, and also attempt to conceptualize what inclusion might look like. They highlight tensions between existing practice in the region, practice in Western countries, and international declarations and agreements. Indeed, these tensions are revisited a number of times in different chapters throughout the book. The need for international agreements to be implemented in a way in which local, cultural variables and values are taken into account is mentioned throughout this first section. This is of utmost importance. What works in one part of the world may not work in other parts of the world. It is, however, important for the Asia-Pacific region to remember that the goals of inclusive education as defined by the most influential international documents such as the Salamanca Statement (UNESCO, 1994a) are universal, and apply equally to this region as to elsewhere. Much of the Asia-Pacific region, including government and other representatives from China, India, Malaysia, the Philippines, Sri Lanka, Thailand, Bangladesh, and Japan joined over 300 delegates from 86 other nations from every region of the world in devising the Salamanca Statement (UNESCO, 1994b). In doing so they provided their tacit agreement with the notion of inclusive education as a universal right, which is desirable regardless of international barriers and cultural differences. It is important, then, that in adapting special education towards a more inclusive approach according to cultural contexts the Asia-Pacific region does not lose sight of its international obligations, and the basic principles behind inclusive education. This point may seem redundant; however, experience in Western countries has shown that in many situations the term "inclusion" has been used to describe a variety of education contexts that are clearly not inclusive, with the justification that they are adapting the philosophy to local contextual variables when, in reality, inclusion is being deliberately avoided (Loreman and Deppeler, 2002). For this reason, dialogue and engagement with the international community needs to continue in order to ensure the Asia-Pacific region progresses in a manner that is in keeping with the spirit of documents such as the Salamanca Statement, and the later Jomtein and Dakar (UNESCO, 1990, 2000) agreements, while at the same time negotiating practice within the local context.

Education systems in the Asia-Pacific region cannot simply copy and adopt, without modification, practices that are viewed as best practice in Western countries simply because they have seemed to work in that part of the world. Indeed, Xu in Chapter 4, has proffered an extremely viable alternative that seems to be working well so far in China. The value of identifying best practices and applying them across even similar cultural contexts (such as the United States) has been brought into question, and critics of this approach argue that best practices represent modernist, linear thinking, and in and of themselves do not take into account local and individual contextual variables.

Practice that seems to work in one context cannot generally be used as a blueprint for practice in other areas. This is particularly true of the relationship between the Asia-Pacific region and Western countries. Significant cultural, demographic, economic, and even religious differences exist between the two regions, and, unless these facts are recognized and accounted for, reform in special education will likely make little progress. Authors in this book continually discuss the need for the Asia-Pacific region to learn from the experience of the West, while at the same time employing Western practices judiciously and modifying them appropriately according to local dynamics. Indeed, the chapters in Section 1 highlight the fact that the movement towards inclusive education in Western countries is far from perfect, and the philosophy of inclusion is not accepted by everyone. While inclusive education is increasingly being found to be an effective educational approach in Western education research (see, e.g. Fredrickson *et al.*, 2004), there are those who do not agree with it. While those in the West who do not support the inclusive approach do so more on philosophical grounds and offer scant research evidence to support their arguments (see, e.g. Kauffman *et al.*, 2002), their views do demonstrate that inclusive education in the West is neither "perfect" nor universally accepted. This further supports the need for the Asia-Pacific region to develop contextually relevant approaches to achieving the common international goal of including all.

Taking into account that all authors in the first section confirm that education reform for special education in the Asia-Pacific region is clearly moving towards a more inclusive approach, Section 2 of this book addresses the preparation of teachers to work in such classrooms. Some recent research in this area has shown that when compared to their Western counterparts, preservice teachers from Asian contexts harbor more negative attitudes towards inclusive education, have less positive sentiments about children with disabilities, and are more concerned about the impact of inclusion on their future teaching (Sharma *et al.*, 2006). Many reasons for this are cited, including prevailing regional and cultural attitudes towards disability. Based on these findings the outlook for the future of inclusive education in the Asia-Pacific region may appear bleak; however, a later study found that with teacher education, which addresses inclusive practice, attitudes towards inclusion and sentiments about children with disabilities improve, and concerns about inclusive education, are reduced (Loreman *et al.*, 2007). Similar findings are also emerging in the Asia-Pacific region (see, e.g. Forlin *et al.* in Chapter 8), It is critical, then, that preservice teacher education maintains a strong, positive focus on providing future teachers with the skills and attitudes they need to succeed in inclusive classrooms. Section 2 of this book not only highlights the need for sound preservice teacher education for inclusion, but also provides ways in which this can be accomplished.

While good preservice teacher education can do much to provide valuable skills, and change attitudes towards disability and inclusion, some research has found that school climate also plays a critical role in continuing positive teacher attitudes towards inclusive education. Positive attitude change will likely not be long term if at the conclusion of their education these new teachers are placed in environments that are resistant to the idea and practice of inclusion. The perpetuation of resistance to inclusion through the cycle of introducing teachers with positive attitudes into resistant environments and thus having those tentative positive attitudes changed, is difficult to counter. Indeed, there are still significant areas of resistance to inclusion in the West despite the idea of inclusion having been around for many years. If the Asia-Pacific region is going to be successful in promoting positive feelings about inclusive education in the face of significant education reform and change, it will need to plan carefully and devise solutions the West has to date largely been unable to develop. Once again, if these solutions are developed in dialogue with the international community, solutions that benefit the world beyond the Asia-Pacific region may be found.

Section 3 of this book takes a school- and classroom-based perspective towards education reform in the Asia-Pacific region by examining practices and strategies that should be considered by schools and education jurisdictions. It provides educators with concrete ways of working towards more inclusive outcomes. Further to this, the role of inclusive education as a catalyst for wider education reform in the region is highlighted. Inclusive education should not be segmented, or seen as an add-on to everything else that occurs in schools. It should be woven throughout all curricular, social, and pedagogical practices in schools. This is one area in which engagement with the international community will be of particular benefit to the Asia-Pacific region. International consultancies, with those who have expertise in the development of inclusive communities and working in inclusive classrooms, may be required. The contributors to this book note that inclusive education has a longer history in other regions of the world than in the Asia-Pacific region, and consultants who have learned lessons from many years of working in the field can help to further develop that expertise in the Asia-Pacific region. This transference of expertise can also undergo cultural negotiation as the knowledge is modified to the differing context.

The issue of resources is woven throughout much of Section 3. When discussing the pragmatics of implementing inclusive education, some consideration of the resource provision is inevitable. This is also a contentious topic in Western countries, even those that are comparatively wealthy, with many saying that inclusive education is inadequately funded (Hodkinson, 2006). Many areas in the Asia-Pacific region are faced with significantly high levels of poverty, accounting for 70 per cent of the world's poor people (ANU Poverty Research Centre, 2006). As such there is a reduced capacity in the region to provide adequate resources to schools. This is an example of how inclusive education can act as a catalyst for wider education reform. While gains have been made, schools in the Asia-Pacific region are still widely under-funded regardless of the presence of students with disabilities (Van Zant, 2006), and as these schools undergo a transformation towards becoming more inclusive environments, resources in general, not just those for special education, can be reconsidered as part of the restructuring that must take place.

Reformulating schools, however, does not create more money, and while existing resources may be used more effectively, these resources are finite and are to some extent dictated by local economies. Thankfully, economies in many areas of the Asia-Pacific region are improving, with exports from the region doubling in the past three years (World Bank, 2007). China, for example, is experiencing unprecedented levels of economic growth. At the time of writing, China's stock market is booming and the World Bank predicts that GDP growth in that country will exceed 10 per cent by the end of the year (Ying, 2007). This new era of prosperity might eventually be reflected in the levels of resources schools are provided with. Even where schools in the Asia-Pacific region continue to suffer from a chronic lack of resources, they can to some extent find relief by restructuring to become more inclusive.

Studies in countries where inclusion is more common consistently show that adopting inclusive education is significantly cheaper than maintaining segregated forms of education (Sobsey, 2005). These savings should remain in the system and be applied to improving conditions for all students. Also, there are those who question the seemingly endless demand for resources in the West (see Ainscow and Sebba, 1996). According to Ainscow and Sebba (1996) the provision of too many resources may reduce a school's capacity to think creatively and may, therefore, do the act of inclusion a disservice rather than a service. Those questioning resource provisions do not advocate the reduction of funding to schools, but rather propose the need for justification of these funds based on a plan involving sound pedagogy. These views might out of necessity be supported by schools and education jurisdictions in the Asia-Pacific region as they find creative ways to deal with resource issues.

Conclusion

The move towards inclusive education in the Asia-Pacific region faces enormous challenges, but if viewed as a catalyst for wider education reform, overcoming these challenges could serve to improve and re-invigorate many aspects of the various regional systems. Where inclusion is successful the classroom context is supported by important factors such as: sound teacher preparation and professional development; appropriate resources; well-conceptualized policy and legislation; strong home and community partnerships; inclusive cultural practices and positive attitudes; together with the consideration of geographic location, local and national economic factors, and the willingness of the entire system to see inclusion work. The Asia-Pacific region can learn from the West, and should be ready to make changes to accept international practices where appropriate. Education systems in the Asia-Pacific region should consider adopting from the West those practices that will work, but they also need to adapt Western practices as appropriate, and devise and trial new ways of working in order to overcome context specific barriers. This is a highly complex task. If the Asia-Pacific region maintains a high level of dialogue and mutual support between its own nations, while at the same time continuing to engage with the wider international community, progress and worthwhile education reform becomes not only possible, but inevitable.

References

Ainscow, M. and Sebba, J. (1996) "International developments in inclusive schooling: Mapping the issues", *Cambridge Journal of Education*, 26(1): 5–18.

Australian National University (ANU) Poverty Research Centre (2006) *Poverty Research Centre*. Online. Available at: http://rspas.anu.edu.au/economics/prc/ (accessed 25 August 2007).

Frederickson, N., Dunsmuir, S., Lang, J. and Monsen, J.J. (2004) "Mainstream–special school inclusion partnerships: Pupil, parent and teacher perspectives", *International Journal of Inclusive education*, 8(1): 37–57.

Hodkinson, A. (2006) "Conceptions and misconceptions of inclusive education – one year on: A critical analysis of newly qualified teachers' knowledge and understanding of inclusion", *Research in Education*, 76: 43–55.

Kauffman, J. M., Bantz, J. and McCollough, J. (2002) "Separate and better: A special public school class for students with emotional and behavioral disorders", *Exceptionality*, 10(3): 149–70.

Loreman, T. and Deppeler, J. (2002) "Working towards full inclusion in education", *The National Issues Journal for People with a Disability*, 3(6): 5–8.

Loreman, T., Forlin, C. and Sharma, U. (2007) "An international comparison of pre-service teacher attitudes towards inclusive education", *Disability Studies Quarterly*, 27(4). Online. Available at http://www.dsq-sds.org/_articles_html/2007/fall/dsq_v27_04_2007_fall_fs_02_loreman.htm

Sharma, U., Forlin, C., Loreman, T. and Earle, C. (2006) "Preservice teachers' attitudes, concerns and sentiments about inclusive education: An international comparison of the novice preservice teacher", *International Journal of Special Education*, 21(2): 80–93.

Sobsey, R. (2005) "Inclusive education research", paper presented at the Whole Schooling Conference, Edmonton, Alberta.

United Nations Educational, Scientific and Cultural Organization (1990) *World Declaration on Education for All and Framework for Action to Meet Basic Learning Needs* (Jomtien Declaration), New York.

United Nations Educational, Scientific and Cultural Organization (1994a) *The Salamanca Statement and Framework for Action on Special Needs Education*, Salamanca, Spain.

United Nations Educational, Scientific and Cultural Organization (1994b) *The World Conference on Special Needs Education: Access and Quality, Final Report*, Salamanca, Spain: Ministry of Education and Science, Madrid.

United Nations Educational, Scientific and Cultural Organization (2000) *The Dakar Framework for Action*, Dakar.

Van Zant, E. (2006) "ADB is helping its developing member countries meet the educational challenges posed by rapid economic change in the region", *Educating Asia: Asian Development Bank Review*, 38(3). Online. Available at: http://www.adb.org/Documents/Periodicals/ADB_Review/2006/vol38–3/educating-asia.asp (accessed 25 August 2007).

World Bank (2007) *East Asia and Pacific Region Overview*. Online. Available at: http://web.worldbank.org/WBSITE/EXTERNAL/COUNTRIES/EASTASIAPACIFICEXT/0,,menuPK:208945~pagePK:146732~piPK:64003010~theSitePK:226301,00.html (accessed 25 August 2007).

Ying, Yu (2007) *Prospects for Growth Remain Good; Policy Could Focus on Liquidating and Rebalancing*. Online. Available at: http://web.worldbank.org/WBSITE/EXTERNAL/COUNTRIES/EASTASIAPACIFICEXT/CHINAEXTN/0,,contentMDK:21351645~menuPK:318956~pagePK:1497618~piPK:217854~theSitePK:318950,00.html (accessed 25 August 2007).

Support materials and activities: Section 3

The following support materials and activities provide additional useful information about effective inclusive practices. The activities are designed to provide authentic approaches to learning that can be contextualized to meet the needs of learners in any given environment.

These websites provide good starting places for further information about developing inclusive schools and classrooms

- The *National Association of Secondary School Principals* (NASSP) Bulletin is available at: http://bul.sagepub.com/
- The *School Effectiveness and School Improvement International Journal of Research, Policy and Practice* is available at: http://www.informaworld.com/smpp/title~content=t714592801
- The *Journal of School Leadership* is available at: http://www.rowmaneducation.com/Journals/JSL/
- The *Federation In Community Support* website: http://www2.ied.edu.hk/fpece/fics/ is a central hub for obtaining information about support services for students with special needs in Hong Kong. It also has extensive links to international websites about special and inclusive education.
- The *Centre for Special Needs and Studies in Inclusive Education* (CSNSIE) operates from the Hong Kong Institute of Education (http://www.ied.edu.hk/csnsie/index.html). It is a useful site for links within the Asia-Pacific region.
- The *Centre for Advancement in Special Education* (CASE) operates from the University of Hong Kong (http://www.hku.hk/case/home.htm). CASE links to a wide range of Asian and international sites and provides links for resources related to special education.
- The National Autistic Society at http://www.nas.org.uk is an excellent site for anyone wanting to develop their understanding of students with ASD, including a number of resources, information sheets and research reports that are free to download.
- This site provides a comprehensive overview of issues relating to ADHD, and includes a section designed specifically for educators interested in

developing their practice to facilitate the inclusion of students with ADHD (http:// www.adhd.com).

- The *Children and Adults with Attention-Deficit/Hyperactivity Disorder* (CHADD) site is a US site for individuals with ADHD and their families, providing information, public advocacy, and support (http://www.chadd.org/).
- The *Educational Administration Quarterly* website provides some articles that can be downloaded for free: http://eaq.sagepub.com/archive/
- A new teacher resource booklet has just been published in Australia on *Improving the Learning Outcomes of Students with Disabilities in the Early, Middle and Post Compulsory Years of Schooling* (October, 2007) and may be downloaded from: http://www.dest.gov.au/sectors/school_education/publications_resources/profiles/learning_outcomes_students_disabilities
- The following sites are central hubs for obtaining information about the *Integrated Play Groups* model training and support services that are available to teachers, families and others devoted to supporting the social inclusion of children with autism spectrum disorders:
    - Autism Institute on Peer Relations and Play: www.autisminstitute.com or www.wolfberg.com
    - San Francisco State University Autism Program: www.sfsu.edu~autism
    - Autism Network for Global Education and Lifelong Support (ANGELS): www.angelscenter.org
    - Friend 2 Friend Social Learning Society: www.friend2friendsociety.org
    - Developmental Pathways for Kids (DPK): www.developmentalpathways.com

Professional development activities for teachers and school leaders considering whole school change for inclusion

1 Review the *Index for Inclusion* and discuss how this could be used to guide a school through a process of inclusive school development (http://inclusion.uwe.ac.uk/csie/indexlaunch.htm). Alternatively review the *Indicators for Inclusion* a Hong Kong version of the *Index* that provides a set of school development instruments aimed at enhancing the capacity of schools in catering for student differences (http://www.edb.gov.hk/FileManager/EN/Content_187/indicators-examples_e.pdf).

2 Review local *Disability Discrimination Acts* or *Equal Opportunity Acts* to identify the legislative requirements for schools and teachers regarding placement decisions for students with disabilities.

3 Establish a school-based coordinating group to review existing policy and practice regarding a whole school approach to inclusive education. Develop a strategic school development plan for becoming more inclusive. Involve all stakeholders including staff, parents, students and community members.

4 Teacher professional development is essential to efforts to improve schools. Read the following article and use it to promote discussion about effective

professional development programs and their impact on teacher learning. Brainstorm directions and strategies for extending your staff's knowledge.

- Borko, H. (2004) *Professional Development and Teacher Learning: Mapping the Terrain,* Educational Researcher, 33, (8): 3–15, American Educational Research Association (full text available from: http://edr.sagepub.com/cgi/content/abstract/33/8/3).

5 Read the following article and discuss how kindergarten to Year 12 educative curriculum materials can be designed to best promote teacher learning in your school.

- Davis, E. A. (2005) *Designing Educative Curriculum Materials to Promote Teacher Learning*, Educational Researcher, 34, (3): 3–14, American Educational Research Association (available online at: http://edr.sagepub.com/cgi/content/abstract/34/3/3).

6 Having read Chapter 9 by Keith Humphreys visit the Publications page on the EQUALS website (www.equals.co.uk) and look at the scheme of work for Science and PSHE. Identify ways in which they might help you to teach.

7 Develop a sensitization program for children to help them understand and make friends with a child with a disability. An activity bank of child to child activities that could be employed in classrooms will make an excellent resource for all teachers in a school.

These texts provide a wealth of practical ideas about effective inclusive practices and are excellent references for teachers and school leaders

Beattie, J., Jordan, L. and Algozzine, B. (2006) *Making Inclusion Work: Effective Practices for All Teachers*, Thousand Oaks, CA: Corwin Press.

Betts, S. W., Betts, D. E. and Gerber-Eckard, L. N. (2007) *Asperger Syndrome in the Inclusive Classroom*, London: Jessica Kingsley.

Cooper, P. and Ideus, K. (1996) *AD/HD: A Practical Guide for Teachers*, London: David Fulton.

Department of Education (2006) *Teaching Children with AD/HD: Instructional Strategies and Practices*, Washington, DC.

Friend, M. and Bursuck, W. D. (2006) *Including Students with Special Needs: A Practical Guide for Classroom Teachers,* Hong Kong: Pearson/Allyn & Bacon.

Lewis, R. B. and Doorlag, D. H. (2006) *Teaching Special Students in General Education Classrooms,* Upper Saddle River, NJ: Pearson/Merrill/Prentice Hall.

Loreman, T., Deppeler, J. and Harvey, D. (2005) *Inclusive Education: A Practical Guide to Supporting Diversity in the Classroom*, Sydney: Allen and Unwin.

Phillipson, S. N. (ed.) (2007) *Learning Diversity in the Chinese Classroom: Contexts and Practice for Students with Special Needs*, Hong Kong: Hong Kong University Press.

Rose, R. and Howley, M. (2007) *The Practical Guide to Special Education Needs in Inclusive Primary Classrooms*, London: Paul Chapman.

Salend, S. J. (2005) *Creating Inclusive Classrooms: Effective and Reflective Practices for All Students,* Upper Saddle River, NJ: Pearson/Merrill/Prentice Hall.

Salvia, J., Ysseldyke, J. E. and Bolt, S. (2007) *Assessment in Special and Inclusive Education,* Boston, MA: Houghton Mifflin.

Seach, D. (1998) *Autistic Spectrum Disorder: Positive Approaches for Teaching Children with ASD*, Stafford, Staffordshire: NASEN.

Toppin, K. and Malone, S. (2005) *The Routledge Falmer Reader in Inclusive Education,* London: Routledge.

Wolfberg, P. J. (2003) *Peer Play and the Autism Spectrum: The Art of Guiding Children's Socialization and Imagination*, Shawnee, KS: Autism Asperger.

Wood, J. (2006) *Teaching Students in Inclusive Settings: Adapting and Accommodating Instruction,* Upper Saddle River, NJ: Merrill/Prentice Hall.

Author index

Subject index